Study Guide

to accompany

Crider • Goethals • Kavanaugh • Solomon

Psychology

Fourth Edition

Sarah A. Rundle

📖 **HarperCollins***CollegePublishers*

Study Guide to accompany Crider/Goethals/Kavanaugh/Solomon PSYCHOLOGY 4e

Copyright © 1993 HarperCollins College Publishers

All rights reserved. Printed in the United States of America. No part of this book may be used or reproduced in any manner whatsoever without written permission with the following exception: testing material may be copied for classroom testing. For information, address HarperCollins College Publishers, 10 E. 53rd St., New York, N.Y. 10022

ISBN: 0-673-46540-3

92 93 94 95 96 9 8 7 6 5 4 3 2 1

CONTENTS

A Message to the Student — iv

Chapter 1: Welcome to Psychology — 1
Answers for Exercises — 190

Chapter 2: Brain and Behavior — 12
Answers for Exercises — 192

Chapter 3: Sensation and Perception — 22
Answers for Exercises — 194

Chapter 4: Motivation and Emotion — 32
Answers for Exercises — 196

Chapter 5: States of Consciousness — 43
Answers for Exercises — 198

Chapter 6: Conditioning and Learning — 53
Answers for Exercises — 200

Chapter 7: Human Memory — 64
Answers for Exercises — 202

Chapter 8: Thinking and Language — 74
Answers for Exercises — 204

Chapter 9: Infancy and Childhood — 84
Answers for Exercises — 206

Chapter 10: Adolescence, Adulthood, and Aging — 95
Answers for Exercises — 208

Chapter 11: Intelligence — 105
Answers for Exercises — 210

Chapter 12: Social Cognition — 116
Answers for Exercises — 212

Chapter 13: Social Influence — 126
Answers for Exercises — 214

Chapter 14: Personality — 138
Answers for Exercises — 216

Chapter 15: Health and Stress — 149
Answers for Exercises — 218

Chapter 16: Major Psychological Disorders — 159
Answers for Exercises — 220

Chapter 17: Treatment of Psychological Disorders — 169
Answers for Exercises — 222

Appendix: Methods and Statistics in Psychology — 179
Answers for Exercises — 224

A MESSAGE TO THE STUDENT

This study guide was prepared to help you get the information from *Psychology* into your long-term memory and to help you make a good grade. But it can only help. You are the one who must attend class, stay awake and alert during class, and spend the time required for effective study.

Effective study begins on the first day of classes. At that time you should survey the situation by doing a course preview, setting up a study plan, and having a notebook ready to collect notes from your reading and from lectures.

Course Preview

The course preview includes reading the class syllabus carefully and becoming acquainted with your text and your study guide.

The syllabus should contain information about the course including a schedule of reading assignments, due dates for assignments, test dates, types of tests to expect, and the method that will be used in determining final grades. If your syllabus does not contain this information, and the instructor does not provide it on the first day of class, it is a good idea to ask about these things.

Becoming acquainted with your text means getting an idea about its content and organization. Look at the Contents. What are the titles of the chapters? How many chapters are there? Are the chapters grouped into units or parts? Look at one of the chapters. Is there a chapter outline on the first page of the chapter? How many levels of headings are used? Are there interim summaries? Is there a chapter summary? How are new terms printed in the text? Are there lists of key individuals, topics, or terms?

If you are reading this, you are already looking at your study guide and have noticed that there is a chapter in the study guide for each chapter in the text. On the first page of each chapter in the study guide, you will find a short discussion related to the material in this chapter. This is followed by learning objectives, essay questions, a completion exercise called "Working with Names and Terms," and two 25-item multiple-choice tests. Answers for all the exercises and tests are at the back of your study guide.

Strategies for Studying

Be an active participant in the learning process.

The best way to be an active participant in the learning process is to write as you read. You might, for example:

1. Use index cards for names and terms, as you might do in learning a foreign language.
2. Make an outline to condense important points from the chapter.
3. Write responses to the learning objectives.
4. Analyze studies that are described in the text. What research method was used? What was the independent variable? What was the dependent variable? What was the result? What does the result mean?
5. Use the organizational schemes discussed below.

Writing things down as you read has at least four important benefits. First, it forces you to attend to what you are reading. Second, it gives you a feeling of accomplishment as you work and of confidence at test time. Third, it provides you with a self-made digest of the text to use in studying for tests. Fourth, it helps you understand and remember what you read.

Organize information you need to remember in a meaningful way.

Good students probably do not have better memories than students who do poorly; they just have their memories more effectively organized. Much of the material in the text can easily be organized into tables, tree diagrams, or flow charts. For example, five perspectives on psychology are discussed in Chapter 1. Information about these perspectives can be readily organized into a table that allows you to put a lot of information on a single sheet of paper. Different areas of specialization within psychology are discussed in Chapter 1, and structures of the nervous system are discussed in Chapter 2. This information fits neatly into tree diagrams. Flow charts are appropriate for material in Chapter 3 which follows the sequence of events that occurs when electomagnetic waves enter your eye or sound waves jiggle your eardrum.

Relate new information to your own experience and to what you already know.

This is especially important in understanding new terms. For example, in your reading you will encounter the term "cognitive dissonance" which is defined as "the state of tension that occurs when a person holds two cognitions that are psychologically inconsistent." Would you recognize cognitive dissonance if it happened to you? Instructors rarely expect students to memorize definitions; they do expect students to understand new terms.

Use visual imagery.

Using visual imagery is making mental movies that you can select and play back at test time. Imagine yourself as a subject in experiments that are described in the text; ride a sound wave into the human ear; or be a patient on Freud's couch. Visual memory is an independent storage system that can greatly enhance the verbal memory we ordinarily use in studying.

Use mnemonics.

Mnemonics are techniques, or tricks, for remembering information that has no inherent pattern or logic. The little verse that helps us remember how many day there are in each month and the music students' use of "Every Good Boy Does Fine" to remember the notes on the lines of the treble clef are examples of mnemonics. In Chapter 2 you will need to remember that the four lobes of the cerebral cortex are frontal, parietal, occipital, and temporal. Can you think of a mnemonic that will help you remember them?

Mnemonics can be stupid or bizarre; their value depends upon whether they are helpful to you. It can be fun to share mnemonics with friends from your psychology class.

Making a Study Plan

You should have a specific, step-by-step plan of attack for the chapters in your text, like the following:

1. Preview the chapter. Look at the chapter outline on the title page for the chapter in your text. Guess what kind of information each major section will contain. Read the chapter summary at the end of the chapter.
2. Read "Think About It" from the first page for the chapter in your study guide.
3. Read the learning objectives from your study guide.
4. Read the first major section of the chapter in your text, writing important names and terms on index cards as you read, or marking the names and terms to make cards later.
5. Write definitions and other pertinent information on the back of the index cards you are preparing.
6. Write responses to the learning objectives that cover the section you have read. Use a table, tree diagram, or flow chart to respond to a learning objective if appropriate.
7. Read the second major section of the chapter, repeating steps 4, 5, and 6. Continue this process for the remainder of the chapter.
8. Review your notes and vocabulary cards.
9. Prepare answers to the essay questions in your study guide and compare your answers with the answers included at the back of the study guide. It is important to write out answers if you will be having essay questions on tests.

10. Do the "Working with Names and Terms" exercise in your study guide. Check your work. Make an index card for any name or term used in the exercise that you may have overlooked.
11. Do Multiple-Choice Test I in your study guide, reading the questions and all the answers carefully. Check your work. Be sure you understand why the keyed answers are correct.
12. If you are not satisfied with your performance on the first Multiple-Choice Test, check your notes and vocabulary cards to see if you have missed an important point, or if you failed to understand some concept.
13. Do Multiple-Choice Test II. Again check your work and be sure you understand the concepts covered by items you missed.
14. After you have completed all the steps in your study plan, give yourself a positive reinforcer, like a rest or a trip to the refrigerator.

Taking Lecture Notes

There are two important objectives in taking lecture notes. The first is to have a record of the important points made by your professor. The second is to be able to read and understand your notes after they have gotten "cold."

Taking notes during a lecture requires dividing your attention between what your professor is saying and your note taking. A good plan is to take abbreviated notes during the lecture and devote the major share of your attention to listening to your instructor. However, this is a good plan only if you return to your notes shortly after class to elaborate and clarify your notes while the lecture is still fresh in your mind. If you want to try this technique, divide the pages in your notebook vertically using the left side for your in-class notes and the right side for your after-class comments.

It is a good idea to read the chapters before they are covered in the lecture. This will generally make the lecture more meaningful. You will also know whether material covered in the lecture is also in the text, and can take this into account in your note taking. Remember that lectures are gone forever unless you tape them, and that your text remains with you for ready reference.

Studying for Tests

There are two major types of tests, and it is important for you to know which type to expect. One type is the objective test. Objective tests include multiple choice, matching, true-false, and completion if a list of answers to choose from is provided. Objective tests require recognition memory--the test taker chooses, rather than produces, the answer.

The other major type of test requires recall memory. This type of test includes essay tests, short answer tests, and completion, if a list of answers is not provided. For these tests, the student must produce the answer. The following suggestions for test preparation are appropriate for either type of test:
1. Read the interim summaries and the chapter summary from your text.

2. Review your vocabulary cards and the notes you took while reading the text. Test yourself on the information as you study.
3. Read the essay questions and the answers from your study guide.
4. Review the vocabulary exercises and the multiple-choice tests in your study guide. Read all the answers to the multiple-choice items and pay special attention to items you missed when you took the tests.
5. Review your lecture notes. Highlight and rehearse information you may need to remember.

For tests that require recall memory, you will need to do some additional memory work. For example, if an essay question on Chapter 1 of your text were, "Describe the five major perspectives in psychology," you would need to be able to recall the names of the five major perspectives. To prepare for essay exams, you might prepare a "list of lists." Mnemonics can be helpful for retrieving the items on your lists.

Strategies for Taking Tests

Let's first consider some general guidelines for test-taking, and then consider strategies for specific types of test items.

General guidelines

1. Read the instructions carefully.
2. Look over the test before beginning. Is there a page missing? Is there a page that is difficult to read?
3. If there are two or more sections in the test, like an objective section and an essay section, budget your time. Read the essay questions first, then do the objective section. There may be items on the objective part of the test that will jog your memory for writing answers to the essay questions.
4. Complete the questions for which you know the correct answers first, then return to the items you found more difficult.
5. After you have taken the first test in a class, look carefully at the items on the test to try to determine what types of material the instructor is most likely to cover on tests. For example, look to see if there are questions on the names of people mentioned in the text, or questions on the content of tables and figures.

Multiple choice

1. Read all the answers carefully before making your choice.
2. Remember that the *best* answer is the correct answer. Some items have more than one reasonable answer among the choices, but one answer should be better than the others.
3. Choose an answer for every item. If items have four alternatives, you have a 25% chance of being right with a "blind" guess. If you can eliminate one or more of the alternatives, your probability of choosing correctly increases.

4. If the last answer is "all of the above," use the following procedure:
   a. If you think two or more of the answers are correct, choose "all of the above."
   b. If you are pretty sure one of the answers is not correct, eliminate that answer and "all of the above" as possibilities.
   c. If you are choosing blindly, choose "all of the above." On most tests it has a probability greater than .25 of being correct.
5. If the last answer is "none of the above," do not choose it unless you are fairly certain there is no correct answer. In writing items, there is a bias for "all of the above" to be correct and "none of the above" to be incorrect.
6. When you are guessing:
   a. Choose "b" or "c" rather than "a" or "d." People who write multiple-choice items have a tendency to want to embed the answer, and thus tend to use "b" and "c" more frequently than "a" and "d."
   b. Choose the longest answer, particularly if it is more precise than the other answers, or if there is a qualifying clause or phrase.

Matching

1. Match the items for which you are reasonably sure of the answers first. Mark off the answers as you use them.
2. Next, match the items you are less certain of, again marking off the answer you use.
3. Guess for the remainder of the items from the reduced set of answers.

Fill-in-the-blanks

1. If a list of names and/or terms to choose from is provided, use the same elimination process described for matching tests.
2. Look for grammatical clues. Should the answer be a noun, a verb, or an adjective? If a noun is appropriate, should it be singular or plural? If a verb is indicated, what number and tense is appropriate?

Essays

1. Read the question very carefully. Your answer should respond to the question. It should not include material that is irrelevant.
2. Take time to think.
3. Organize the points you intend to make before you start writing. A brief outline will help you present your answer in a logical way.
4. If you know any terms or names that are appropriate to the topic of your essay, be sure to use them. People who score essay questions often look for key terms in answers. If you can recall relevant information from an earlier chapter, it is very impressive and should get you a few extra points.

Work hard, study smart, and have a good term!

Chapter 1

WELCOME TO PSYCHOLOGY

Learning Objectives

After studying this chapter, you should be able to:

1. Define psychology as it is viewed today and identify the four major goals of psychology.

2. Describe the essential features of the scientific method.

3. Differentiate between single-blind and double-blind research procedures.

4. Describe the advantages and limitations of naturalistic observation.

5. Describe the major uses of case studies in psychology.

6. Outline the purposes and limitations of survey research.

7. Contrast correlational and experimental approaches to research.

8. Define the correlation coefficient and describe its limitations.

9. Discriminate between a positive and a negative correlation.

10. Differentiate between dependent and independent variables.

11. Differentiate between control and experimental groups.

12. Differentiate between the concerns of internal and external validity in experiments.

13. Describe the advantages of multimethod approaches in psychology.

14. Identify the disciplines from which the science of psychology emerged.

15. Outline the contributions of Wundt, James, and Hall in the emergence of psychology as an academic discipline.

16. Describe the procedure and goal of introspection.

17. Outline and contrast the five current major perspectives within psychology, and identify the individuals prominently associated with each perspective.

18. Describe the major specialties of both academic and practicing psychologists.

19. Describe the ethical considerations involved in psychological experiments that use human and animal subjects.

Working with Names and Terms

From the alphabetized list below choose the name or term that answers the question, using each name and term only once. Answers are at the back of your study guide.

behavioral	introspection
case study	James, William
catharsis	law of effect
cognitive	Maslow, Abraham
conditioned reflex	multi-method approach
confounded	Neisser, Ulric
correlational	neuroscience
dependent	operational definition
double-blind	psychodynamic
Hall, G. Stanley	random assignment
humanistic	Sperry, Roger
independent	statistical analysis

_____ 1. What was the experimenter doing when he put subjects who drew a black marble in the experimental group and subjects who drew a white marble in the control group?

_____ 2. Which perspective is responsible for "mental processes" being added to the definition of psychology in recent years?

_____ 3. What technique was being used when neither the children, their parents, nor the experimenter knew which twin was brushing with brand X and which twin was brushing with brand Y?

_____ 4. Which perspective rejected the study of activities such as thinking and problem solving on the grounds of their being unobservable and unmeasurable?

_____ 5. What term is used by psychodynamic psychologists to describe the reduction of emotional feelings that results from expressing the feelings?

_____ 6. What psychologist is known as the great organizer?

_____ 7. What cognitive psychologist observed that all our knowledge of reality comes from our interpretation of sensory events?

_____ 8. What term did Pavlov use to describe the responses made by the dogs he used in his studies?

_____ 9. What term is used to describe an experiment in which some variable other than the independent variable has influenced the dependent variable?

_____ 10. What is the perspective of a psychologist who describes himself as a biopsychologist?

_____ 11. What method is most likely to be used to study the effects of a person's injury to the brain on the person's behavior and mental processes?

_____ 12. What psychologist shared the perspective of Carl Rogers and is best known for his hierarchy of motives?

_____ 13. What term is used to describe research in which several types of studies are used to investigate a problem or hypothesis?

_____ 14. What was the experimenter doing when he said that "learning" is the rats' making five consecutive correct choices in the maze?

_____ 15. Which perspective has been most active in the encounter group movement?

_____ 16. What type of variable was "food versus no food outside the puzzle box" in Thorndike's research with cats?

_____ 17. What must an experimenter do before she can claim that the results of her study are unlikely to have occurred by chance?

_____ 18. What principle says that we tend to repeat behaviors for which we are rewarded and to avoid behaviors for which we are punished?

_____ 19. What research method that was used by Wundt has been revived and modified by contemporary cognitive psychologists?

_____ 20. What is the perspective of the psychologist who said that one of his patient's has problems with authority figures because of his repressed hostility toward his father?

_____ 21. What research method was being used by the psychologist who said that her study showed a relationship between being exposed to loud music and hearing loss, but that further research must be done before it can be concluded that exposure to loud music causes hearing loss?

_____ 22. What type of variable is the "amount of saliva" that Pavlov measured in his research?

_____ 23. Who founded a laboratory at Harvard in 1875 and wrote a classic text entitled *Principles of Psychology*?

_____ 24. What neuroscientist won the Nobel Prize for research showing that the two hemispheres of the brain perform different functions?

Essay Questions

Suggested answers for the essay questions are included at the back of your study guide.

1. Different philosophical views characterize the different perspectives of psychology. One of the questions on which the perspectives disagree concerns the "basic nature of human nature." Compare the psychodynamic, behavioral, and humanistic views on the basic nature of humans.

2. Discuss advantages and disadvantages of the five methods of research discussed in the text.

3. An experimenter has the hypothesis that caffeine has an adverse effect on problem-solving performance. Identify the independent and dependent variables and discuss how the experimenter might operationally define them.

4. The text describes a study by Liebert and Baron investigating the effects of TV violence on aggressive behavior in children. Relate this study to the four goals of psychology--that is, how does it fulfill each of the four goals?

Multiple-Choice Test I

For the multiple-choice items, choose the best of the answers provided. Check your work with the answers provided at the back of your study guide, and be sure you understand why the keyed answers are correct.

1. Psychology differs from philosophy and religion in that it emphasizes _____ in its search for truth about behavior and mental processes.
   a. intuition and authority
   b. inductive and deductive reasoning
   c. empiricism and scientific methodology
   d. description and theory

2. Research that made it possible to identify people who are susceptible to substance abuse in early childhood would fulfill the goal of
   a. prediction.
   b. empiricism.
   c. internal validity.
   d. catharsis.

3. In the study that Liebert and Baron did on the relationship between TV violence and aggressive behavior in children, they operationally defined "aggression" in terms of
   a. hurting another child.
   b. teachers' ratings of aggressiveness.
   c. expressing the intention to hurt another child.
   d. assaulting an inflatable doll.

4. The single-blind procedure is used to prevent bias on the part of the _____ from affecting the dependent variable; the double-blind procedure is used to prevent bias on the part of the _____ from affecting the dependent variable.
   a. experimental group; control group
   b. control group; experimental group
   c. subjects; experimenter
   d. experimenter; subjects

5. Statistical analyses of data are used to
   a. describe data.
   b. guide inferences made from data.
   c. determine the probability that results are due to chance.
   d. do all of the above.

6. To test the hypothesis that women are more likely than men to obey the law, a psychology student hid behind a tree and noted the sex of people who stopped or failed to stop at a stop sign on a residential street. The student used the research method called
   a. survey research.
   b. correlational research.
   c. naturalistic observation.
   d. experimentation.

7. A psychologist who believes that the best way to understand human behavior is to study one individual or a few individuals intensively would be most likely to use the research method called
   a. naturalistic observation.
   b. correlational research.
   c. the case study method.
   d. experimentation.

8. A psychologist who wanted to collect data on the sexual behavior of high school students in the United States would be most likely to use the research method called
   a. survey research.
   b. correlational research.
   c. naturalistic observation.
   d. experimentation.

9. To show that there is a relationship between the heights and weights of male college students, one would use the research method called
   a. discriminate analysis.
   b. correlation.
   c. factor analysis.
   d. analysis of variance.

10. The weight of automobiles is related to their fuel consumption. The correlation between weight and miles per gallon is _____; the correlation between weight and the amount of fuel it takes to travel 100 miles is _____.
    a. positive; positive
    b. positive; negative
    c. negative; positive
    d. negative; negative

11. The limits of the values correlation coefficients can have are
    a. plus infinity and minus infinity.
    b. 0 and +10.00.
    c. -10.00 and +10.00.
    d. -1.00 and +1.00.

12. If there is a high positive or negative correlation between variable A and variable B, it could mean
    a. variable A causes variable B.
    b. variable B causes variable A.
    c. variable A and variable B are both influenced by variable C.
    d. any of the above.

13. In the study in which Hinz and Tomhave studied responses to facial expressions, the facial expressions of the experimenter's assistants defined the _____ variable, and the facial expressions of the subjects who responded to the facial expressions of the experimenter's assistants defined the _____ variable.
    a. independent; dependent
    b. dependent; independent
    c. subject; experimenter
    d. experimenter; subject

14. The important reason why most psychologists prefer the experimental method over the correlational method when it is possible to do an experiment is that
    a. fewer subjects are required for experimental research.
    b. cause-and-effect relations can be inferred from experimental results.
    c. variables can be operationally defined in experimental research.
    d. experimental results do not require statistical analysis.

15. If a farmer did an experiment to determine whether a hormone would cause his chickens to lay bigger eggs, the independent variable in his study would be
    a. the breed of chickens used in the study.
    b. the weight of the eggs laid by the experimental and control chickens.
    c. the procedure used to assign the chickens to two groups.
    d. the administration of the hormone only to chickens in the experimental group.

16. Random assignment is used to
    a. divide subjects into groups for experiments.
    b. choose variables for correlational research.
    c select questions for survey research.
    d. identify subjects for naturalistic observation.

17. An experiment that used children from a representative public school as subjects would probably have more external validity than the same experiment using children from an exclusive private school as subjects because
    a. the public school children could be randomly assigned to groups.
    b. the results would have greater generalizability.
    c. the study with public school children could be longitudinal.
    d. the probability of confounding would be lower.

18. The nineteenth century physiologist who did ground-breaking research on the nervous system and the sensory systems was
    a. Ulric Neisser.
    b. Wilhelm Wundt.
    c. Abraham Maslow.
    d. Hermann von Helmholtz.

19. William James was to psychology in the United States as _____ was to psychology in Germany.
    a. Hermann von Helmholtz
    b. Sigmund Freud
    c. Ulric Neisser
    d. Wilhelm Wundt

20. The physiological roots of psychology express themselves today in the _____ perspective.
    a. psychodynamic
    b. neuroscience
    c. behavioral
    d. cognitive

21. "Unconscious motives," "repression," and "catharsis" are concepts associated with the _____ perspective.
    a. behavioral
    b. humanistic
    c. cognitive
    d. psychodynamic

22. Freud was to psychoanalysis as _____ was to behaviorism.
    a. Carl Rogers
    b. Ivan Pavlov
    c William James
    d. John B. Watson

23. The strategies you use to process and remember the information in your textbook would be of most interest to psychologists who prefer the _____ perspective.
    a. cognitive
    b. behavioral
    c. neuroscience
    d. humanistic

24. "Free will," "inherent goodness," and "self-actualization" are central themes of the _____ perspective.
    a. psychodynamic
    b. behavioral
    c. humanistic
    d. cognitive

25. All of the following have traditionally been considered specialties within the area of experimental psychology *except*
    a. sensation and perception.
    b. motivation and emotion.
    c. learning and memory.
    d. personality and social.

Multiple-Choice Test II

For the multiple-choice items, choose the best of the answers provided. Check your work with the answers provided at the back of your study guide, and be sure you understand why the keyed answers are correct.

1. In fulfilling the goals of psychology, gathering data is to description as formulating theories is to
    a. prediction.
    b. statistical analysis.
    c. hypothesis generation.
    d. explanation.

2. Which of the following might an experimenter use as an operational definition of "memory"?
    a. deciding whether certain specific words occurred in a story
    b. reproducing a geometrical shape
    c. finding objects that subjects have seen being hidden
    d. Any of the above could be used as an operational definition of "memory."

3. In scientific research, the first formal step is to
    a. generate a hypothesis.
    b. operationalize the variables.
    c. randomly assign the subjects to groups.
    d. ensure against experimenter bias.

4. Scientists who study the behavior of animals in their natural environment are called _____, and they are most likely to use the method of _____.
    a. epistomologists; case studies
    b. epistemologists; naturalistic observation
    c. ethologists; case studies
    d. ethologists; naturalistic observation

5. In a study testing the effectiveness of a new drug for the treatment of major depression, the experimenter who assessed the mental condition of subjects after the treatment did not know which subjects had the new drug and which subjects had not had it. This suggests that the study used
   a. the method of naturalistic observation.
   b. random assignment of subjects.
   c. the double-blind procedure.
   d. an introspective dependent variable.

6. Clinical psychologists are most likely to use the research method called
   a. case studies.
   b. correlational research.
   c. experimentation.
   d. survey research.

7. A psychologist who studies the behavior and mental processes of people who have had brain damage as a result of an accident use the research method called
   a. naturalistic observation.
   b. correlational research.
   c. experimentation.
   d. the case study method.

8. If class attendance is related to the grades students make in a course, one would expect that there would be a _____ correlation between grades and number of classes attended and a _____ correlation between grades and number of classes not attended.
   a. positive; positive
   b. positive; negative
   c. negative; positive
   d. negative; negative

9. A curious student in a statistics class calculated the correlation coefficient for the relationship between the weight of female students and the average number of calories they consumed daily. If she calculated correctly, she is most likely to have gotten a correlation of
   a. +1.67.
   b. +.56.
   c. -.68.
   d. -1.00.

10. A curious psychology professor found that there was a negative and sizeable correlation between the grades students made and how far the students sat from the professor's podium. (High grades were related to short distances, low grades to longer distances.) What could the professor conclude?
    a. There is a relationship between grades and where students choose to sit.
    b. Good students usually prefer to sit close to the professor.
    c. Professors are partial to students who sit at the front of the room.
    d. Students who sit near the front of the room find it easier to attend to the lecture.

11. In an experiment, "treatment" is to the _____ variable as the "effect of the treatment" is to the _____ variable.
    a. experimenter; subject
    b. subject; experimenter
    c. independent; dependent
    d. dependent; independent

12. In the study that Hinz and Tomhave did on responses to facial expressions, the subjects did not know they were participants in an experiment, and the person who observed the subjects' responses could not see the facial expression of the experimenter's assistant. Thus it can be inferred that
    a. experimenter bias may have affected the results.
    b. the dependent variable was poorly defined.
    c. the method being used was correlational research.
    d. the double-blind procedure was used.

13. If a farmer did an experiment to determine whether a hormone would cause his chickens to lay bigger eggs, the dependent variable in his study would be
    a. the breed of chickens used in the study.
    b. the weight of the eggs laid by the experimental and control chickens.
    c. the procedure used to assign the chickens to two groups.
    d. the administration of the hormone only to chickens in the experimental group.

14. If an experiment has an experimental group and a control group, the experimenter will generally use _____ to assign subjects to groups.
    a. voluntary choice
    b. unbiased judges
    c. statistical procedures
    d. random assignment

15. The important factor in establishing the internal validity of an experiment is
    a. operationalizing the variables.
    b. ruling out effects of confounding variables.
    c. having more than one control group.
    d. using a homogenous group of subjects.

16. Socrates is to the philosophical roots of psychology as Hippocrates is to the _____ roots of psychology.
    a. physiological
    b. sociological
    c. epistemological
    d. ethological

17. Both Wilhelm Wundt and William James did all of the following *except*
    a. establish a laboratory.
    b. write a psychology text.
    c. teach psychology courses.
    d. organize a professional association for psychologists.

18. One man obtained the first Ph.D in psychology in the United States, organized the American Psychological Association, founded the first psychology journal in this country, and hosted visits to this country by Freud and Jung. His name was
    a. G. Stanley Hall.
    b. William James.
    c. Edward Thorndike.
    d. Abraham Maslow.

19. The idea that humans are basically irrational and selfish is associated with the _____ perspective.
    a. psychodynamic
    b. behavioral
    c. humanistic
    d. cognitive

20. Ivan Pavlov and Edward Thorndike are important precursors of the _____ perspective.
    a. psychoanalytic
    b. neuroscience
    c. cognitive
    d. behavioral

21. The belief that psychologists should study only those phenomena that can be observed and measured was a central theme of
    a. biopsychology.
    b. behaviorism.
    c. cognitive psychology.
    d. humanistic psychology.

22. Learning and conditioning are central to the _____ perspective; memory and thought are central to the _____ perspective.
    a. behavioral; cognitive
    b. behavioral; psychodynamic
    c. psychodynamic; humanistic
    d. humanistic; cognitive

23. The establishment of encounter groups and the development of human potential are associated with the _____ perspective.
    a. behavioral
    b. humanistic
    c. cognitive
    d. psychodynamic

24. Academic psychology includes all of the following *except*
    a. clinical psychology.
    b. developmental psychology.
    c. personality and social psychology.
    d. experimental psychology.

25. The *Ethical Principles for Psychologists* are primarily concerned with
    a. qualifications of mental health professionals.
    b. protection of the rights of subjects who participate in research.
    c. standards for truth and accuracy in reporting research results.
    d. personal conduct of therapists in their relationships with patients.

Chapter 2

BRAIN AND BEHAVIOR

Learning Objectives

After studying this chapter, you should be able to:

1. Identify the two types of cells in the brain and explain the function of each type.

2. List the three major functions of the brain.

3. Describe the structures and functions of the central and peripheral nervous systems.

4. Differentiate between the functions of the autonomic and somatic nervous systems.

5. Describe the functions of the three types of neurons, and the basic structure of all neurons.

6. Differentiate between resting and action potentials and describe the ionic event that initiates an action potential.

7. Describe the process of synaptic transmission.

8. Discuss the factors that influence the firing of one neuron.

9. Describe the role of endorphins in the brain.

10. Describe the function of the endocrine system, and the relationship between the nervous system and the endocrine system.

11. Describe the contribution of Gall's phrenology to the study of the brain.

12. Outline the location and functions of Broca's and Wernicke's areas of the brain.

13. Describe the sensory and motor functions of each of the lobes of the cerebral cortex.

14. Describe the functions of the association areas of the frontal, parietal, and temporal lobes.

15. List the major structures of the limbic system and describe the functions associated with each structure.

16. Describe the major components and functions of the central core.

17. Describe a brain graft and the potential for this technique in the treatment of Parkinson's disease.

18. Describe the ethical controversy surrounding the use of brain grafts.

19. Explain the differences among the EEG, CAT scan, MRI, and PET scan, and describe the uses of each device.

20. Describe the unusual characteristics of the split-brain patient and their implications for the understanding of human consciousness.

21. Outline the specializations of the cerebral hemispheres.

Working with Terms and Names

From the alphabetized list below, choose the name or term that answers the question, using each name and term only once. Answers are at the back of your study guide.

all-or-none response	hippocampus
amygdala	hormones
aphasia	limbic system
Berger, Hans	Penfield, Wilder
brain graft	sodium ions
convolutions	soma
corpus callosum	somatic
dendrite	somatosensory cortex
endocrine	spinal reflex
endorphins	synapse
Fechner, Gustave	thalamus
Gall, Franz	visual agnosia

_____ 1. To what division of the nervous system do the neurons in your hands belong?

_____ 2. What system other than the nervous system is involved in communication within the body?

_____ 3. What term is used to describe the fact that the impulse on a neuron does not vary in intensity or speed?

4. What moves through the membrane of an axon from the outside to the inside when an action potential is generated?

5. What substances produced by the body have effects similar to the effects of morphine?

6. What term is used to refer to the wrinkles that occur on the surface of the cerebral cortex?

7. What is the name of the structure that connects the hemispheres of the cortex?

8. Whose ideas about phrenology introduced the concept of localization of functions in the brain?

9. What is the name of the procedure in which tissue from a human fetus is implanted into the *substantia nigra* of a person suffering from Parkinson's disease?

10. What structure in the central core of the brain performs the functions of a complex switchboard?

11. What term is used to refer to the space that neurotransmitters cross in their journey from an axon terminal to a receptor on another neuron?

12. Who used electrical stimulation in his attempt to determine the functions of different parts of the brain?

13. What is the name given to the part of a neuron that has receptors for receiving messages from other neurons?

14. What German philosopher and physicist may have been the first to speculate concerning the effect of separating the two hemispheres of the brain?

15. What type of behavior could occur even if a person's spinal cord were severed at the neck?

16. What term is used to describe the problem of the man who mistook his wife's head for his hat?

17. Which part of a neuron lies between the dendrites and the axon and manufactures nutrients for the neuron?

18. What structure in the limbic system is most deeply involved in aggressive behavior?

_____ 19. What name is given to the chemical substances that are released by the endocrine glands?

_____ 20. What structure in the limbic system is most likely to be strongly activated when you are storing information in your memory?

_____ 21. What term is used to refer to difficulty in the production or comprehension of language?

_____ 22. What name is given to the part of the brain that includes the hypothalamus, the amygdala, and the hippocampus?

_____ 23. Whose interest in telepathy led him to study psychiatry and to do pioneering work on the electroencephalogram?

_____ 24. What area of the brain receives the neural communication telling you that a fly has landed on the tip of your nose?

Essay Questions

Suggested answers for the essay questions are included at the back of your study guide.

1. Something warm falls into your lap while you are eating at an Italian restaurant. Describe the route of the neural impulses that occur from the moment the chunk of meatball falls in your lap until the moment you reach down to remove it.

2. Explain what neurotransmitters do and how they affect behavior and mental processes.

3. Imagine that you are a psychology major who has decided to specialize in the neuroscience perspective. Explain why you have chosen this perspective as you would explain it on your application for graduate school.

4. Describe methods that are used to identify the functions of specific areas of the brain.

5. Describe in sequence the processes that occur as a neural impulse moves from the axon terminal of one neuron to an axon terminal of the next neuron.

Multiple-Choice Test I

For the multiple-choice items, choose the best of the answers provided. Check your work with the answers at the back of your study guide, and be sure you understand why the keyed answers are correct.

1. When the brain receives information that the food in your mouth is hot and sweet, the nervous system is performing its _____ function
   a. perceptive
   b. somatic
   c. autonomic
   d. sensory

2. The spinal cord is part of the _____ nervous system.
   a. somatic
   b. peripheral
   c. central
   d. autonomic

3. Sensory neurons and motor neurons are connected by
   a. glial cells.
   b. synapses.
   c. association neurons.
   d. spinal ganglia.

4. Which of the following concerning spinal reflexes is *not* true?
   a. The impulses involved travel very rapidly.
   b. They involve both sensory and motor neurons.
   c. They can occur without intervention by the cerebral cortex.
   d. They are regulated by structures in the brain stem.

5. During the resting potential of a neuron, molecules of neurotransmitters can be found
   a. at receptor sites.
   b. surrounding the soma.
   c. in synaptic vesicles.
   d. outside the semipermeable membrane.

6. The process that determines whether a neuron will fire when both excitatory and inhibitory potentials are being received is most similar to
   a. throwing a balloon at a brick wall.
   b. mixing blue and yellow paint.
   c. adding positive and negative numbers.
   d. pulling the trigger of a gun.

7. The "all-or-none response" is associated with the behavior of
   a. sodium ions.
   b. brainstem functions.
   c. endocrine glands.
   d. neurons.

8. Acupuncture, jogging, and pregnancy have all been associated with the body's production of
   a. endorphins.
   b. norepinephrine.
   c. dopamine.
   d. GABA.

9. Neurotransmitters are
   a. excitatory.
   b. inhibitory.
   c. either excitatory or inhibitory.
   d. neither excitatory nor inhibitory.

10. The pituitary gland is called the "master gland" and is located close to the
    a. central fissure.
    b. somatosensory cortex.
    c. hypothalamus.
    d. kidneys.

11. Phrenology was based on the assumption that
    a. behavior affects the development of the brain.
    b. there is localization of functions in the brain.
    c. all neurons are association neurons.
    d. all of the above are true.

12. Difficulty in production of language is associated with _____ area; difficulty in comprehension of language is associated with _____ area.
    a. Wernicke's; Wernicke's
    b. Wernicke's; Broca's
    c. Broca's; Wernicke's
    d. Broca's; Broca's

13. The limbic system is most heavily involved in
    a. emotional behavior.
    b. cerebral reflexes.
    c. sensory integration.
    d. control of bodily functions.

14. If you were to compare a human brain to a sheep brain, you would find
    a. that the cortex of the human brain is more convoluted.
    b. that the ratio of brain weight to body weight is greater for humans.
    c. that the cortex accounts for a larger proportion of the human brain.
    d. all of the above.

15. A woman who had "sensory neglect syndrome" used eyebrow pencil and mascara on her right eye but not on her left eye. One would suspect that she has a tumor or lesion in her
    a. occipital lobe.
    b. corpus callosum.
    c. medial geniculate nucleus.
    d. somatosensory cortex.

16. The man who continued to wash his hands until he had used up an entire cake of soap would be suspected of having damage to the association area of his _____ lobes.
    a. frontal
    b. occipital
    c. temporal
    d. parietal

17. The limbic system includes all of the following *except* the
    a. thalamus.
    b. hypothalamus.
    c. hippocampus.
    d. amygdala.

18. The investigator who said "these alpha waves suggest that she was alert but relaxed" was using information from
    a. positron emission tomography (PET).
    b. electroencephalography (EEG).
    c. magnetic resonance imaging (MRI).
    d. computer-assisted axial tomography (CAT).

19. Research of Olds and Milner suggested that pleasure centers of the brain are in the
    a. cerebellum.
    b. hypothalamus.
    c. hippocampus.
    d. somatosensory cortex.

20. Damage to the brain differs most dramatically from damage to other parts of the body in that it is
    a. usually fatal.
    b. self-propagating.
    c. difficult to detect.
    d. permanent.

21. The purpose of brain grafts for people who are suffering from Parkinson's disease is
    a. to provide nutrients to damaged areas of the brain.
    b. to prevent the reabsorption of inhibitory neurotransmitters.
    c. to stimulate regeneration of neurons.
    d. to increase the supply of dopamine in the brain.

22. Studies of people with split brains have been made possible as a result of surgically severing the corpus callosum to relieve the symptoms of
    a. epilepsy.
    b. visual agnosia.
    c. agoraphobia.
    d. Parkinson's disease.

23. Who won the Nobel prize for his research on the question that was first proposed by Gustave Fechner?
    a. Roger Sperry
    b. Hans Berger
    c. Ulric Neisser
    d. Wilder Penfield

24. The left hemisphere of the brain appears to be dominant in all of the following *except*
    a. analytical ability.
    b. spatial ability.
    c. verbal ability.
    d. mathematical ability.

25. Which of the following statements is most accurate concerning the two hemispheres of the brain?
    a. The right hemisphere is dominant in most people.
    b. Highly creative people have an unusually well-developed right hemisphere.
    c. The difference between the hemispheres is primarily in the frontal lobes.
    d. The hemispheres interact to perform complex functions.

Multiple-Choice Test II

For the multiple-choice items, choose the best of the answers provided. Check your work with the answers in the back of your study guide, and be sure you understand why the keyed answers are correct.

1. When your brain sends the message that results in your writing your name, it is performing its _____ function.
   a. motor
   b. autonomic
   c. prehensile
   d. somatic

2. The neurons that connect the brain and spinal cord with the involuntary muscles of your heart and stomach are part of the _____ nervous system.
   a. somatosensory
   b. autonomic
   c. somatic
   d. visceral

3. If the dendrites of a neuron can be compared to the branches of a tree, the _____ can be compared to the trunk of the tree.
   a. soma
   b. nodes
   c. synapse
   d. axon

4. Which of the following is *not* true of a neuron's resting potential?
   a. The semipermeable membrane prevents sodium ions from passing through.
   b. Protein ions are trapped inside the cell membrane.
   c. The sodium, potassium, and protein ions are all negatively charged.
   d. The balance between positive and negative charges is very delicate.

5. The relationship between the receptors found on dendrites and molecules of neurotransmitters is most similar to
   a. locks and keys.
   b. bullets and guns.
   c. baseballs and mitts.
   d. magnets and metals.

6. We can tell the difference between a slap on the back and a light touch on the back because more intense stimulation causes
   a. neural impulses to travel faster.
   b. neurons to produce larger action potentials.
   c. more neurons to fire.
   d. all of the above.

7. Neurotransmitters are responsible for synaptic transmission in
   a. the peripheral nervous system.
   b. the spinal cord.
   c. the brain.
   d. all of the above.

8. Research suggests that neurotransmitters may be involved in
   a. learning and memory.
   b. mental disorders.
   c. regulation of blood pressure.
   d. all of the above.

9. Recent research suggests that neurotransmitter functions are altered by
   a. fluorescent lights.
   b. drugs.
   c. protein deficiency.
   d. hair sprays.

10. The endocrine system is comprised of _____ that produce _____.
    a. vesicles; neurotransmitters
    b. glands; neurotransmitters
    c. vesicles; hormones
    d. glands; hormones

11. Both Broca's area and Wernicke's area are located in the _____ hemisphere of the cerebral cortex. Broca's area is in the frontal lobe and Wernicke's area is in the _____ lobe.
    a. left; temporal
    b. left; parietal
    c. right; temporal
    d. left; parietal

12. The ability to produce nonsensical sentences with little difficulty suggests a lesion in _____ area; lack of ability to comprehend language suggests a lesion in _____ area.
    a. Wernicke's; Wernicke's
    b. Wernicke's; Broca's
    c. Broca's; Broca's
    d. Broca's; Wernicke's

13. If you could look at the brain of a brontosaurus, you would probably find that the largest structure is the
    a. amygdala.
    b. corpus callosum.
    c. somatosensory cortex.
    d. brain stem.

14. If you ran your finger over your head from the top of your nose to the top of your neck, you would pass over the frontal lobe first, the _____ lobe next, and the _____ lobe last.
    a. temporal; occipital
    b. parietal; occipital
    c. occipital; temporal
    d. temporal; parietal

15. The temporal lobe is to hearing as the _____ lobe is to vision.
    a. occipital
    b. frontal
    c. cerebral
    d. parietal

16. Penfield found that electrical stimulation to the _____ produced muscular twitches in his patients.
    a. motor cortex
    b. somatosensory area
    c. superior temporal lobe
    d. central fissure

17. Memory is to the association area of the temporal lobe as _____ is to the association area of the parietal lobe.
    a. control of bodily movements
    b. personality
    c. emotional control
    d. sensory integration

18. The psychosurgery that was performed on Julia was first suggested by Heinrich Kluver and Paul Bucy. The psychosurgery involved making a lesion in Julia's
    a. motor cortex.
    b. right frontal lobe.
    c. amygdala.
    d. hypothalamus.

19. To produce complex motor movements, the motor cortex works in conjunction with the
    a. cerebellum.
    b. thalamus.
    c. hippocampus.
    d. medulla oblongata.

20. The procedure that displays activity in parts of the brain by monitoring the use of glucose is called
    a. nuclear magnetic resonance (NMR).
    b. magnetic resonance imaging (MRI).
    c. computer-assisted axial tomography (CAT).
    d. positron emission tomography (PET).

21. Procedures in which tissue from the adrenal medulla has been implanted to an area of the brain called the *substantia nigra* has been used to treat _____ disease.
    a. Parkinson's
    b. Huntington's
    c. Crutzfeld-Jakob
    d. Alzheimer's

22. What is the primary ethical problem with the use of brain grafts?
    a. Patients often get worse instead of better.
    b. Many people feel that any form of psychosurgery is unethical.
    c. Some researchers believe that the best tissue for implants is from human fetuses.
    d. Implanted tissue from another person may affect the integrity of the self.

23. What would you do to try to determine whether Horatio has a split brain?
    a. Ask him to identify any object that comes in pairs, like shoes or bookends.
    b. Ask him to match the words and the melodies of songs.
    c. Have him feel a key with his left hand and tell you what it is.
    d. Have him order a handful of nails according to length.

24. The terms "analyzer" and "synthesizer" are used to refer to the
    a. brain and spinal cord.
    b. frontal and occipital lobes.
    c. left and right hemispheres.
    d. hippocampus and temporal lobe.

25. One of the controversies that has arisen as a result of research on hemispheric specialization concerns whether
    a. results from animal studies can be generalized to humans.
    b. PET scans support hemispheric specialization.
    c. there are sex differences in hemispheric superiority.
    d. neurotransmitters are responsible for hemispheric specialization.

Chapter 3

SENSATION AND PERCEPTION

Learning Objectives

After reading this chapter, you should be able to:

1. Discriminate between sensation and perception.

2. Compare and contrast absolute thresholds, signal detection theory, and difference thresholds.

3. Briefly explain Weber's Law.

4. Describe the three physical characteristics of visual stimuli and their corresponding psychological properties.

5. Identify the structures through which visual information passes successively from receptor to cortex.

6. Outline the Young-Helmholtz trichromatic, the Hering opponent-process, and the composite theories of color vision.

7. Describe the three physical characteristics of the auditory stimulus and their corresponding psychological properties.

8. Trace the sequence of transmission of a sound wave from the external world to the hair cells.

9. Outline the place and frequency theories of hearing.

10. Compare and contrast conduction deafness and nerve deafness.

11. Describe the mechanisms that mediate the senses of taste and smell.

12. Describe the receptor mechanisms for the skin senses.

13. Outline the essential features of the spinal pain-gate theory.

14. Contrast kinesthesis and equilibrium.

15. Describe the three primary components of perception: selection, organization, and interpretation.

16. Differentiate among the Gestalt organizing principles of figure-ground, similarity, proximity, closure, good continuation, and simplicity.

17. Identify the binocular and monocular cues for depth perception.

18. Describe the phenomena of size, shape, and color constancy.

19. Explain the experience of an illusion.

20. Describe the influence of expectation, motivation, and early experience on perception.

Working with Names and Terms

From the alphabetized list below, choose the name or term that answers the question, using each name and term only once. Answers are at the back of your study guide.

aerial haze
amplitude
attention
binocular disparity
closure
complementary
cones
cornea
dichromat
fovea
Helmholtz, Hermann von
Hering, Ewald

kinesthesis
olfactory mucosa
ossicles
oval window
papillae
rods
shape constancy
signal detection
transduction
Wald, George
Weber, Ernst
Wundt, Wilhelm

_____ 1. What theory recognizes that the absolute threshold is affected by response bias?

_____ 2. What cue for three-dimensional vision depends upon a slight difference between the images on our two retinas?

_____ 3. What term is used to refer to the bumps on the tongue where taste buds are found?

_____ 4. What process results in chemical molecules being converted to neural impulses by the olfactory system?

_____ 5. Which basic law of form perception accounts for our overlooking typos and omitted letters when we proofread a paper we've written?

_____ 6. What type of photoreceptors do nocturnal animals, like rats and owls, have on their retinas?

_____ 7. What term do we use to refer to the selection process in perception?

_____ 8. Who proposed the idea that the size of the j.n.d. increases with the size of the reference stimulus?

_____ 9. Where in the auditory system does the medium sound waves travel in change from air to fluid?

_____ 10. Where are the receptors for your sense of smell?

_____ 11. What cue for three-dimensional vision is enhanced by smog?

_____ 12. What are the three small bony structures called the malleus, incus, and stapes?

_____ 13. Whose work supported the trichromatic theory of color vision by identifying three types of cones on the retina?

_____ 14. What is the first structure light encounters as it enters the eye?

_____ 15. What explains why we perceive a plate as round even though its image on the retina is oval?

_____ 16. What term is used to describe a person who cannot distinguish between red and green?

_____ 17. Who proposed theories to explain both color vision and pitch perception?

_____ 18. What area on the retina has excellent acuity?

_____ 19. Who originated the opponent-process theory of color vision?

_____ 20. What sense makes it possible for you to touch the tip of your nose with the tip of your finger, even in the dark?

_____ 21. Whose research using a metronome provided clues that we organize sensory information into specific forms and patterns?

_____ 22. What characteristic of wave forms is associated with brightness in vision and loudness in audition?

_____ 23. Where is iodopsin found?

_____ 24. What is the relationship between two colors that produce gray when they are mixed together?

Essay Questions

Suggested answers for the essay questions are included at the back of your study guide.

1. If a number of people witnessed an argument that culminated in a fight, they would disagree in their reports of the incident. How do you explain this?

2. An artist is standing on a hilltop and is going to paint a picture of the rural landscape she sees. How can the artist create the illusion of depth in the picture?

3. Discuss your opinion concerning whether humans would be better off if our senses were more sensitive than they are.

4. Describe sensations experienced as you lunch on a hamburger and orange soda pop.

Multiple-Choice Test I

For the multiple-choice items, choose the best of the answers provided. Check your work with the answers at the back of your study guide, being sure you understand why the keyed answers are correct.

1. A subject is sitting in a soundproof room wearing earphones. When a light comes on, the subject tells the experimenter whether or not she heard a tone. the experimenter is measuring the subject's
   a. auditory orientation.
   b. subliminal hearing.
   c. absolute threshold.
   d. vestibular sensitivity.

2. Signal detection is an improvement over the traditional concept of the absolute threshold because it
   a. eliminates sources of internal noise.
   b. decreases the variability of sensory responses.
   c. defines the absolute threshold as a probability of detection.
   d. recognizes the influence of response bias.

3. When you switch a light bulb from 100 watts to 150 watts, the increase in brightness if not as great as when you switch the light bulb from 50 watts to 100 watts. This difference in perceived brightness is best explained by
   a. Weber's law.
   b. Emmett's law.
   c. signal detection theory.
   d. Hering's constant.

4. The minimum amount of stimulus change needed for two stimuli to be distinguishable is called
   a. the difference threshold.
   b. the detectability limen.
   c. Weber's constant.
   d. Fechner's unit.

5. If a visual stimulus is described as having a wavelength of 500 nanometers, the stimulus would be perceived as
   a. very bright.
   b. very dim.
   c. green.
   d. white.

6. Light is focused on the retina by
   a. the cornea.
   b. the lens.
   c. the pupil.
   d. all of the above.

7. The saturation of a hue could be *decreased* by
   a. increasing the amplitude of the wave forms.
   b. adding light of a complementary hue.
   c. decreasing the band width of the wave forms.
   d. doing any of the above.

8. The j.n.d. for colors will be the lowest if the stimulus is projected
   a. on the fovea.
   b. in the area where the optic nerve leaves the retina.
   c. on the periphery of the retina.
   d. directly onto ganglion cells.

9. The Young-Helmholtz theory of color vision is supported by research showing
   a. that the hue of afterimages is complementary to the hue of the stimulus.
   b. that almost all dichromats confuse red and green.
   c. that there are three types of cones on the retina.
   d. all of the above.

10. The current view is that color vision is best explained by
    a. the trichromatic theory of Young and Helmholtz.
    b. the opponent-process theory of Hering.
    c. a composite of the trichromatic theory and the opponent-process theory.
    d. Hubel and Wiesel's concept of hypercomplex cells.

11. Wavelength is to color in vision as frequency is to _____ in audition.
    a. loudness
    b. amplitude
    c. complexity
    d. pitch

12. The psychological property of sounds that make it possible to tell whether a 500-hertz tone was played by a piano or a trumpet is
    a. timbre.
    b. saturation.
    c. complexity.
    d. reverberation.

13. The basilar membrane is located
    a. in the middle ear.
    b. in the cochlea.
    c. behind the tympanic membrane.
    d. between the ossicles.

14. The theories of hearing proposed by Helmholtz and by Békésy claim that we perceive pitch because different areas of the basilar membrane are sensitive to different frequencies. Their theories are called _____ theories.
    a. localization
    b. place
    c. specificity
    d. frequency

15. If an infection interferes with the ability of the ossicles to transmit sound waves properly, a person will experience _____ deafness.
    a. conduction
    b. transduction
    c. inner ear
    d. mechanical

16. Amoore's stereochemical theory of olfaction claims that the molecules of the seven basic odors
    a. attach themselves to different areas of the olfactory membrane.
    b. produce different patterns of excitatory and inhibitory impulses.
    c. fit particular receptors in the olfactory mucosa.
    d. stimulate the release of different neurotransmitters by olfactory receptors.

17. Which of the following sensory receptors are replaced about every 11 days?
    a. hair cells on the basilar membrane
    b. cones in the fovea
    c. hair cells in the semicircular canals
    d. taste receptors on the tongue

18. All of the following are basic sensations of the skin senses *except*
    a. hot.
    b. cold.
    c. touch.
    d. pain.

19. According to the current state of research and theory about pain and its control, which of the following is *least* likely to be accurate?
    a. Pain signals must pass through a "neuronal gate" in the spinal cord.
    b. Receptors specifically for pain are widely distributed on the body's surface.
    c. Perception of pain can be affected by a wide variety of psychological factors.
    d. Neurotransmitters called "endorphins" are involved in the control of pain.

20. Damage to the semicircular canals would be most serious problem for a(n)
    a. oral hygienist.
    b. ditch digger.
    c. tightrope walker.
    d. animal trainer.

21. The Gestalt principles of perceptual organization include all of the following *except*
    a. simplicity.
    b. closure.
    c. proximity.
    d. interposition.

22. The cue for depth and distance that we get from the muscles that move the eyes is a _____ cue that is called _____.
    a. binocular; retinal disparity
    b. binocular; convergence
    c. monocular; retinal disparity
    d. monocular; convergence

23. The retinal image of the cat is larger than the retinal image of the dog that is chasing the cat, but the viewer perceives that the dog is larger. This is an example of
    a. Emmett's law.
    b. Weber's law.
    c. size constancy.
    d. interposition.

24. Which of the following illusions is a result of physical distortion of the stimuli?
    a. the size of the people in the Ames room
    b. the illusory lake covering the highway in the distance
    c. the tree that seems taller after it has been cut down.
    d. the impossible figures of Escher.

25. People sometimes misinterpret the behavior of others, such as their gestures, tone of voice, or eye contact. These misinterpretations could occur because of _____ of the viewer.
    a. the motivation
    b. the perceptual set
    c. the past experience
    d. any of the above

Multiple-Choice Test II

For the multiple-choice items, choose the best of the answers provided. Check your work with the answers at the back of your study guide, and be sure you understand why the keyed answers are correct.

1. What happens when transduction occurs in a sensory system?
    a. Environmental energy is transformed into neural impulses.
    b. Other sensory systems are alerted to the presence of a stimulus.
    c. Signals from the thalamus are received by the somatosensory cortex.
    d. Receptor cells become polarized.

2. When a person's hearing is being tested, tones of different frequencies are increased in amplitude until the person reports hearing the tones. This type of hearing test measures a person's _____ for the tones.
    a. absolute threshold
    b. subliminal perception
    c. vestibular sensitivity
    d. transduction potential

3. What would you experience if you were looking at a star whose brightness is at your absolute threshold?
   a. You would have to concentrate to see the star continuously.
   b. The star would appear to vary in its distance from you.
   c. The star would become brighter as you continued to fixate on it.
   d. First you would see the star, and then you wouldn't.

4. There are 10 lighted candles in a room, and a viewer can just barely detect a difference in brightness when another candle is lit. If there were 50 candles in the room, Weber's law tells us that _____ more candle(s) will have to be lit before the viewer can detect a difference in brightness.
   a. one
   b. two
   c. five
   d. ten

5. If a subject is repeatedly asked if she can detect the difference between a reference stimulus and a comparison stimulus, the experimenter is measuring her
   a. Weber's constant.
   b. difference threshold.
   c. transduction differential.
   d. absolute threshold.

6. The wavelength of electromagnetic energy is largely responsible for our perception of
   a. saturation.
   b. complexity.
   c. brightness.
   d. hue.

7. A physicist is most likely to describe wavelengths of light waves in terms of their
   a. hue.
   b. saturation.
   c. purity.
   d. complexity.

8. Rods transmit neural impulses to _____; cones transmit neural impulses to _____.
   a. bipolar cells; bipolar cells
   b. bipolar cells; ganglion cells
   c. ganglion cells; bipolar cells
   d. ganglion cells; ganglion cells

9. The absolute threshold for brightness will be lowest if the stimulus is projected
   a. on the fovea.
   b. near the blind spot.
   c. on the periphery of the retina.
   d. in an area where there are many bipolar cells.

10. The opponent-process theory of color vision is supported by research showing
    a. that there are three types of cones on the retina.
    b. that the hue of afterimages is complementary to the hue of the stimulus.
    c. that almost all dichromats confuse blue and green.
    d. all of the above.

11. Current views concerning theories of color vision suggest that _____ theory applies at the retina, and that _____ applies at the thalamus.
    a. trichromatic; trichromatic
    b. trichromatic; opponent-process
    c. opponent-process; trichromatic
    d. opponent-process; opponent-process

12. Wave amplitude is the primary determinant of _____ in vision and _____ in audition.
    a. hue; pitch
    b. hue; brightness
    c. brightness; pitch
    d. brightness; loudness

13. A 100-hertz tone at 100 decibels would be perceived as _____ in pitch and _____ in loudness.
    a. high; high
    b. high; low
    c. low; high
    d. low; low

14. The retina in the visual system is most similar to the _____ in the auditory system.
    a. tympanic membrane
    b. basilar membrane
    c. oval window
    d. round window

15. Theories of hearing that claim we perceive pitch because the basilar membrane vibrates in synchrony with the frequency of the stimulus are called _____ theories.
    a. literal
    b. monotonic
    c. synchrony
    d. frequency

16. Nerve deafness or inner ear deafness can be a result of
    a. diseases during pregnancy.
    b. exposure to loud noises or loud music.
    c. old age.
    d. any of the above.

17. It has been proposed that molecules of neurotransmitters fit different receptor sites on neurons as keys fit locks. A similar idea has been proposed by Amoore to explain how we perceive
    a. pain.
    b. gravity.
    c. odors.
    d. tastes.

18. There are no taste buds on the _____ of the tongue.
    a. middle
    b. tip
    c. back
    d. sides

19. The demonstration showing that simultaneous exposure to cold and warm stimuli produces the sensation of hot supports the theory that sensations from the skin are produced by
    a. patterns of stimulation.
    b. receptor cells that produce variable action potentials.
    c. Pacinian corpuscles and receptors located in hair follicles.
    d. receptor cells that can release either excitatory neurotransmitters or inhibitory neurotransmitters.

20. A person with poor kinesthetic sensitivity would be *least* likely to be a(n)
    a. astronomer.
    b. gymnast.
    c. reporter.
    d. florist.

21. All of the following are basic types of perceptual organization *except*
    a. form perception.
    b. perceptual constancies.
    c. figure-ground perception.
    d. depth and distance perception.

22. Who would be most likely to apply the Gestalt principles of perceptual grouping in his or her work?
    a. the coach of a volleyball team
    b. the author of a cookbook
    c. the president of a large shoe company
    d. the director of a marching band

23. David Hubel and Thorsten Wiesel found simple, complex, and hypercomplex cells in the visual cortex of a cat. They suggested that these cells are involved in
    a. form perception.
    b. depth and distance perception.
    c. color vision.
    d. misperception of stimuli.

24. As you come over the hill and look at the long stretch of highway ahead, you notice that the highway appears to get narrower as it recedes from you. This is a _____ cue to the perception of depth and distance called _____.
    a. monocular; linear perspective
    b. monocular; convergence
    c. binocular; linear perspective
    d. binocular; convergence

25. Expectations, motivation, and experience are most influential in the _____ process of perception.
    a. analysis
    b. synthesis
    c. interpretation
    d. organization

Chapter 4

MOTIVATION AND EMOTION

Learning Objectives

After studying this chapter, you should be able to:

1. Define motivation.

2. Present the historical perspective on the term instinct and discuss the main features of instinct theory.

3. Identify the major tenet of sociobiology.

4. Discuss the concepts of drive, drive reduction, and homeostasis in the context of drive theory.

5. Outline the main features of arousal theory.

6. Discuss the main argument of opponent-process theory.

7. Discuss the main tenets of incentive theory.

8. Identify the physiological factors involved in hunger, eating, and satiety.

9. Discuss the various factors that are involved in the development of human obesity, and in dieting and weight reduction.

10. Describe the behaviors and causes associated with two eating disorders: anorexia and bulimia.

11. Describe the four phases of the sexual response in men and women.

12. Describe the role of androgens in physiological sexual differentiation.

13. Discuss the role of experience, external stimuli, and attitudes in sexual behavior and motivation.

14. Discuss the possible factors that contribute to homosexual orientation.

15. Outline Freud's theory of human motivation.

16. Describe the need theories of Murray and Maslow.

17. Review the research on the need for achievement.

18. Compare and contrast intrinsic and extrinsic motivations.

19. Describe attempts to increase work motivation and job satisfaction.

20. Define emotion, and describe ways of classifying emotions.

21. Discuss the bodily changes associated with emotions.

22. Discuss the James-Lange theory of emotion, and Cannon's criticism of this theory.

23. Describe the two-factor theory of emotions.

24. Describe the varied ways emotions may be expressed, and identify universal versus culture specific expressions.

25. Describe the research on the facial feedback hypothesis.

Working with Names and Terms

From the alphabetized list below, choose the name or term that answers the question, using each name and term only once. Answers are at the back of your study guide.

anterior
autonomic
extrinsic
Darwin, Charles
fitness
fixed-action pattern
homeostasis
Hull, Clark
incentive
James, William
Johnson, Virginia
Kinsey, Alfred

Maslow, Abraham
Murray, Henry
opponent-process
Plutchik, Robert
refractory
Schachter, Stanley
set point
sexually dimorphic
sociobiology
testosterone
ventromedial
Wilson, Edmund

_____ 1. Who claimed that facial expressions have evolved in humans because they are adaptive?

_____ 2. Who compiled a list of 20 human social motives?

_____ 3. What hormone belongs to the class of hormones called androgens?

_____ 4. What is measured by the number of children you produce to carry your genes to the next generation?

_____ 5. What theory of motivation emphasizes the chocolate cake instead of the hunger drive?

_____ 6. Who developed a three-dimensional classification of emotions?

_____ 7. What type of motivation is satisfied by money, praise, and a reserved parking space?

_____ 8. Whose research and publications pioneered the study of sexual behavior in America?

_____ 9. What biological process resembles a thermostat in that its function is to keep physiological processes at an optimum level?

_____ 10. Who collaborated with James Singer in a famous experiment designed to test the two-factor theory of motivation?

_____ 11. Whose theory of emotion claims that you don't feel afraid until you start running out of the burning building?

_____ 12. What term is used to refer to a person's "natural weight"?

_____ 13. Who collaborated with William Masters in studying the physiological aspects of sexual intercourse?

_____ 14. What part of the hypothalamus is apparently involved in telling us it is time to stop eating?

_____ 15. What theory of motivation attempts to explain behaviors like drug addiction and skydiving?

_____ 16. Whose theory of motivation emphasized the concepts of "drive" and "drive reduction"?

_____ 17. Who was the originator of sociobiology and claimed that the primary goal of a group is to protect its genes from extinction?

_____ 18. Whose view of motivation claims that people cannot be concerned with motives like belongingness and self-esteem if they are hungry and homeless?

_____ 19. What term is used to describe species whose members are either male or female?

_____ 20. What term has replaced "instinct" in the vocabulary of ethologists?

_____ 21. What name is given to the interval that immediately follows orgasm and resolution in males?

_____ 22. What division of the nervous system regulates the physiological components of emotion?

_____ 23. What perspective claims that altruistic behavior is selfishly motivated to preserve the genes of the group?

_____ 24. What part of the hypothalamus appears to be larger in homosexual males than it is in heterosexual males?

Essay Questions

Suggested answers for the essay questions are included at the back of your study guide.

1. How does the sexual behavior of humans differ from the sexual behavior of other animals?

2. Write a short article refuting the claim that people are obese because they lack will power.

3. Describe a good job in terms of its effectiveness in satisfying the motives of workers.

4. Discuss benefits that can be derived from smiling.

Multiple-Choice Test I

For the multiple choice items, choose the best of the answers provided. check your work with the answers at the back of your study guide, and be sure you understand why the keyed answers are correct.

1. The definition of motivation states that motivation arouses and activates an organism and
   a. increases the probability of survival of both the individual and the species.
   b. maintains the integrity of the organism's psychological and biological systems.
   c. preserves the homeostasis of the organism.
   d. directs the organism toward a specific goal.

2. A book entitled *The Selfish Gene* is most likely to take the _____ approach to understanding behavior.
   a. sociobiological
   b. drive reduction
   c. opponent-process
   d. psychodynamic

3. In Hull's drive theory of motivation, one of the important concepts is
   a. deficiency.
   b. homeostasis.
   c. fixed-action pattern.
   d. sign stimuli.

4. The opponent-process theory of motivation says that people initially use drugs to experience a high, and that they continue to use them to
   a. recapture the experience of being high.
   b. escape the unpleasant experience of withdrawal.
   c. maintain a constant level of emotional arousal.
   d. conform to the behavior of peers.

5. The incentive theory of motivation emphasizes that the power of an incentive to motivate behavior depends upon
   a. the temporary state and enduring goals of the person.
   b. acquired habits and cultural norms.
   c. the value of the incentive and the expectation of obtaining it.
   d. the difference between the current state of arousal and the optimum state of arousal.

6. Why did the fat rat pictured in the text get so obese?
   a. Researchers removed its ventromedial hypothalamus.
   b. Large quantities of insulin were injected into its blood stream.
   c. It was prevented from engaging in any physical activity.
   d. It ate soggy chocolate chip cookies.

7. Study of Danish adoption records suggests that the physiological mechanisms that regulate body weight are determined by
   a. heredity.
   b. the prenatal environment.
   c. eating habits.
   d. activity level.

8. The research of Joyce Slochower showed that obese people, compared with normal-weight people, are more likely to
   a. eat more when others are present.
   b. overeat when they are stressed.
   c. spend more time thinking about food.
   d. have occupations that involve little or no physical activity.

9. Which of the following statements is most accurate?
   a. The longer a person diets, the easier it becomes to lose weight.
   b. Exercise is of little value in weight reduction because the appetite that results cancels the calories consumed.
   c. Dieters' appetites decrease as they continue to diet.
   d. Most dieters gain back all the weight they lost by dieting.

10. The text suggests that exercise is an important aspect of weight loss because it
    a. may lower the set point.
    b. raises metabolic rate.
    c. burns off calories.
    d. does all of the above.

11. The four stages proposed by Masters and Johnson are excitement, plateau, orgasm, and
    a. refraction.
    b. relaxation.
    c. resolution.
    d. withdrawal.

12. What effect does the presence of androgens have in prenatal development?
    a. They determine the sexual orientation of males.
    b. They determine the sexual orientation of females.
    c. They trigger development of male sex organs.
    d. They trigger development of female reproductive organs.

13. Freud thought that constraints imposed by reality and morals can result in _____ of the energy generated by the sex drive into activities that are realistic and moral.
    a. sublimation
    b. redirection
    c. displacement
    d. cathecting

14. In their studies on the need for approval, Douglas Crowns and David Marlowe found that the strength of this need is related to
    a. aggressiveness.
    b. conformity.
    c. self-esteem.
    d. achievement motivation.

15. How did David McClelland measure nAch?
    a. He observed people while they were participating in group discussions.
    b. He analyzed the stories people told about pictures.
    c. He asked people to set goals for a variety of activities.
    d. He measured how long people continued to work at an impossible task.

16. Research has shown that people with a high need for achievement tend to choose tasks that are _____ difficult; people with high fear of success tend to choose tasks that are _____ difficult.
    a. very; very
    b. very; moderately
    c. moderately; very
    d. moderately; moderately

17. Using college students as subjects, Deci and Ryan did an experiment in which students in the experimental group were paid a dollar for solving each of four puzzles. What hypothesis was being tested?
    a. People evaluate their performance by comparing it with the performance of others.
    b. Persistence at a task is increased if rewards are given frequently.
    c. Money is not valued as highly as praise in some situations.
    d. Extrinsic rewards reduce intrinsic motivation.

18. What does Z-theory emphasize?
    a. good relations between labor and management
    b. pleasant work environments
    c. job security and company loyalty
    d. opportunity and personality responsibility

19. The sympathetic and parasympathetic nervous systems are the two divisions of the _____ nervous system.
    a. peripheral
    b. somatic
    c. affective
    d. autonomic

20. A sophisticated polygraph can record
    a. electrical activity of the brain.
    b. signals from the autonomic nervous system.
    c. activity of skeletal muscles.
    d. all of the above.

21. Which of the following criticisms did Walter Cannon make of William James' theory of emotion?
    a. People cannot accurately perceive the activity of visceral organs.
    b. The autonomic nervous system is cortically controlled.
    c. The patterns of autonomic nervous system activity are very complex.
    d. Cannon made all of the above criticisms.

22. Research has supported William James' belief that
    a. physiological arousal precedes subjective awareness of emotion.
    b. people can perceive changes in autonomic activity accurately.
    c. different emotions produce different patterns of autonomic activity.
    d. the thalamus plays a major role in integrating the components of emotion.

23. There is evidence that emotional responses can be intensified if the emotion-provoking event occurs when is person's arousal level is already high for some other reason, like caffeine consumption. This evidence supports the _____ theory of emotion.
    a. Eysenck-Solomon
    b. two-factor
    c. Cannon-Bard
    d. James-Lange

24. There were two independent variables in the Schachter and Singer study on two-factor theory. One independent variable concerned whether or not subjects were informed of the effects of epinephrine. The other independent variable concerned
    a. the behavior of the confederates.
    b. the sex of the subjects.
    c. the amount the subjects were paid.
    d. the quantity of epinephrine injected.

25. The advice in the song that says "smile when you're feeling blue" is supported by the
    a. research of Schachter and Singer.
    b. cross-sectional study of Ekman and Friesen.
    c. facial feedback hypothesis.
    d. Cannon-Bard theory of emotion.

Multiple-Choice Test II

For the multiple-choice items, choose the best of the answers provided. Check your work with the answers at the back of your study guide, and be sure you understand why the keyed answers are correct.

1. The internal signal that tells a salmon that it is time to return to its birthplace is called a(n)
    a. instinct activator.
    b. genetic marker.
    c. sign stimulus.
    d. action-pattern releaser.

2. Defining hunger in terms of the number or hours an organism has been deprived of food is an example of how Hull's theory allowed psychologists to
    a. distinguish between physiological and social motives.
    b. distinguish between arousal and activation.
    c. quantify the dependent variable in experiments.
    d. operationalize the concept of drive.

3. The inverted-U function that is associated with the arousal theory of motivation shows the relationship between level of arousal and
   a. performance on various tasks.
   b. activity level.
   c. homeostasis.
   d. subjective state of the organism.

4. Push is to the drive theory of motivation as pull is to the _____ theory of motivation.
   a. incentive
   b. arousal
   c. opponent-process
   d. instinct

5. Research suggests that the experience of hunger is related to
   a. contractions of stomach muscles.
   b. blood sugar level.
   c. autonomic activity.
   d. all of the above.

6. Set point is most closely related to
   a. body structure.
   b. insulin production.
   c. metabolic rate.
   d. calorie intake.

7. What happens when a person loses weight by dieting?
   a. The set point is lowered.
   b. Insulin production decreases.
   c. Metabolic rate goes down.
   d. All of the above occur.

8. Joyce Slochower did a study comparing obese and normal-weight subjects. Her dependent variable was
   a. the amount of work done to earn a candy bar.
   b. the number of cashew nuts eaten.
   c. the calorie content of subjects' ten favorite foods.
   d. the amount of time spent thinking about food.

9. The research of Judith Rodin demonstrated how different foods affect
   a. production of insulin.
   b. metabolic rate.
   c. functions of the hypothalamus.
   d. energy level.

10. Harry Harlow's study using rhesus monkeys as subjects emphasized the importance of _____ on adult sexual behavior.
    a. androgens and estrogens
    b. self-exploration and stimulation
    c. social contact
    d. visual stimulation

11. It has been suggested that homosexuality is causally related to
    a. poor relationships with same-sex parents.
    b. stress during pregnancy.
    c. fantasies of same-sex friends during masturbation.
    a. all of the above.

12. Recent evidence indicates that _____ play a strong role in determining sexual orientation.
    a. psychodynamic conflicts
    b. biological factors
    c. early sexual experiences
    d. conditioning and learning

13. *Eros* and *thanatos* as defined by Freud are most accurately associated with
    a. sex and aggression.
    b. love and hate.
    c. sex and reproduction.
    d. selfishness and altruism.

14. Which of the following attributes are parents of children with high achievement motivation most likely to encourage in their children?
    a. task orientation and persistence
    b. high self-esteem and assertiveness
    c. independence and self-sufficiency
    d. extraversion and fair-mindedness

15. Janis has high nAch, and being good at math is important to her. She has just gotten a score of 84 on a math test. What does the Self-Evaluation Maintenance Model suggest that she will do?
    a. She will ask her friends what score they made on the test.
    b. She won't tell anyone what score she got.
    c. She will decide that math really isn't so important.
    d. She will accuse the teacher of giving a test that is too difficult.

16. Rational-economic motives are _____; self-actualization motives are _____.
    a. intrinsic; extrinsic
    b. extrinsic; intrinsic
    c. innate; learned
    d. learned; innate

17. All of the following are components of emotion *except*
    a. expressive.
    b. physiological.
    c. subjective.
    d. cognitive.

18. As examples of complex or mixed emotions, the text cites
    a. jealousy and disappointment.
    b. anxiety and apprehension.
    c. boredom and annoyance.
    d. all of the above.

19. When you are frightened, activity of your sympathetic nervous system will result in
    a. dilation of your pupils.
    b. increased activity of the salivary and tear glands.
    c. increased intestinal activity.
    d. all of the above.

20. Electrocardiograms are to heart rate as electroencephalograms are to
    a. the electrodermal response.
    b. finger pulse volume.
    c. pupillary dilation and constriction.
    d. electrical activity of the brain.

21. Which of the following criticism of the use of polygraphs in criminal investigations was made by the authors of the text?
    a. They detect guilt in guilty people less than half the time.
    b. Polygraphs are accurate, but the people who administer them are often biased.
    c. They frequently detect guilt in innocent people.
    d. Their test-retest reliability is very low.

22. Cannon and Bard both claimed that the integrative center for emotion is in the
    a. adrenal cortex.
    b. thalamus.
    c. limbic system.
    d. frontal lobe of the cortex.

23. Compared to other theories of emotion, the two-factor theory emphasizes
    a. patterns of neural activity.
    b. behavioral consequences of emotion.
    c. cognitive factors.
    d. the expressive component.

24. Darwin's belief that facial expressions have evolved as adaptive mechanisms in humans was supported by the _____ research of Ekman and Friesen.
    a. longitudinal
    b. cross-cultural
    c. physiological
    d. ethological

25. Ekman and his colleagues did a series of experiments in which subjects learned to pose the facial expressions of several emotions. The results of the studies provided strong support for the
    a. Cannon-Bard theory of emotion.
    b. James-Lange theory of emotion.
    c. two-factor theory of emotion.
    d. facial feedback hypothesis.

Chapter 5

STATES OF CONSCIOUSNESS

Learning Objectives

After studying this chapter, you should be able to:

1. Distinguish among subconscious, unconscious, and preconscious mental processes.

2. Describe the role of selective attention in consciousness.

3. Differentiate between the characteristics of effortful and automatic information processing.

4. Describe the physiological and behavioral characteristics of both REM and NREM sleep.

5. Describe the cyclical NREM-REM patterns observed during a normal night's sleep.

6. Describe the characteristics of the major sleep disorders: insomnia, sleepwalking, narcolepsy, and sleep apnea.

7. Summarize the effects of REM sleep deprivation.

8. Distinguish between two theories of dreaming: wish fulfillment and the activation-synthesis hypotheses.

9. Describe the procedures used in meditation and the characteristics of the altered state induced by meditation.

10. Outline the essential elements of hypnotic induction.

11. Describe the perceptual, behavioral, and memory changes that can be observed during hypnosis.

12. Define hypnotic susceptibility. What appears to be its major determinant?

13. Contrast the state and nonstate theories of hypnosis.

14. Describe the general characteristics of compounds that are called psychoactive drugs.

15. Outline the four major classes of psychoactive drugs and identify at least two specific drugs in each class.

Working with Names and Terms

From the alphabetized list below, choose the name or term that answers the question, using each name and term only once. Answers are at the back of your study guide.

activation-synthesis	Hofman, Albert
amnesia	hypermnesia
analgesics	introspection
anesthesia	James, William
Benson, Herbert	latent content
circadian rhythm	Mesmer, Anton
confabulation	mindfulness
delta	narcolepsy
depersonalization	psychoactive
dichotic listening	sleep apnea
dissociated consciousness	sleep spindles
hallucinogens	state

HALLUCINOGENS
LSD
1. What name is used to describe drugs like LSD, mescaline, and psilocybin?

ANTON MESMER
ANIMAL MAGNETISM→HYPNOSIS
2. Who brought hypnosis to the attention of the public and proposed the theory of "animal magnetism"?

(MINDFULNESS)
CON$\frac{s}{N}$: understanding & remember
3. What state should you be in as you concentrate on understanding and remembering the material in your text?

NARCOLEPSY
sudden sleeping spells
4. What sleep disorder could result in a person's being a menace on the highway?

ANALGESICS
opium
5. What class of drugs do opium and its derivatives belong to?

ACTIVATION-SYNTHESIS
dream theory: random neural firing
6. What hypothesis claims that dreams are the result of the brain's attempt to make sense of random neural firing?

SLEEP APNEA
breathing funny
7. What disorder is characterized by intervals in which there is suspension of breathing?

(CIRCADIAN RHYTHM)
biligical & behavioral cycle controlled by biological clock
8. What name is given to the biological and behavioral cycle that appears to be controlled by an internal biological clock?

9. What is a person experiencing when he or she does not respond to sensory stimuli, even stimuli that would ordinarily be painful?

ANESTHESIA — no sensory stimuli response

10. What name is given to drugs that alter conscious experience by altering the chemical activity of the brain?

PSYCHOACTIVE — alter conscious experience by altering chemical activity in brain

11. What method of research was used by Wilhelm Wundt and William James and later rejected because there was no way to objectively confirmed or measure the results of the research?

INTROSPECTION — Wundt & James

12. What state of consciousness did the Hilgards suggest to describe the situation in which the nonhypnotized self is a "hidden observer" of the hypnotized self?

DISSOCIATED CONSCIOUSNESS — "hidden observer"

13. Who was the first psychologist to propose that consciousness has evolved in humans because it has survival value?

WILLIAM JAMES — survival value of consciousness

14. What aspect of dreams did Freud cite as symbolic representation of material from the unconscious?

LATENT CONTENT — symbolic representation of material from consciousness

15. What theory claims that hypnosis is different than normal waking consciousness?

STATE — hypnosis is different than normal waking consciousness

16. What term is used to describe inaccurate memories that are perceived by the person as accurate?

CONFABULATION — inaccurate memories thought to be accurate

17. What is the condition in which a person is temporarily unable to recall certain events?

AMNESIA — temporarily unable to recall certain events

18. Whose extensive study of meditative techniques led him to propose that all forms of meditation have four essential ingredients?

HERBERT BENSON — meditation 4 ingredients

19. What would you be likely to observe on the EEG of a person who is in Sleep Stage 2?

SLEEP SPINDLES — stage 2; EEG

20. What method has been used to study selective attention in the laboratory?

DICHOTIC LISTENING — selective attention

21. What state would you be in if you experienced your body as separate from your self?

DEPERSONALIZATION — body separate from self

22. What Swiss chemist discovered LSD?

ALBERT HOFMAN — LSD man

23. What type of brain waves occur when a person is in a state of deep sleep?

DELTA — deep sleep waves

HYPERAMNESIA 24. What do law enforcement people hope will happen when a person who has witnessed a crime is hypnotized?

Essay Questions

Suggested answers for the essay questions are included at the back of your study guide.

1. Distinguish between conscious processes, preconscious processes, and unconscious processes in terms of the functions they perform and the type of memory storage involved in each.

2. The text discusses Freud's psychoanalytic theory of dreams and the activation-syntheses hypothesis of Hobson and McCarley. Describe the two theories and give your opinion of each of them.

3. The majority of drug users have a "drug of preference." Why are there individual differences in drug preferences?

4. Discuss the question of whether hypnosis should be used for memory enhancement in criminal investigations.

Multiple-Choice Test I

For the multiple-choice items, choose the best of the answers provided. Check your work with the answers at the back of your study guide, and be sure you understand why the keyed answers are correct.

1. The "stream of consciousness" as described by William James is compatible with his belief that
    a. the self has continuity.
    (b.) we cannot focus attention on one stimulus for more than a few seconds.
    c. mental processes are affected by variations in our physiological state.
    d. people tend to ignore external stimuli in favor of subjective events.

2. Unconscious mental processes play a prominent role in the theorizing of
    (a.) Sigmund Freud.   c. Wilhelm Wundt.
    b. William James.   d. John Watson.

3. Consciousness is best described as having a(n)
    a. external orientation.   (c.) limited capacity.
    b. internal orientation.   d. unlimited capacity.

4. The "cocktail party phenomena" illustrates the process of
   a. becoming intoxicated.
   b. subliminal communication.
   c. introspection.
   d. selective attention. *(circled)*

5. "Interpretation of ambiguous sentences" and "priming" are techniques used to investigate
   a. hypnotic suggestion.
   b. marijuana intoxication.
   c. unconscious processing. *(circled)*
   d. meditative concentration.

6. Mindlessness can occur when a person
   a. brushes his or her teeth.
   b. drives an automobile.
   c. eats a hot dog.
   d. does any of the above. *(circled)*

7. The text reports a study done by Shiffrin and Schneider in which subjects searched through sets of letters for target letters. What was their dependent variable?
   a. dream deprived versus not dream deprived
   b. number of target letters
   c. time to complete the task *(circled)*
   d. type of EEG activity

8. The study of sleep began when
   a. EEG machines were developed. *(circled)*
   b. Wundt established his laboratory.
   c. pilots were being trained during World War II.
   d. doctors became interested in the cause or causes of insomnia.

9. During REM sleep
   a. physiological arousal occurs.
   b. it is relatively difficult to awaken a person.
   c. inhibition of muscular activity occurs.
   d. all of the above occur. *(circled)*

10. Because the brain and internal organs are highly activated during REM sleep, REM sleep is often referred to as _____ sleep.
    a. paradoxical *(circled)*
    b. active
    c. pseudo
    d. micro

11. Research has shown
    a. that dreams occur in response to environmental stimuli.
    b. that all people dream. *(circled)*
    c. that periods of dreaming often last only a few seconds.
    d. all of the above.

12. Anxiety, depression, and drugs are frequently causal factors in
    a. sleep apnea.
    b. narcolepsy.
    c. insomnia. *(circled)*
    d. all of the above.

13. The characteristics of dreams that most psychologists agree upon include all of the following *except*
    a. the space-time relationships of dreams are fantastic.
    b. dreams are often emotionally charged.
    c. dreams have a delusional quality.
    (d.) sex is the most frequent theme of dreams.

14. The activation-synthesis hypothesis of J. Allan Hobson and Robert McCarley is best described as a(n) _____ theory.
    a. evolutionary
    b. psychoanalytic
    c. cognitive
    (d.) neuropsychological

15. Alpha waves tend to dominate brain wave patterns when people are
    (a.) meditating.
    b. taking amphetamines.
    c. dreaming.
    d. hypnotized.

16. All of the following are techniques used to prepare subjects for hypnotic induction *except*
    a. focused attention.
    (b.) trusting attitude.
    c. reduced reality testing.
    d. imaginative involvement.

17. Which of the following is an example of a positive hallucination such as might be experienced by a hypnotized person?
    a. The person does not perceive the odor of a rotten potato.
    (b.) A piece of bread tastes like chocolate candy.
    c. The person cannot remember hitting her husband.
    d. All of the above are examples of positive hallucinations.

18. Spontaneous amnesia is most likely to occur after
    a. long sessions of meditation.
    b. attacks of narcolepsy.
    (c.) being awakened from hypnosis.
    d. dream deprivation.

19. In a study done by Dywan and Bowers, the tendency of hypnotized subjects to report inaccurate memories demonstrated
    (a.) confabulation.
    b. narcolepsy.
    c. dissociated consciousness.
    d. hypermnesia.

20. In the Hilgards' research, hypnotized subjects were simultaneously aware of two levels of pain. This research supported the Hilgards' concept of
    a. subconscious processes.
    b. hypermnesia.
    c. depersonalization.
    (d.) the hidden observer.

21. All of the following drugs are derived from plants *except*
    a. ethyl alcohol.
    b. barbiturates.
    c. heroin.
    (d.) marijuana.

22. Anesthesia followed by coma is most likely to occur when a person overdoses on
    a. LSD.
    b. barbiturates.
    c. cocaine.
    d. mescaline.

23. All of the following have been identified as neurotransmitters *except*
    a. benzodiazepine.
    b. epinephrine.
    c. serotonin.
    d. acetylcholine.

24. What type of drugs has the greatest effect on perception?
    a. psychedelics
    b. analgesics
    c. stimulants
    d. sedatives

25. What drug causes a mixture of stimulant and psychedelic effects?
    a. LSD
    b. cocaine
    c. PCP
    d. mescaline

Multiple-Choice Test II

For the multiple-choice items, choose the best of the answers provided. Check your work with the answers at the back of your study guide, and be sure you understand why the keyed answers are correct.

1. With which of the following statements would William James *disagree*?
    a. Consciousness evolved in humans because it has survival value.
    b. Normal waking consciousness is only one of many possible forms of consciousness.
    c. Religious ecstasy and mental illness are alternative forms of consciousness.
    d. People have the ability to focus attention on a single stimulus for long periods.

2. Unconscious processes include such things as
    a. driving a car.
    b. brushing your teeth.
    c. secreting hormones.
    d. all of the above.

3. With which of the following statements would Freud *disagree*?
    a. Unconscious processes occupy a small proportion of mental capacity.
    b. Unconscious processes can be detected in everyday use of language.
    c. Unconscious processes appear in symbolic form in dreams.
    d. Unconscious processes are associated with sexual and aggressive drives.

4. The term currently used to refer to what William James called the "searchlight of consciousness" is
    a. preconsciousness.
    b. confabulation.
    c. selective attention.
    d. shadowing.

5. Subjects in dichotic listening studies are most likely to hear the message being delivered to the unshadowed ear if the message
   a. is repeated several times.
   b. includes their own name.
   c. is in a foreign language.
   d. is from a familiar book or story.

6. Mindlessness is most likely to be observed in the performance of a typist who is
   a. highly skilled.
   b. unskilled.
   c. using an analgesic.
   d. using a stimulant.

7. The text reports a study done by Shiffrin and Schneider in which subjects searched through sets of letters for target letters. What was the independent variable in the study?
   a. dream deprived versus not dream deprived
   b. number of target letters
   c. time to complete the task
   d. type of EEG activity

8. Shiffrin and Schneider did a study in which subjects searched through sets of letters for target letters. The results of their study showed that
   a. marijuana affects performance on simple tasks.
   b. hypnotic suggestion can increase motivation to perform boring tasks.
   c. meditation can increase attention span.
   d. automatic processing requires extensive practice.

9. The EEG allows researchers to study
   a. hypnotic sensibility.
   b. alcohol intoxication.
   c. selective attention.
   d. stages of sleep.

10. Eugene Aserinsky and Nathaniel Kleitman were the first to notice that
    a. hypermnesia occurs when people are hypnotized.
    b. rapid eye movements occur when people are dreaming.
    c. a passive attitude is basic to all forms of meditation.
    d. skill at a task can result in automatic processing.

11. During a night's sleep, the length of stages of deep sleep _____, and the length of intervals between periods of REM sleep _____.
    a. increases; increases
    b. increases; decreases
    c. decreases; increases
    d. decreases; decreases

12. Why do sleep researchers believe that sleeping at night was adaptive for our ancestors during our evolutionary history?
    a. It kept them from being eaten by predators and having accidents.
    b. It contributed to the preservation of the species by encouraging procreation.
    c. It gave their bodies and minds time to rejuvenate.
    d. It caused them to look for sheltered places so they would be safe while sleeping.

13. Sleepwalking occurs most frequently among _____; sleep apnea occurs most frequently among _____.
    a. adolescents; overweight men
    b. adolescents; overweight women
    c. children; overweight men
    d. children; overweight women

14. "The latent content of your dreams suggests that you have a repressed desire to hurt and humiliate your brother." This type of interpretation of dreams is associated with the _____ perspective.
    a. humanistic
    b. psychoanalytic
    c. cognitive
    d. behavioral

15. Which of the following is *not* among the essential ingredients of meditation as described by Herbert Benson?
    a. a contemplative personality
    b. a quiet environment
    c. a passive attitude
    d. a mental device

16. Meditation is most likely to be used clinically for the treatment of
    a. alcoholism.
    b. narcolepsy.
    c. anxiety disorders.
    d. depression.

17. A dentist using hypnosis to anesthetize a patient wants the patient to experience
    a. depersonalization.
    b. hypermnesia.
    c. paradoxical sleep.
    d. negative hallucinations.

18. Hypnosis has been used to
    a. relieve pain.
    b. control addictive behavior.
    c. enhance memory.
    d. do all of the above.

19. Confabulation is a problem that can occur when
    a. dreams are used to explore unconscious motivation.
    b. hypnosis is used to enhance memory.
    c. sleeping pills are taken regularly.
    d. the effects of PCP dissipate.

20. Research suggests that people who are highly susceptible to hypnotic suggestion have
    a. a capacity for deep involvement in imaginative activities.
    b. a high susceptibility to drug addiction, particularly psychedelics.
    c. passive and introverted personalities.
    d. strong motivation to please others, especially authority figures.

21. Evidence from EEG studies supports the _____ theory of hypnosis.
    a. conscious
    b. nonconscious
    c. nonstate
    d. state

22. Which of the following is an analgesic?
    a. mescaline
    b. heroin ✓
    c. barbiturates
    d. cocaine

23. Tranquilizers like Valium and Halcion belong to the class of psychoactive drugs called
    a. barbiturates.
    b. analgesics.
    c. stimulants.
    d. sedatives. ✓

24. To reduce anxiety or induce sleep, doctors used to prescribe barbiturates. Currently, they are more likely to prescribe _____ for these problems.
    a. epinephrine
    b. amphetamines
    c. dopamine
    d. benzodiazepines ✓

25. Depersonalization is most likely to be experienced as a result of using
    a. LSD. ✓
    b. PCP.
    c. cocaine.
    d. heroin.

Chapter 6

CONDITIONING AND LEARNING

Learning Objectives

After studying this chapter, you should be able to:

1. Describe the essential components of the definition of learning.

2. Differentiate between classical and operant conditioning.

3. Outline the procedures used to produce classical conditioning in the laboratory.

4. Describe the temporal relationships between the CS and US that most effectively promote learning.

5. Describe the major phenomena in classical conditioning: acquisition, extinction, spontaneous recovery, generalization, and discrimination.

6. State the law of effect.

7. Describe the major contribution of B. F. Skinner to the study of conditioning.

8. Differentiate between positive and negative reinforcement.

9. Differentiate between negative reinforcement and punishment.

10. Describe the procedures used to shape a response.

11. Differentiate between primary and conditioned reinforcers.

12. Outline the four basic schedules of partial reinforcement.

13. Compare the rates of extinction for behaviors that are continuously reinforced and those that are reinforced on a partial schedule.

14. Differentiate between escape and avoidance learning.

15. Indicate the ways in which punishment can be used most effectively to modify behavior.

16. Describe the side effects of using punishment.

17. Describe preparedness and the limitations imposed on learning by instinctual drift.

18. Identify the types of behaviors that humans may be biologically prepared to acquire.

19. Describe how ethologists may study learning differently than psychologists.

20. Indicate how the cognitive approach to learning differs from the stimulus-response approach.

21. Discriminate between insight learning and observational learning.

22. Describe the conditions that promote the development of learned helplessness.

Working with Names and Terms

From the alphabetized list below, choose the name or term that answers the question, using each name and term only once. Answers are at the back of your study guide.

associative
Bernstein, Ilena
chaining
conditioned reinforcers
discriminative stimulus
extinction
fixed interval
Garcia, John
generalization
Hollis, Karen
insight
instinctual drift

instrumental conditioning
learned helplessness
Mowrer, O. H.
negative punishment
negative reinforcement
observational
operant conditioning
preparedness
reflexive
shaping
Tolman, Edward
variable ratio

__REFLEXIVE__   1. What type of behavior can be classically conditioned?
classical conditioning

__CONDITIONED REINFORCERS__   2. What term is used to refer to rewards that have no intrinsic survival value?
rewards with no intrinsic survival value

__JOHN GARCIA__   3. Whose work on taste aversions was applied to protect sheep from coyotes?
taste aversions

__VARIABLE RATIO__ 4. What kind of reinforcement schedule is in effect for the flower vendors who gets a dollar for every bouquet she sells?

__GENERALIZATION__ 5. What process are we demonstrating when we answer telephones even though they ring at different frequencies and amplitudes?

__DISCRIMINATIVE STIMULUS__ 6. What term used in operant conditioning is appropriate for the dial tone that tells you it is time to make the response that may be reinforced with an answer?

__INSTINCTUAL DRIFT__ — animal's natural biological reactions interfere with learning 7. What term is used to describe the phenomenon that occurs when an animal's natural biological reactions interfere with learning?

__INSIGHT__ — Köhler's chimps 8. What type of learning was demonstrated by Köhler's chimpanzees?

__SHAPING__ — desired response reinforced by experimenter 9. What process is used to get a subject to make the desired response so that the response can be reinforced by the experimenter?

__EDWARD TOLMAN__ — animal expectancies 10. Who was the early proponent of cognitive learning who claimed that animals have "expectancies"?

__INSTRUMENTAL CONDITIONING__ / operant conditioning 11. What is the other name for operant conditioning?

__EXTINCTION__ 12. What process results in a decrease in the probability that a response will occur, even though the response was well learned?

__Ilena Bernstein__ — chemo guy 13. Who demonstrated that children undergoing chemotherapy developed an aversion for mapletoff ice cream?

__CHAINING__ — relatively simple responses combine with complex behavior 14. What term is used to refer to the process in which several relatively simple responses are combined into a more complex behavior?

__ASSOCIATIVE__ — classical & operant conditioning 15. What type of learning are both classical conditioning and operant conditioning?

__KAREN HOLLIS__ — naturalistic observation & laboratory experimentation complementary in learning 16. Whose work with tropical fish demonstrated that naturalistic observation and laboratory experimentation are complementary in the study of learning?

__FIXED INTERVAL__ 17. Which reinforcement schedule is in effect for employees who are paid every Friday afternoon?

OBSERVATIONAL 18. What type of learning is demonstrated by the three-year-old who stands at the steering wheel of a car and "drives"?

OPERANT
CONDITIONING
THORNDIKE
19. What type of learning did Thorndike's work with cats and puzzle boxes introduce into psychology?

PREPAREDNESS
learning behaviors that have survival value
20. What is the genetic bias that results in animals' readiness to learning behaviors that have survival value?

NEGATIVE PUNISHMENT 21. What type of consequence is being used when a child cannot watch TV for a week because she bit her sister?

O. H. MOWRER
avoidance learning
22. Who proposed the theory that avoidance learning involves both classically conditioned fear and an instrumentally conditioned response to the fear?

LEARNED HELPLESSNESS
cannot escape or avoid an aversive stimulus
23. What is likely to happen when an organism is put into a situation where it cannot escape or avoid an aversive stimulus?

NEGATIVE REINFORCEMENT 24. What type of consequence is occurring when a drink relieves an alcoholic of unpleasant withdrawal symptoms?

Essay Questions

Suggested answers for the essay questions are included at the back of your study guide.

1. Little Allison acquired a conditioned fear of dogs after being bitten by a neighbor's collie. Identify the US, UR, CS, and CR in the situation, and explain how Allison's fear might generalize.

2. Both positive and negative emotional responses can be classically conditioned. Explain how Margo's attitude toward the new roommate she has just met might be affected by Margo's classically conditioned responses.

3. Write a short article for parents concerning the use of punishment as a method of controlling the behavior of their children.

4. Well-meaning parents frequently misuse reinforcement in dealing with their children. Explain how this can happen.

Multiple-Choice Test I

For the multiple-choice items, choose the best of the answers provided. Check your work with the answers at the back of your study guide, and be sure you understand why the keyed answers are correct.

1. An association between a response and its consequences is made in _____ conditioning; an association between two stimuli is made in _____ conditioning.
    a. stimulus; response
    b. response; stimulus
    c. classical; operant
    d. operant; classical

2. When Kim's dog hears the can opener operating, he runs to the kitchen and begins to drool. "Running to the kitchen" is a(n) _____ conditioned behavior; "drooling" is a(n) _____ conditioned behavior.
    a. operantly; operantly
    b. operantly; classically
    c. classically; operantly
    d. classically; classically

3. When Little Albert showed fear in the presence of a rabbit and of Santa's whiskers, he was demonstrating
    a. backward conditioning.
    b. higher-order conditioning.
    c. generalization.
    d. spontaneous recovery.

4. Kim noticed that her dog came to the kitchen and drooled with decreasing frequency after she began feeding him dry food. What is occurring?
    a. discrimination
    b. extinction
    c. shaping
    d. inhibition

5. What is the basic assumption of operant conditioning?
    a. Associations occurs between events that are temporally contiguous.
    b. Seeking reinforcement has survival value.
    c. Animals are genetically programmed to seek pleasure and avoid pain.
    d. Behavior is influenced by its consequences.

6. Operant conditioning differs from classical conditioning in that in operant conditioning
    a. generalization and discrimination occur.
    b. cognitive processes are not involved.
    c. voluntary responses are learned.
    d. learning occurs more rapidly.

7. Skinner says that reinforcers
    a. cannot be operationally defined.
    b. provide pleasure or satisfaction.
    c. increase the probability of a response.
    d. have survival value.

8. A mother uses "television-watching privileges" to control the behavior of her children. What did she do when she negatively reinforced her son, Henry?
   a. She let him watch a program he doesn't like.
   b. She banned TV watching for two days.
   c. She let his sister choose the programs.
   (d.) She lifted the ban on TV watching early.

9. Which of the following is an example of negative punishment?
   a. a fine for a traffic violation
   b. withdrawal of attention from a child
   c. losing money in the stock market
   (d.) All of the above are examples of negative punishment.

10. The processes below all occur in both classical and operant conditioning *except*
    (a.) shaping.
    b. spontaneous recovery.
    c. generalization.
    d. discrimination.

11. Little Anita stopped screaming for "goodies" at the grocery store when her mother stopped buying them, no matter how long or how loudly Anita screamed. The mother used _____ to stop Anita's screaming.
    a. punishment
    (b.) extinction
    c. negative punishment
    d. negative reinforcement

12. A person's ability to operate the appliances in a strange kitchen is an example of the role _____ plays in human behavior.
    a. shaping
    (b.) generalization
    c. chaining
    d. discrimination

13. The most important aspect of Fred Keller's "Personalized System of Instruction" is
    a. chaining of responses.
    b. active participation.
    (c.) immediate feedback.
    d. primary reinforcement.

14. What important point is made in the case of Wendy, the child who spent too much time out of her seat at school?
    (a.) Reinforcers and punishers should be identified by observing their effect on behavior.
    b. Punishment is ineffective if it is not immediate and intense.
    c. Positive reinforcement is usually more effective than negative reinforcement in controlling the behavior of children.
    d. Secondary reinforcement is most effective when it is given by a person who is liked and/or respected.

15. Pauses occur after reinforcement when _____ schedules of reinforcement are used. Rate of responding is higher when _____ schedules of reinforcement are used.
    a. fixed; interval
    (b.) fixed; ratio
    c. variable; interval
    d. variable; ratio

16. Little Anita's mother used to give in and buy her a "goodie" occasionally when Anita screamed at the grocery store. Now her mother refuses to buy "goodies" no matter how long and how loudly Anita screams. The fact that Anita continues to scream even though it is not longer reinforced is most likely to be an example of
    a. lack of stimulus control.
    b. perseveration.
    c. the partial reinforcement effect.
    d. spontaneous recovery.

17. The shuttle box devised by O. H. Mowrer and Neal Miller is used to study
    a. partial reinforcement.
    b. chaining.
    c. negative reinforcement.
    d. punishment.

18. Punishment is most likely to be effective if it is
    a. intense and immediate.
    b. intense and delayed.
    c. mild and immediate.
    d. mild and delayed.

19. It can be inferred from the text that it would by most appropriate to physically punish a child for
    a. temper tantrums.
    b. fighting with other children.
    c. refusing to obey parents.
    d. running into the street.

20. Garcia and his associates did a study in which rats learned a taste aversion to saline solution as a result of its being paired with a high dose of X-rays. This study suggests
    a. that conditioning can occur after a single trial.
    b. that biological factors affect the formation of associations.
    c. that a long interval can occur between the CS and the US.
    d. all of the above.

21. Ilena Bernstein demonstrated taste aversion learning in humans. The unconditioned stimulus in her study was
    a. benzodiazepine.
    b. chemotherapeutic drugs.
    c. mapletoff ice cream.
    d. radiation treatments.

22. A study by Ohman, Eriksson, and Olofssen demonstrated that preparedness may be involved in humans' fear of
    a. high places.
    b. spiders.
    c. snakes.
    d. thunder and lightning.

23. Reports such as those of Garcia and the Brelands have resulted in ethologists questioning
    a. the ability of animals to learn through classical conditioning.
    b. the ability of animals to learn through operant conditioning.
    c. the concept of biological preparedness.
    d. the value of studying animal learning in the laboratory.

24. Tolman objected to the concept of S-R learning as described by Pavlov and Thorndike because he believed
    a. that cognitive processes are involved in learning. ✓
    b. that mechanisms of learning are species specific.
    c. that results from animal studies should not be generalized to humans.
    d. all of the above.

25. A study described in the text demonstrated how _____ influenced children to donate money to the March of Dimes.
    a. positive reinforcement
    b. negative reinforcement
    c. observational learning ✓
    d. expectancies

Multiple-Choice Test II

For the multiple-choice items, choose the best of the answers provided. Check your work with the answers at the back of your study guide, and be sure you understand why the key answers are correct.

1. Learning is defined as a change in _____ that results from _____.
   a. behavior; education
   b. behavior; experience ✓
   c. mental structures; education
   d. mental structures; experience

2. In classical conditioning, the conditioned stimulus should be
   a. neutral. ✓
   b. intense.
   c. familiar.
   d. all of the above.

3. Conditioning will occur most rapidly if the CS occurs
   a. just before the US. ✓
   b. with the UR.
   c. just after the US.
   d. with the CR.

4. Kim's dog runs to the kitchen and drools when it hears the sound of the can opener, but just goes back to sleep when Kim uses the food processor or the knife sharpener. The dog's failure to respond to the sound of these other appliances suggests that it has developed
   a. second-signal responses.
   b. higher-order conditioning.
   c. discrimination. ✓
   d. inhibition of response.

5. When a conditioned response recurs after it has undergone extinction, it is said that _____ has occurred.
   a. reinstitution of response
   b. reconditioning
   c. spontaneous recovery ✓
   d. disinhibition of response

6. Research has suggested that classical conditioning may be involved in all of the following *except*
   a. instinctive behavior.
   b. drug addiction.
   c. fears and phobias.
   d. reactions of the immune system.

7. Thorndike's "law of effect" refers to the importance of _____ in learning.
   a. practice and repetition
   b. environmental circumstances
   c. consequences of behavior
   d. genetic predispositions

8. Negative reinforces include such things as
   a. low grades on tests.
   b. pills that relieve pain.
   c. unwanted attention.
   d. all of the above.

9. When little Anita's mother buys her a "goodie," she stops screaming. Anita uses _____ to control her mother's behavior.
   a. positive reinforcement
   b. negative reinforcement
   c. punishment
   d. negative punishment

10. To get animals like seals to learn to perform tricks, animal trainers use the process called
    a. generalization.
    d. discrimination learning.
    c. counterconditioning.
    d. shaping.

11. Timothy whines and cries to "get his own way" at home but not at school. For Timothy, being at home is a _____ stimulus for crying.
    a. discriminative
    b. conditioned
    c. disinhibitory
    d. reinforced

12. Dieters are often instructed to eat only at the dining table and *not* in front of TV, at a desk, or in bed. The purpose of this is
    a. successive approximation to normal eating habits.
    b. negative reinforcement of eating between meals.
    c. stimulus control of eating behavior.
    d. chaining of responses that inhibit eating.

13. *The experimental analysis of behavior* emphasizes
    a. the physiological aspects of learning.
    b. the identification of effective reinforcers and punishers.
    c. the importance of biological preparedness.
    d. the role of operant conditioning in mental disorders.

14. A rat that has been reinforced with food for bar pressing will continue to press the bar to hear the "click" of the food mechanism, even though no food is released. The "click" has become a
    a. negative reinforcer.
    b. conditioned reinforcer.
    c. higher-order stimulus.
    d. symbolic reinforcer.

15. To help children learn relatively complex behaviors, like brushing their teeth, getting dressed, or feeding the dog, parents often use the procedure called
    a. chaining.
    b. higher-order conditioning.
    c. analysis of behavior.
    d. delayed conditioning.

16. The boss comes around two or three times a day and pays each worker one dollar for each bushel of beans the worker has picked. The workers are on a _____ schedule of reinforcement.
    a. fixed interval
    b. fixed ratio
    c. variable interval
    d. variable ratio

17. The "partial reinforcement effect" explains why
    a. children acquire language rapidly.
    b. superstitious behaviors persist.
    c. gamblers get discouraged.
    d. absenteeism is high on Mondays.

18. The idea that both classical and operant conditioning are involved in avoidance learning is expressed by
    a. two-process theory.
    b. Skinner's hypothesis.
    c. the interactive effect.
    d. sequential conditioning.

19. Research suggests that children who are being punished at school by failure, criticism, and rejection are likely to become
    a. withdrawn and inhibited.
    b. fearful of going to school.
    c. aggressive.
    d. any of the above.

20. The Brelands' article on "The Misbehavior of Organisms" told how _____ can interfere with learning.
    a. prior conditioning
    b. extraneous stimuli
    c. instinctual behavior
    d. preparedness

21. In the study done by Karen Hollis with gouramies, the red light was a(n) _____ stimulus.
    a. conditioned
    b. unconditioned
    c. discriminative
    d. generalized

22. Tinklepaugh's monkey supported Tolman's ideas about learning because the monkey's behavior indicated that it had
    a. judgment.
    b. expectancies.
    c. insight.
    d. discrimination.

23. Köhler disagreed with Thorndike's belief that
    a. cognitive processes are involved in animal learning.
    b. biological preparedness influences what animals can learn.
    c. there are species-specific differences in the mechanisms of learning.
    d. intelligent behavior results from random trial and error.

24. The S-R view of learning is challenged by studies showing that animals
    a. learn by observing others.
    b. demonstrate insight.
    c. have expectancies.
    d. do all of the above.

25. In the study by Seligman and Maier, dogs developed "learned helplessness" as a result of being
    a. forced to make difficult decisions.
    b. conditioned on a variable-interval schedule.
    c. unable to escape an aversive stimulus.
    d. punished for performing a behavior that was previously reinforced.

Chapter 7

HUMAN MEMORY

Learning Objectives

After studying this chapter, you should be able to:

1. Define encoding and distinguish between effortful and effortless encoding.

2. Compare maintenance and elaborative rehearsal.

3. Describe the functions, capacities, and durations of the sensory memory, short-term memory, and long-term memory systems.

4. Outline the experiment conducted by George Sperling that led to the discovery of sensory memory.

5. Discuss how information is transferred from sensory memory to short-term memory via pattern recognition and attention.

6. Describe a memory-span task and discuss how Miller used this procedure to identify the capacity of short-term memory.

7. Outline the study conducted by Peterson and Peterson that established the duration of a short-term memory trace.

8. Describe the operations that control the transfer of information from short-term to long-term memory.

9. Contrast semantic coding with imagery coding.

10. Distinguish between procedural and declarative memory, as well as semantic and episodic memory.

11. Describe how the retrieval of information is influenced by the schematic organization of that information.

12. Distinguish between the processes of memory construction and memory distortions.

13. Describe the research on the accuracy of recall for eyewitnesses.

14. Compare and contrast how information is lost from memory through the four major theories of forgetting: encoding failure, decay, interference, and retrieval failure.

15. Differentiate between retroactive and proactive interference.

16. Describe the importance of cues in retrieving information from long-term memory.

17. Outline five suggested techniques for improving memory.

18. Compare the two mnemonic techniques: the method of loci and the keyword method.

19. Identify the brain structures that play a prominent role in the physiology of memory.

20. Discuss the chemistry of amnesia, highlighting the role of neurotransmitters, hormones, and other drugs thought to affect memory.

Working with Names and Terms

From the alphabetized list below, choose the name or term that answers the question, using each name and term only once. Answers are at the back of your study guide.

acetylcholine	Loftus, Elizabeth
anterograde amnesia	maintenance
Bahrick, Harry	method of loci
Bartlett, Frederick	Miller, George
chunking	Paivio, Alan
Ebbinghaus, Herman	proactive interference
elaborative	procedural
encoding failure	retrieval failure
engram	schema
episodic	short-term
flashbulb memory	Sperling, George
Lashley, Karl	vasopressin

HERMAN EBBINGHAUS (forgetting) 1. Who memorized thousands of nonsense syllables in his study of forgetting?

HARRY BAHRICK (long-term memory guy) 2. Who did studies assessing long-term memory for faces and names of classmates, Spanish vocabulary, and algebra?

Answer	#	Question
METHOD OF LOCI	3.	What mnemonic might use landmarks on the route from the bus stop to the classroom as associates of to-be-remembered information?
FRED BARTLETT	4.	Who showed that memory is constructive by asking subjects to recall a story named "The War of the Ghosts"?
LIZ LOFTUS	5.	Whose work has shown that constructive memory may be involved in eyewitness testimony?
CHUNKING	6.	What can be used to increase the capacity of short-term memory?
SCHEMA	7.	What term would Frederick Bartlett use to refer to "all I know about eating in cafeterias"?
SHORT-TERM	8.	What memory system is most similar to "consciousness"?
ACETYLCHOLINE	9.	What neurotransmitter appears to be in short supply in the brains of people suffering from Alzheimer's disease?
ENCODING FAILURE	10.	What theory of forgetting says we can't retrieve what was never stored?
GEORGE MILLER	11.	Who used the term "magical number 7 ± 2" to describe the capacity of short-term memory?
ELABORATIVE	12.	What type of rehearsal do we use when we integrate new information into existing schemata?
FLASHBULB MEMORY	13.	What term did Brown and Kulik use to describe the remarkable recollections people had of what they were doing when they heard that President Lincoln had been shot?
ENGRAM	14.	What term is used to describe the physical change that occurs in the brain when a memory is stored?
KARL LASHLEY	15.	Who declared that "learning is just not possible" after 30 years of trying to localize memory in the brain?
AL PAIVIO	16.	Who has emphasized the importance of imagery as a strategy for remembering?
GEORGE SPERLING	17.	Who demonstrated characteristics of visual sensory memory using what he called the "partial report" method?

| MAINTENANCE | 18. What type of rehearsal do we use to keep information circulating in short-term memory? |

| EPISODIC | 19. What memory resembles a personal diary? |

| ANTEROGRADE AMNESIA | 20. What condition did H. M. have as a result of having his hippocampus surgically removed? |

| PROCEDURAL | 21. What memory includes your program for roller skating and swimming? |

| RETRIEVAL FAILURE | 22. What theory of forgetting says that information in long-term memory is not available because the access to it has been lost? |

| PROACTIVE INTERFERENCE | 23. What could make it more difficult to learn Italian in college because you studied Spanish in high school? |

| VASOPRESSIN | 24. What hormone was suggested by James McGaugh to improve memory? |

Essay Questions

Suggested answers for the essay questions are included at the back of your study guide.

1. Explain how the three memory systems work as a student is reading from a textbook.

2. Describe and give examples of the content of procedural, semantic, and episodic memory.

3. Kester cannot remember the first name of his third-grade teacher. How would his forgetting be explained by each of the four theories of forgetting?

4. As people get older, they have increasing difficulty remembering. Explain this using retrieval failure theory and interference theory.

5. A friend complains that although she reads the assignments for her classes, she is failing most of her tests. What advice would you give her about increasing the effectiveness of her studying.

Multiple-Choice Test I

For the multiple-choice items, choose the best of the answers provided. Check your work with the answers at the back of your study guide, and be sure you understand why the keyed answers are correct.

1. To refer to placing information in memory, psychologists use the term
   a. processing.
   b. integration.
   c. purposive rehearsal.
   (d.) encoding.

2. When subjects create bizarre images or make up sentences to help them remember pairs of words, they are using _____ processing and _____ rehearsal.
   a. automatic; elaborative
   b. automatic; maintenance
   (c.) effortful; elaborative
   d. effortful; maintenance

3. Craik and Tulving demonstrated that subjects were more likely to recall information if they used
   a. maintenance rehearsal.
   (b.) elaborative rehearsal.
   c. the method of loci.
   d. the SQ3R method.

4. The study in which Jacqueline Sachs showed that subjects store the meaning rather than the verbatim content of sentences demonstrated that people use
   (a.) semantic coding.
   b. grammatical markers.
   c. automatic processing.
   d. maintenance rehearsal.

5. The "trash" that gets into our memories, like the ditty from a TV commercial, illustrates how what psychologists call _____ can occur.
   a. elaborative rehearsal
   (b.) automatic processing
   c. incidental engrams
   d. unintentional learning

6. Sensory memory has a _____ capacity and a _____ duration.
   (a.) large; short
   b. large; long
   c. small; short
   d. small; long

7. Short-term memory has a capacity that is _____ and a duration that is _____ than sensory memory.
   a. larger; shorter
   b. larger; longer
   c. smaller; shorter
   (d.) smaller; longer

8. What was the distractor task that subjects performed in the study by Lloyd and Margaret Peterson?
   a. reading words
   b. sorting beads
   c. copying geometric figures
   (d.) counting backward

9. Declarative memory includes _____ memory and _____ memory
   a. procedural; representational
   (c.) procedural; semantic
   c. episodic; semantic
   d. representational; semantic

10. Which of the following would be in episodic memory?
    a. My friend Terry had a baby on the Tuesday after Easter in 1992.
    b. Columbus discovered America in 1492.
    c. February will have 29 days in the year 2000.
    (d.) I had Cheerios for breakfast the day of the Challenger disaster.

11. What did William James conclude after having memorized *Paradise Lost*?
    a. Forgetting is best explained by decay of memory traces.
    b. Elaborative rehearsal is a necessary condition for long-term retention.
    c. Long-term memory has an unlimited capacity.
    (d.) Exercise does not improve memory.

12. There is evidence that contextual cues can be provided by
    a. hormones.
    (b.) drugs.
    c. engrams.
    d. dreams.

13. When Margo was asked to name all the foods she likes, she began by naming vegetables she likes, then proceed to name fruits and dairy products. "Vegetables," "fruits," and "dairy products" are what psychologists call
    a. organizers.
    (b.) retrieval cues.
    c. recall prompts.
    d. engrams.

14. The availability of distinctive cues has been used to explain what Brown and Kulik call
    (a.) flashbulb memory.
    b. constructive memory.
    c. the tip-of-the-tongue phenomenon.
    d. the state-dependent effect.

15. When we elaborate on memories by making inferences from the memories or from our experience, _____ has occurred.
    a. reminiscence
    (b.) memory construction
    c. schematization
    d. reconstructive recollection

16. "Ordering in a restaurant," "fishing for trout," and "enrolling in classes" are examples of what Bartlett called
    a. icons.
    b. contexts.
    (c.) schemata.
    d. engrams.

17. Imagine that Ebbinghaus has just learned another list of nonsense syllables. He takes a short walk, then tries to recall the nonsense syllables on the list. The forgetting that has occurred after only 20 minutes is most likely to be the result of
    (a.) proactive interference.
    b. decay.
    c. encoding failure.
    d. retroactive interference.

18. What theory of forgetting best explains why many people are unable to remember whose picture is on $20 bills?
    a. interference
    b. retrieval failure
    c. decay
    d. encoding failure *(circled)*

19. The absent-minded professor parks his car in the same parking lot every day. The difficulty he often has finding his car could result from encoding failure or _____ interference.
    a. anterograde
    b. proactive *(circled)*
    c. retrograde
    d. retroactive

20. What is the customary independent variable in studies designed to demonstrate interference?
    a. number of trial required to learn the last list
    b. number of items recalled from the tested list
    c. whether or not subjects learn a second list *(circled)*
    d. number of items on the list that is tested

21. Why is it a good idea to go to sleep immediately after studying for a test?
    a. It gives your brain time to organize what you have learned.
    b. It minimizes interference. *(circled)*
    c. It gives memory traces time to reverberate.
    d. It facilitates regeneration of acetylcholine.

22. Mnemonics include such things as
    a. the SQ3R method.
    b. the method of loci. *(circled)*
    c. the method of distinctive cues.
    d. all of the above.

23. H. M., the man who was observed by William Scoville and Brenda Milner, had anterograde amnesia after having his _____ surgically removed.
    a. cerebellum
    b. left parietal lobe
    c. hippocampus *(circled)*
    d. thalamus

24. James McGaugh's research showed that two hormones, _____, improve memory in animals.
    a. thyroxin and adrenaline
    b. serotonin and dopamine
    c. GABA and acetylcholine
    d. vasopressin and norepinephrine *(circled)*

25. Paul Gold suggested that the chemical messenger through which hormones affect memory functions is
    a. glucose. *(circled)*
    b. epinephrine.
    c. acetylcholine.
    d. hemoglobin.

Multiple-Choice Test II

For the multiple-choice items, choose the best of the answers provided. Check your work with the answers at the back of your study guide, and be sure you understand why the keyed answer are correct.

1. The idea that there are three separate memory stores is associated with the
   a. levels-of-processing theory of memory.
   b. information processing model of memory.
   c. parallel-processing approach to memory.
   d. artificial intelligence analogy.

2. Lynn Hascher and Rose Zachs did a study showing that _____ occurred when subjects were asked how many times particular words appeared in a list.
   a. automatic processing
   b. effortful processing
   c. maintenance rehearsal
   d. elaborative rehearsal

3. If you look up a telephone number and repeat it over and over until you have dialed it, you have used
   a. maintenance rehearsal.
   b. semantic encoding.
   c. automatic processing.
   d. iconic memory.

4. Elaborative rehearsal differs from maintenance rehearsal in that elaborative rehearsal involves
   a. visual imagery.
   b. effortful processing.
   c. analysis of meaning.
   d. repetition.

5. Allen Paivio demonstrated that recall for pairs of words is enhanced if subjects use
   a. retrieval cues.
   b. constructive memory.
   c. maintenance rehearsal.
   d. imagery coding.

6. The research of George Sperling showed that _____ memory has a large capacity and a short duration.
   a. visual short-term
   b. auditory short-term
   c. visual sensory
   d. auditory sensory

7. If information is not rehearsed, it will remain in short-term memory for about 20
   a. milliseconds.
   b. seconds.
   c. minutes.
   d. hours.

8. Memory span tasks suggest that our short-term memories have a capacity of about _____ items
   a. seven
   b. ten
   c. twelve
   d. seventeen

9. Procedural memory stores information about how to
   a. speak grammatically.
   b. use a telephone directory.
   c. bake a cake.
   d. feed the dog.

10. Information like "the hypothalamus is part of the limbic system" and "William James wrote *Principles of Psychology*" should be stored in your _____ memory.
    a. representational
    b. semantic
    c. procedural
    d. episodic

11. John Jenkins and Karl Dallenbach did a study in which subjects either slept or continued normal waking activities after learning a list of ten nonsense syllables. They interpreted their results as supportive of the _____ theory of forgetting.
    a. replacement
    b. decay
    c. interference
    d. retrieval failure

12. Subject in an experiment were asked to learn two lists of words (List 1 and List 2). If the subjects are asked to recall List 1, _____ interference is being tested; if they are asked to recall List 2, _____ interference is being tested.
    a. anterograde; retrograde
    b. retrograde; anterograde
    c. proactive; retroactive
    d. retroactive; proactive

13. The tip-of-the-tongue phenomenon as described by Roger Brown and David McNeill demonstrates how forgetting can be the result of
    a. replacement.
    b. interference.
    c. retrieval failure.
    d. encoding failure.

14. Harry Bahrick and Lynda Hall tested people's memory for high school math courses 50 years later. They concluded that some of their subjects had forgotten very little because they had
    a. stored distinctive retrieval cues for accessing math information.
    b. used elaborative rehearsal to organize and structure the information.
    c. retrieved the information periodically over a period of several years.
    d. careers that involved the use of math.

15. Alexander Luria described the case of the journalist "S." What problem did "S" have?
    a. He couldn't forget anything.
    b. Images in his visual sensory memory faded very slowly.
    c. His short-term memory had a very small capacity.
    d. He couldn't store new long-term memories.

16. The patient, M. D., could sort pictures of animals and vehicles into categories, but he could not sort pictures of fruits and vegetables. His case supports the idea that
    a. elaborative rehearsal is a necessary condition for long-term memory.
    b. short-term memory and long-term memory are anatomically distinguishable.
    c. the destruction of brain tissue in Alzheimer's disease is not random.
    d. information in long-term memory is highly organized.

17. When we return to a house where we once lived or to a school we attended in the past, memories of people and events associated with these places are revived. This is an example of how retrieval can be assisted by
    a. contextual cues.
    b. spontaneous probes.
    c. associative bonds.
    d. irradiation of effect.

18. Frederick Bartlett suggested that distortion of memories occurs when the memories do *not* fit our
    a. frame of reference.
    b. world view.
    c. schemata.
    d. contextual constructs.

19. It has been suggested that experts in a field have excellent memory for information relevant to their field because they
    a. selectively attend to relevant information at a subconscious level.
    b. have distinctive retrieval cues for the information.
    c. have well-developed schemata for integrating the information.
    d. can chunk the information when it is being processes in short-term memory.

20. Loftus and Zanni did a study in which the independent variable was different verbs used to describe an automobile accident. The study demonstrated how
    a. eyewitness testimony can be distorted.
    b. contextual cues can enhance recollection of an event.
    c. schemata influence the testimony of witnesses.
    d. visual imagery can be an adjunct to constructive memory.

21. The "keyword method" is especially useful for remembering
    a. dates of important events.
    b. shopping lists.
    c. the location of personal possessions.
    d. vocabulary of a foreign language.

22. The "3Rs" in the SQ3R are
    a. read, reread, recall.
    b. read, reflect, remember.
    c. read, repeat, recap.
    d. read, recite, review.

23. The case of H. M. supports the idea that
    a. short-term memory and long-term memory are anatomically separate systems.
    b. long-term memory functions are performed by association areas in the cortex.
    c. memories are organized in the brain.
    d. acetylcholine is involved in learning and memory.

24. Based on studies of people with anterograde amnesia, Larry Squire has suggested that the hippocampus is crucial for _____ memory.
    a. declarative
    b. short-term
    c. procedural
    d. sensory

25. Brain researchers have discovered that people suffering from Alzheimer's disease have a shortage of the neurotransmitter _____ in their brains.
    a. vasopressin
    b. acetylcholine
    c. sucrose
    d. thyroxin

Chapter 8

THINKING AND LANGUAGE

Learning Objectives

After studying this chapter, you should be able to:

1. List the varied skills included in the definition of thinking.

2. Describe the process of concept formation, highlighting the relative contributions of "teaching" and "experience" to the acquisition of a concept.

3. Define a hierarchy and describe how it is used to integrate concepts.

4. Discuss the nature of problem-solving ability, describing the stages outlined by Newell and Simon.

5. Differentiate between algorithms and heuristic strategies of problem solving.

6. Describe the impact of mental set, functional fixedness, and confirmation bias on problem-solving ability.

7. Distinguish between deductive and inductive reasoning.

8. Define a syllogism and examine some common errors in the process of syllogistic reasoning.

9. Describe the role of utility and probability in decision making.

10. Describe how the representativeness, anchoring, and availability heuristics may lead to faulty decisions.

11. Identify the aspects of human intelligence that have yet to be successfully programmed on a computer.

12. Describe the three criteria (meaningfulness, generativity, and displacement) that comprise natural language.

13. Differentiate among the three characteristics of spoken language (phonology, syntax, and semantics).

14. Outline the stages of language development from early babbling to complex sentence constructions.

15. Describe the ways language development has been quantified.

16. Compare and contrast the three theories of language development, including the major strengths and weaknesses of each perspective.

17. Explain the linguistic relativity hypothesis and describe why many contemporary psychologists no longer value this theory.

18. Review the research on language behavior in chimps, and describe the current controversy over whether or not chimps trained in sign language truly possess a language.

Working with Names and Terms

From the alphabetized list below, choose the name or term that answers the question, using each name and term only once. Answers are at the back of your study guide.

algorithm	heuristics
anchoring	inductive
availability	mean length of utterance
Chomsky, Noam	morphemes
Collins, Allan	Rosch, Eleanor
conformation bias	semantics
connotative	Simon, Herbert
deductive	subgoal analysis
displacement	Tversky, Amos
framing	utility
functional fixedness	von Frisch, Karl
generativity	Whorf, Benjamin

_____ 1. Who claimed that the language of a culture determines how people perceive and interpret their world?

_____ 2. What index is commonly used to measure children's language development?

_____ 3. What block to problem solving is demonstrated by the man who couldn't drive a nail without a hammer?

_____ 4. What name is given to the smallest meaningful elements of a language?

_____ 5. What heuristic predicts that people at a party will be influenced by the first "guesser" when they are asked to estimate the number of beans in a jar?

_____ 6. What linguist claimed that the ability to acquire language is innate in humans?

_____ 7. What aspect of language makes it possible for us to communicate about things that happened long ago or far away?

_____ 8. What heuristic is illustrated by people's mistakenly believing that it is more dangerous to travel by airplane than by automobile because airplane crashes get more publicity than automobile accidents?

_____ 9. Who suggested that natural language concepts are acquired by identifying prototypes and also collected cross-cultural data that challenged the linguistic-relativity hypothesis?

_____ 10. Who collaborated with M. Ross Quillian in studies supporting the hypothesis that concepts are organized in hierarchies in human memory?

_____ 11. What problem-solving strategy are people most likely to use when they divide 73,621 by 163?

_____ 12. What could cause the results gotten in survey research to be biased?

_____ 13. What is the term that refers to the block in problem solving that involves difficulty rejecting your first hypothesis?

_____ 14. Who was associated with Daniel Kahneman in identifying heuristics people use in decision making?

_____ 15. What term is used to refer to the study of the meaning of words and sentences?

_____ 16. What type of reasoning do lawyers and judges use when they apply a law to a particular case?

_____ 17. What problem-solving strategy is being used when a person solves a complex problem by partitioning the problem into a set of ordered steps?

_____ 18. What type of meaning refers to the emotional and affective aspects of a word?

_____ 19. What term is used to refer to the values we assign the alternatives in a decision-making situation?

_____ 20. What problem-solving strategy would you use to avoid generating the 720 permutations for a six-letter anagram?

_____ 21. What term is used to describe the idea that a finite number of words can be combined to produce an almost infinite number of sentences?

_____ 22. What type of reasoning is required to solve analogies and series-completion problems?

_____ 23. What biologist studied and described the language of bees?

_____ 24. Who collaborated with Alan Newell in devising a three-stage model for solving complex problems?

Essay Questions

Suggested answers for the essay questions are included at the back of your study guide.

1. Describe functional fixedness and mental set and give an example of each.

2. Explain how the representativeness heuristic and the availability heuristic might be used by a campaign manager in a presidential election.

3. The letters in the word ASPIRE can be rearranged to form another word. How would you use an algorithm to solve the problem? How would you use heuristics?

4. Explain how a child might form an appropriate concept for the word "animal."

5. Discuss three advantages language has given humans in the struggle for survival.

Multiple-Choice Test I

For the multiple-choice questions, choose the best of the answers provided. Check your work with the answers at the back of your study guide, and be sure you understand why the keyed answers are correct.

1. Natural concepts include such things as
   a. red.
   b. round.
   c. rabbit.
   d. all of the above.

2. The work of Eleanor Rosch and her colleagues has stimulated work on
   a. deductive reasoning.
   b. decision-making strategies.
   c. natural concepts.
   d. misleading heuristics.

3. The research of Collins and Quillian suggested that _____ are used to integrate concepts.
   a. hierarchies
   b. associative bonds
   c. generalization and discrimination
   d. neural networks

4. In the model proposed by Newell and Simon, the formulation of hypotheses in problem solving occurs in the _____ stage.
   a. preparatory
   b. organizational
   c. second
   d. analytic

5. If you lost one of your favorite yellow sox and searched for it by systematically looking from one end of the house to the other, you would be using _____ to solve your problem.
   a. trial and error
   b. an algorithm
   c. the availability heuristic
   d. the anchoring heuristic

6. What problem-solving strategy is most appropriate for calculating your income tax?
   a. the anchoring heuristic
   b. framing
   c. subgoal analysis
   d. working backward

7. Titalia had only 18 denarii left after three different tax collectors each took 25 percent of her money on her way from the city to her own village. What problem-solving strategy would you use to determine how many denarii she had when she left the city?
   a. trial and error
   b. working backward
   c. inference
   d. contradiction

8. Which of the following demonstrates functional fixedness?
   a. "If we can't find a corkscrew, we can't have wine with dinner."
   b. "If God had intended for people to fly, he would have given them wings."
   c. "I've gotten along so far without a microwave oven, so why get one now?"
   d. "There is no use arguing with me because I've already made up my mind."

9. If you keep looking in the same place for an object just because that is where you expect the object to be, you are demonstrating
   a. cognitive dissonance.
   b. functional fixedness.
   c. negative framing.
   d. confirmation bias.

10. Hjlom said that in his country all murderers are executed, and since Kbimn Uwala was executed, he must have murdered someone. Kjlom made an error in his
    a. major premise.
    b. minor premise.
    c. inductive reasoning.
    d. deductive reasoning.

11. How did prehistoric people learn about natural phenomena, like the changing of the seasons and the movement of the stars?
    a. deductive reasoning.
    b. inductive reasoning.
    c. by applying algorithms.
    d. by applying heuristics.

12. Standardized tests that include analogies and series-completion problems assess people's
    a. inductive reasoning.
    b. deductive reasoning.
    c. familiarity with algorithms.
    d. familiarity with heuristics.

13. Michael has a high forehead and wears thick glasses. The interviewer who hired him because she perceived him as intelligent may have been influenced by the _____ heuristic.
    a. availability
    b. anchoring
    c. representativeness
    d. confirmation

14. A pitchman at a county fair asked his audience to estimate the cost of the vegetable slicer he was demonstrating. The pitchman had a confederate who quickly responded "$25," which was three times the cost of the gadget. The pitchman was exploiting the _____ heuristic to set a high price for his merchandise.
    a. availability
    b. confirmation
    c. representativeness
    d. anchoring

15. People perceive that the divorce rate among entertainers is much higher than for the rest of the population. This perception is influenced by the _____ heuristic.
    a. representativeness
    b. availability
    c. confirmation
    d. anchoring

16. Programming a computer to use heuristics to solve anagrams is an example of
    a. computer cognition.
    b. higher-order processing.
    c. artificial intelligence.
    d. electronic simulation.

17. In languages, a limited number of words and rules for combining them can produce an almost infinite number of sentences. This feature of language is called
    a. generativity.
    b. permutability.
    c. replacement.
    d. substitution.

18. The grammar of a language refers to
    a. its phonology.
    b. its syntax.
    c. its semantics.
    d. all of the above.

19. The smallest units of sounds in a spoken language are called
    a. letters.
    b. diphthongs.
    b. morphemes.
    d. phonemes.

20. The words "beast" and "animal" are synonyms but differ in the emotional responses they elicit. For this reason, a linguist would say that there is a difference in the _____ meaning of the two words.
    a. connotative
    b. denotative
    c. implicit
    d. explicit

21. A child's first word is most likely to be a _____ that has a _____ quality.
    a. noun; static
    b. noun; dynamic
    c. verb; static
    d. verb; dynamic

22. The most common index for assessing the language development of children is based on
    a. the number of words in their vocabulary.
    b. their ability to use bound morphemes (-s, -ed, -ing, etc.).
    c. the average length of the "sentences" they use.
    d. the extent to which they can communicate with others.

23. The theory that humans are innately equipped for acquisition of language is best supported by research showing that
    a. there are universals in language development.
    b. Broca's area is in the left cerebral hemisphere.
    c. language and thought are closely related.
    d. bilingualism in children is not uncommon.

24. The linguistic-relativity of Benjamin Whorf says that
    a. thought structures language.
    b. language structures thought.
    c. syntax determines semantics.
    d. phonology determines syntax.

25. Allen and Beatrice Gardner used _____ conditioning to teach Washoe to use _____ for communicating.
    a. operant; American sign language
    b. operant; plastic symbols
    c. classical; American sign language
    d. classical; plastic symbols

Multiple-Choice Test II

For the multiple-choice items, choose the best of the answers provided. Check your work with the answers at the back of your study guide, and be sure you understand why the keyed answers are correct.

1. Which of the following is most likely to be considered a "fuzzy concept"?
   a. round
   c. big
   c. three
   d. white

2. Which of the following is most likely to be the prototypical bird for people living in the United States?
   a. eagle
   b. chicken
   c. robin
   d. gull

3. Based on the research of Collins and Quillian, which of the following questions would subjects answer fastest?
   a. Do whales lay eggs?
   b. Do robins sing?
   c. Do tables eat?
   d. Do turkeys fly?

4. In Newell and Simon's model of problem solving, the first stage involves
   a. subgoal analysis.
   b. classification of problem type.
   c. evaluation of strategies.
   d. hypothesis generation.

5. What problem-solving strategy do doctors use in diagnosing illnesses?
   a. algorithms
   b. framing
   c. subgoal analysis
   d. heuristics

6. The Tower of Hanoi problem is an example of how _____ can be useful in problem solving.
   a. an algorithm
   b. framing
   c. subgoal analysis
   d. working backward

7. People who cannot devise new and better ways of performing tasks or solving problems have an obstacle in their thought processes called
   a. intellectual rigidity.
   b. functional inflexibility.
   c. cognitive dissonance.
   d. mental set.

8. If you have used a dime to tighten a screw or your hair dryer to defrost your radiator, you do *not* have
   a. functional fixedness.
   b. cognitive dissonance.
   c. isolated schemata.
   d. perceptual set.

9. The juror weighed the evidence against the defendant more heavily than the evidence in her favor because he had decided she was guilty the moment he saw her heavy makeup and flashy clothes. The juror had an obstacle in his thinking processes called
   a. mental set.
   b. negative framing.
   c. cognitive dissonance.
   d. confirmation bias.

10. Harold said, "If Jeannie is sick, she wouldn't come to work, so since she isn't at work, she must be sick." Harold has made an error in his
    a. major premise.
    b. minor premise.
    c. deductive reasoning.
    d. inductive reasoning.

11. When his wife worked late more and more frequently, Tory used _____ in deciding that she may have a boyfriend.
    a. deductive reasoning
    b. inductive reasoning
    c. intuitive thinking
    d. operational thinking

12. Psychologists say that the outcome of decision making is based on
    a. probability and utility.
    b. rewards and punishment.
    c. emotion and cognition.
    d. goals and aspirations.

13. In the decision making process, "utility" refers to
    a. money.
    b. satisfaction.
    c. security.
    d. any of the above.

14. Tversky and Kahneman suggested that people are influenced by stereotypes in making decisions. They call this the _____ heuristic.
    a. confirmation
    b. anchoring
    c. availability
    d. representativeness

15. Research on "framing" has shown that decision making is sometimes based on
    a. the way in which a question is worded.
    b. the context in which the decision is made.
    c. the person who describes the alternatives.
    d. the probability of occurrence of the alternatives.

16. The essential characteristics of language include all of the following *except*
    a. generativity.
    b. displacement.
    c. phonology.
    d. meaning.

17. What characteristic of language makes it possible for us to learn about Attila the Hun and Julius Caesar?
    a. generativity
    b. abstraction
    c. displacement
    d. regeneration

18. The work "dislikes" has _____ morphemes.
    a. two
    b. three
    c. four
    d. seven

19. The set of rules that specify how the morphemes of a language can be combined to form grammatical utterances is called the _____ of the language.
    a. syntax
    b. semantics
    c. morphology
    d. grammar

20. The branch of semantics that is concerned with how meaning is affected by intonation and context is called
    a. pragmatics.
    b. semiotics
    c. morphology.
    d. dialectics.

21. In comparing individual children, the greatest difference among the children is most likely to be in
    a. the types of things they talk about.
    b. the order in which syntactic rules are acquired.
    c. they types of word combinations they use.
    d. the rate at which they acquire language.

22. By the time they are five years old, most children use _____ in their speech.
    a. pronouns
    b. tag questions
    c. embedded sentences
    d. all of the above

23. In his theorizing about language development, Piaget emphasized the relationship between language and
    a. physical development.
    b. cognition.
    c. parental models.
    d. schemata.

24. In the research that challenged Whorf's linguistic-relativity hypothesis, Eleanor Rosch tested the hypothesis that there is a positive correlation between
    a. the number of color words in languages and the ability of members of the language community to discriminate colors.
    b. the size of people's vocabularies and their mastery of formal operational thought.
    c. perceived kinship and the availability of words to describe relationships (uncle, cousin, etc.).
    d. the language environment of children and the rate at which they acquire their native language.

25. Researchers who have worked at developing language skills in primates have claimed that their students can
    a. invent new combinations of words.
    b. teach language to a friend.
    c. refer to past and future events.
    d. do all of the above.

Chapter 9

INFANCY AND CHILDHOOD

Learning Objectives

After studying this chapter, you should be able to:

1. Describe the three primary questions studied in developmental psychology: continuity vs. discontinuity, stability vs. change, and nature vs. nurture.

2. Differentiate between cross-sectional and longitudinal methods of studying development.

3. Define the basic terminology of inheritance, including genes, DNA, and dominant and recessive genes.

4. Compare and contrast the influence of heredity and environment on development.

5. Differentiate between a genotype and phenotype.

6. Outline the sequence of prenatal development, including the zygote, embryo, and fetus.

7. Discuss the impact of the environment on prenatal development, including critical periods.

8. Outline the sequence of motor development in infants.

9. Describe the visual and auditory perceptual abilities of infants.

10. Discuss the concept of object permanence and the development of symbolic thought during Piaget's sensorimotor period of cognitive development.

11. Discuss the characteristics of Piaget's preoperational period of cognitive development and explain the concepts of conservation and reversibility.

12. Discuss the characteristics of Piaget's concrete operational period of cognitive development and describe the sequence of the mastery of conservation.

13. Outline the development of formal operational thinking and describe the potassium iodide test, contrasting the performances of a 9-year-old and a 14-year-old child.

14. Discuss criticisms of Piaget's theory.

15. Describe the information processing approach to the study of cognitive development.

16. Identify how the processes of attention and memory change from infancy to childhood.

17. Compare and contrast the parents' role in fostering development with the infant's role.

18. Describe the development of attachments with others during infancy.

19. Describe the four dimensions of child rearing: control, demands for maturity, clarity of communication, and nurturance.

20. Describe the effects of maternal employment and day care on children's cognitive and social development.

21. Identify the primary areas of documented gender differences.

22. Examine the development of gender roles in children, contrasting the psychoanalytic, social learning, cognitive-developmental, gender schema, and sociobiological perspectives.

Working with Names and Terms

From the alphabetized list below, choose the name or term that answers the question, using each name or term only once. Answers are at the back of your study guide.

Baumrind, Diana
continuity
critical period
cross-sectional
dominant
fetus
Freud, Sigmund
gender constancy
gender schema
genes
Gesell, Arnold
Harlow, Harry

Kohlberg, Lawrence
longitudinal
nature
object permanence
placenta
preoperational
reversibility
sensorimotor
sociobiology
teratogen
visual cliff
zygote

_____ 1. During which of Piaget's periods of development does the concept of object permanence develop?

_____ 2. What perspective emphasized the role of genetics in the determination of the sexual behavior of males and females?

_____ 3. What principle says that if you can make a ball of clay into the shape of a hot dog, you can reshape the clay into a ball?

_____ 4. Who was the Yale psychologist who charted norms for physical and motor development in the first half of the twentieth century?

_____ 5. What stage has Jennifer entered when she realizes that girls will always be females and that boys will always be males regardless of the clothes they wear or the activities they prefer?

_____ 6. Whose work with rhesus monkeys demonstrated the importance of holding and caressing in the development of attachment?

_____ 7. What type of gene will invariably be expressed in a person's phenotype?

_____ 8. What position is taken by people who emphasize the role of heredity in the determination of personality and behavior?

_____ 9. What research method would be used to study the stability of personality traits from childhood through adulthood?

_____ 10. What theory says that children assimilate culturally defined sex roles as they acquire the concepts of male and female?

_____ 11. Who claimed that the process of identification with the same-sex parent is an important factor in the development of gender roles?

_____ 12. What term is used to refer to an unborn child when a woman's pregnancy is obvious to others?

_____ 13. What apparatus was developed by Eleanor Gibson and Richard Walk to study depth perception in young organisms?

_____ 14. What name is given to an interval during which a developing organism is especially sensitive to a particular teratogen?

_____ 15. Who proposed a theory of gender role development based on Piaget's theory of cognitive development?

_____ 16. Which of Piaget's periods of development includes the acquisition of language?

_____ 17. What concept is missing in the infant who behaves as if objects that are out of sight cease to exist?

_____ 18. What research method was the psychologist using when she compared the short-term memory capacities of 5-year-old children and 10-year-old children?

_____ 19. What name is given to the segments of deoxyribonucleic acid that we have in our cells?

_____ 20. What general term is used to refer to substances that can permeate the membranes of the placenta and disrupt the development of a fetus?

_____ 21. Who analyzed child-rearing practices and related these practices to children's behavior?

_____ 22. What position is taken by psychologists who believe that the course of development occurs in a smooth progression rather than in a series of spurts and plateaus?

_____ 23. Where does the transfer of nutrients from mother to fetus occur?

_____ 24. What is created when a sperm cell and an ovum meet?

Essay Questions

Suggested answers for the essay questions are included at the back of your study guide.

1. Explain why it is difficult to collect data from infants and young children, and discuss how developmental psychologists have resolved this problem.

2. Describe the cross-sectional and longitudinal methods of research. Discuss the advantages and disadvantages of each, and describe a research question that would be appropriate for each of the methods.

3. Explain how researchers determine whether a child has mastered the concept of conservation, and discuss cognitive skills that are precursors of conservation.

4. Your text discusses three enduring controversies concerning human development. Describe the controversies and give a specific example of how each of them applies to some aspect of development.

Multiple-Choice Test I

For the multiple-choice items, choose the best of the answers provided. Check your work with the answers at the back of your study guide, and be sure you understand why the keyed answers are correct.

1. An important step leading to early research on child development was
   a. the ideas of Freud concerning infant sexuality.
   b. the advent of compulsory public education.
   c. the norms charted by Arnold Gesell.
   d. the publication of baby biographies.

2. Piaget's theory of cognitive development is most accurately described as taking the _____ positions.
   a. discontinuity and nature
   b. discontinuity and nurture
   c. continuity and nature
   d. continuity and nurture

3. The old saying, "As the twig is bent, so grows the tree," expresses the _____ view of human development.
   a. nature
   b. nurture
   c. continuity
   d. discontinuity

4. Compared to the longitudinal method, the cross-sectional method has the advantage of
   a. being faster and simpler.
   b. being experimental rather than correlational.
   c. providing data on several aspects of development.
   d. avoiding experimenter bias.

5. In the nature versus nurture controversy, most psychologists take the position that
   a. nature dominates nurture.
   b. nurture dominates nature.
   c. nature and nurture interact.
   d. nature and nurture are independent.

6. Genes that are dominant will express themselves in
   a. the genotype.
   b. the phenotype.
   c. both the genotype and the phenotype.
   d. neither the genotype nor the phenotype.

7. Which of the following is the correct order?
   a. zygote, fetus, embryo
   b. zygote, embryo, fetus
   c. embryo, fetus, zygote
   d. embryo, zygote, fetus

8. The symptoms of fetal alcohol syndrome include
   a. intellectual impairment.
   b. deformity of the hands and face.
   c. bodily tremors.
   d. all of the above.

9. Because the central nervous system is especially sensitive to disruption by teratogens during the early weeks of pregnancy, these early weeks are referred to as a _____ for development of the central nervous system.
   a. vulnerable state
   b. high-risk interval
   c. susceptible phase
   d. critical period

10. The text describes studies investigating the pitch perception of young infants. The studies used _____ as the dependent variable.
    a. heart rate
    b. head turning
    c. notes on a piano
    d. human voices

11. Research suggests that infants have depth perception
    a. at birth.
    b. shortly after birth.
    c. before they are old enough to crawl.
    d. by the time they are able to stand without support.

12. Piaget claimed that during the sensorimotor period, infants acquire
    a. the concept of reversibility.
    b. the ability to imitate the behavior of others.
    c. the ability to think symbolically.
    d. all of the above.

13. When a child has acquired the concept of reversibility, the child has entered the stage that Piaget called the _____ period.
    a. formal operational
    b. preoperational
    c. symbolic operational
    d. concrete operational

14. Piaget's work showed that children in the period of concrete operations are *unable* to
    a. systematically generate and test hypotheses.
    b. apply the concept of reversibility.
    c. use symbolic representation in cognitive processes.
    d. do any of the above.

15. The information processing theory of cognitive development differs from Piaget's theory in its emphasis on
    a. individual differences.
    b. genetic determinants.
    c. continuity.
    d. qualitative change.

16. Research suggests that children are _____ years old before they selectively attend to the relevant aspects of a situation.
    a. 2 or 3
    b. 4 or 5
    c. 6 or 7
    d. 8 or 9

17. The first of the many love relationships humans experience is
    a. adience.
    b. attachment.
    c. caretaker preference.
    d. imprinting.

18. The interaction of fathers with their infant children is most likely to involve
    a. holding and cuddling.
    b. verbal exchanges.
    c. feeding and bathing.
    d. physical play.

19. Baumrind's research showed that the parents of children who are dependent and passive score low on all the dimensions of child rearing *except*
    a. control.
    b. demands for maturity.
    c. clarity of communication.
    d. nurturance.

20. Which of the following is true of the children of mothers who work outside the home, compared to the children of mothers who do not work outside the home?
    a. They are less mature and more dependent.
    b. They have fewer stereotypes about sex roles.
    c. They are more likely to have behavior problems at school.
    d. They are more likely to feel insecure and rejected.

21. Concerning gender differences in intellectual ability, the text reports that males and females are intellectually similar, but that
    a. males are overrepresented at the extremes.
    b. females are overrepresented at the extremes.
    c. males reach their full intellectual capacity earlier than females.
    d. females reach their full intellectual capacity earlier than males.

22. Which of the following is accurate concerning gender roles?
    a. They are strongly influenced by culture.
    b. They are apparent by the age of two years.
    c. They are difficult to change.
    d. All of the above are accurate concerning gender roles.

23. In Kohlberg's cognitive theory of gender-role development, children at the stage he calls _____ understand the reality of gender but rely on superficial signs, like clothing, to determine the gender of others.
    a. gender recognition
    b. gender constancy
    c. gender stability
    d. gender identity

24. Sociobiologists claim that the primary goal of human sexual behavior is to
    a. experience pleasure.
    b. insure the survival of our genes.
    c. bolster our egos.
    d. insure the survival of our species.

25. Research on animals has shown that testosterone levels are correlated with _____ behavior.
    a. altruistic
    b. aggressive
    c. dependent
    d. compliant

Multiple-Choice Test II

For the multiple choice items, choose the best of the answers provided. Check your work with the answers at the back of your study guide, and be sure you understand why the keyed answers are correct.

1. Which of the following is (are) among the three enduring questions that confront students of human development?
    a. cross-sectional versus longitudinal research
    b. clinical versus experimental data
    c. continuity versus noncontinuity in development
    d. all of the above.

2. A person is expressing the idea of stability in development when she says that the newly elected mayor
    a. resembles his father, who was a member of the state legislature.
    b. has been a politician ever since he learned to talk.
    c. will fulfill the promises he made while campaigning.
    d. has learned to control his emotions.

3. The old saying, "You can't make a silk purse out of a sow's ear," expresses the _____ view of human development.
    a. nature
    b. nurture
    c. continuity
    d. discontinuity

4. A group of children with high IQs was identified and retested annually for many years. This study used the _____ method.
    a. cross-sectional
    b. life-span
    c. longitudinal
    d. repeated measures

5. In determining characteristics such as intelligence, it is most accurate to say that genes
   a. are much more important than environmental factors.
   b. are much less important than environmental factors.
   c. determine the phenotype but not the genotype.
   d. establish a potential range of reactions.

6. If eye color is determined by a single pair of genes, then one can predict that invariably
   a. two brown-eyed parents will have children with brown eyes.
   b. two blue-eyed parents will have children with blue eyes.
   c. a brown-eyed parent and a blue-eyed parent will have children with blue eyes.
   d. a brown-eyed parent and a blue-eyed parent will have children with brown eyes.

7. Teratogens include such things as
   a. drugs, such as heroin.
   b. pollutants, such as lead.
   c. disease organisms, such as the rubella (German measles) virus.
   d. all of the above.

8. To determine whether a child's intellectual and physical development is proceeding normally, parents and pediatricians frequently compare the child's level of development with
   a. epidemiological data.
   b. maturational standards.
   c. norms.
   d. composite guidelines.

9. Between birth and the age of two years, the number of neurons in the brain _____, and the weight of the brain _____.
   a. remains the same; triples
   b. remains the same; doubles
   c. increases dramatically; triples
   d. increases dramatically; doubles

10. Infants are most interested in the visual investigation of
    a. hands.
    b. faces.
    c. geometric forms.
    d. colored objects.

11. The idea that qualitative changes in cognitive processes result in identifiable periods or stages in intellectual development was proposed by
    a. Sigmund Freud.
    b. Arnold Gesell.
    c. John Watson.
    d. Jean Piaget.

12. The child who says she can get more cookie by breaking a cookie in two is in what Piaget called the _____ period.
    a. sensorimotor
    b. preoperational
    c. anthropomorphic
    d. egocentric

13. The term "conservation" is used by Piaget to refer to the ability to make logical judgments concerning
    a. number.
    c. weight.
    c. length.
    d. all of the above.

14. When children are able to compare the world as it is with the world as it could be, they are in what Piaget called the _____ period of cognitive development.
    a. abstract representational
    b. mature intellectual
    c. formal operational
    d. deductive logical

15. On what basis have Gelman and other investigators criticized Piaget's work?
    a. His work ignores individual differences in the rate of cognitive development.
    b. His theory is not supported by research.
    c. His work fails to disclose cognitive skills children possess.
    d. He used only the longitudinal method in his studies.

16. The development of selective attention and memory strategies are most likely to be studied by psychologists who prefer the _____ approach to cognitive development.
    a. information processing
    b. behavioral
    c. Piagetian
    d. discontinuity

17. The research of Harry Harlow demonstrated the importance of _____ in attachment.
    a. eye contact
    b. contact comfort
    c. maternal relaxation
    d. verbal exchanges

18. Infants' active role in the attachment process involves
    a. crying.
    b. smiling.
    c. gazing.
    d. all of the above.

19. The research of Diana Baumrind showed the effect of _____ on children's personalities and behavior.
    a. day care
    b. attachment in infancy
    c. child-rearing practices
    d. single parenting

20. The text reports that some psychologists are concerned about the effect of extended day care on the _____ of infants and young children.
    a. quality of the attachment relationship
    b. rate of intellectual development
    c. development of self-esteem
    d. maintenance of physical health

21. Of the following, which personality trait shows the most stable and enduring difference between males and females?
    a. altruism
    b. aggression
    c. dependence
    d. empathy

22. The social learning theory of gender role development emphasizes
    a. biological determinants.
    b. gender identity.
    c. classical conditioning.
    d. reinforcement and imitation.

23. Kohlberg's theory suggests that gender stability and gender constancy develop primarily as a result of
    a. observation and imitation.
    b. reinforcement for sex-appropriate behavior.
    c. cognitive processes.
    d. biological maturation.

24. The theory of gender that recognizes the importance of both social learning and cognitive processes is called _____ theory.
    a. two-process
    b. interactive
    c. gender-schema
    d. gender-identity

25. Sociobiologists claim that to achieve the goal of survival of our genes, males have evolved to be _____ in their sexual relationships and females have evolved to be _____ in their sexual relationships.
    a. promiscuous; selective
    b. aggressive; compliant
    c. selfish; unselfish
    d. selective; compliant

Chapter 10

ADOLESCENCE, ADULTHOOD, AND AGING

Learning Objectives

After studying this chapter, you should be able to:

1. Define adolescence and compare the divergent perspectives on this "uniquely troubling time."

2. Compare and contrast physical growth spurts in adolescent boys and girls.

3. Differentiate between primary and secondary sex characteristics, including menarche in girls.

4. Define moral realism and contrast this stage with that of autonomous morality.

5. Describe Kohlberg's six stages of moral development.

6. Discuss criticisms of Kohlberg's theory, highlighting the distinction between moral judgment and moral behavior.

7. Describe how emerging adolescent cognitive skills can be impaired by personal needs.

8. Describe Erikson's stage of identity versus role confusion, and discuss what is meant by the development of a negative identity.

9. Refute the stereotype of adolescent "storm and stress" with data on adolescent/parent relationships.

10. Describe the influence of peer relationships in adolescence.

11. Describe the recent trends in adolescent sexuality and two possible negative consequences of that activity: pregnancy and AIDS.

12. Define adulthood and describe the physical developments that occur during this period.

13. Discuss cognitive development during adulthood.

14. Discuss social and personal development during adulthood, including factors leading to satisfaction in both family life and career.

15. Describe the physical changes that occur during the later years of adulthood.

16. Discuss cognitive development during old age, describing the difference in results obtained when using cross-sectional or longitudinal studies.

17. Compare the decrement model and the personal development model of old age.

18. Discuss the challenges of aging, noting especially the challenges of ill health, dementia, and Alzheimer's disease.

19. Discuss the concept of bereavement and describe the five stages in the terminally ill person's attitude toward death as identified by Kubler-Ross.

Working with Names and Terms

From the alphabetized list below, choose the name or term that answers the question, using each name and term only once. Answers are at the back of your study guide.

Alzheimer, Alois
cross-sectional
decrement model
dementia
empty nest
Erikson, Eric
filtering
foreclosure
Freud, Sigmund
Gilligan, Carol
Hall, G. Stanley
intimacy
Kalish, Richard
Kohlberg, Lawrence
Kübler-Ross, Elisabeth
longitudinal
Marcia, James
metacognitive skills
moral realism
Neugarten, Bernice
Piaget, Jean
role confusion
secondary sexual characteristics
self-accepted principles

_____ 1. What research method should one use if one wants to study the stability of intelligence or other personality traits?

_____ 2. Who criticized the theories of both Erikson and Kohlberg as being sweeping generalizations based on observations of white male subjects?

_____ 3. What term is used to refer to the ability to monitor and evaluate our own thinking and reasoning?

_____ 4. What term would Erikson use to refer to an 18-year-old male who has not found direction or purpose for his life?

_____ 5. What is the positive outcome of the stage that immediately follows Erikson's stage of "identity versus identity confusion"?

_____ 6. Whose research first established a link between cognitive development and moral reasoning?

_____ 7. Who proposed that people accept their own death during the final stage of dying?

_____ 8. Whose study of 2000 adults challenged the idea that childhood experiences forecast adult behavior?

_____ 9. What identity status describes the adolescent who accepts without question the plans her parents have made for her?

_____ 10. Whose theory of personality development focuses on a conflict or crisis in each of the eight stages of life?

_____ 11. What term is used to describe the home of a couple whose children are married and live in another state?

_____ 12. What early twentieth century psychologist proposed that adolescence is a period of great "storm and stress"?

_____ 13. What expert on late adult development claims that older people are often happy because they focus their energy on matters of true importance?

_____ 14. Whose emphasis on the importance of developing a clear and independent sense of self during adolescence is reflected in Erikson's emphasis on identity formation?

_____ 15. What term is used to refer to such things as growth of pubic hair, development of breasts in girls, and deepening of the voice in boys?

_____ 16. What theory describes steps people go through in the process of mate selection?

_____ 17. What term did Piaget use to describe the response of a child who says that the boy who broke three cups while helping his mother is naughtier than the boy who broke one cup as he tried to sneak a cookie from the kitchen cabinet?

_____ 18. Whose work led him to propose four different "status" categories in adolescents' search for identity?

_____ 19. According to Kohlberg, at what level of moral development should college students be?

_____ 20. What term do psychologists currently use to refer to the mental deterioration that occurs in Alzheimer's disease?

_____ 21. What research method has produced results suggesting that intelligence steadily declines after the age of 50?

_____ 22. What theory views old age as a period of decline in health, intelligence, and vitality?

_____ 23. Whose theory is based on Piaget's work and identifies six stages of moral reasoning?

_____ 24. Who identified a brain disease that occurs most frequently among older people

Essay Questions

Suggested answers for the essay questions are included at the back of your study guide.

1. Adolescents are responsible for a disproportionate share of criminal activity in the United States. How do you account for this?

2. If you wanted to rate young people on their progress in establishing an identity, what criteria would you use as indicators of progress?

3. Discuss your views concerning whether adolescence is a distinct stage in the human life cycle.

4. A large proportion of the data on adolescents and adulthood comes from surveys and questionnaires and from correlational research. Explain why there are problems with these types of data.

Multiple-Choice Test I

For the multiple-choice items, choose the best of the answers provided. Check your work with the answers at the back of your study guide, and be sure you understand why the keyed answers are correct.

1. The research of Bernice Neugarten on adults challenged the accuracy of the idea that
    a. there are gender differences in moral reasoning.
    b. childhood experiences irrevocably determine the course of development.
    c. there are identifiable life stages after adolescence.
    d. identity formation occurs during adolescence and early adulthood.

2. Primary sexual characteristics in females include all of the following *except* the
    a. ovaries.
    b. vagina.
    c. breasts.
    d. uterus.

3. Research has shown that it is socially advantageous for males to
    a. mature early.
    b. mature late.
    c. have an older sister.
    d. have a younger sister.

4. Carl realizes that his younger sister meant to be helpful when she tried to give his rabbit a bath. Carl is at the stage of moral reasoning that Piaget called _____ morality.
    a. autonomous
    b. conventional
    c. principled
    d. realistic

5. Allison said Heinz should steal the drug because if he doesn't, his wife's family will get mad and scream at him. Allison is at what Kohlberg called the _____ level of moral reasoning.
    a. realistic
    b. hedonistic
    c. retributional emphasis
    d. premoral

6. Kohlberg's theory of moral reasoning has been criticized on the basis of
    a. being based on an all-male sample.
    b. dealing with judgments rather than behavior.
    c. assuming implicitly that certain kinds of moral reasoning are superior to others.
    d. all of the above.

7. The text observes that the new-found cognitive skills of adolescents are *not* apparent in adolescents' ability to
    a. deal with political and social realities.
    b. distinguish between love and lust.
    c. evaluate social risks.
    d. make sophisticated moral judgments.

8. To refer to the type of identity confusion that occurs when adolescents become involved in drug abuse or delinquent behavior, Erikson used the term
   a. foreclosure.
   b. negative identity.
   c. moratorium.
   d. peer conformity.

9. A young male that James Marcia would assign "foreclosure status" would be most likely to
   a. go to medical school.
   b. experiment with drugs.
   c. commit suicide.
   d. run away from home.

10. Adolescents are most likely to have conflicts with parents concerning
    a. politics and religion.
    b. rules and chores.
    c. sex roles and gender differences.
    d. goals and aspirations.

11. The increase in adolescent sexual intercourse that has occurred in recent years is most pronounced among
    a. girls.
    b. boys.
    c. minorities.
    d. homosexuals.

12. Which of the following statements is most accurate concerning adolescent sexual practices?
    a. The majority of teenage pregnancies are terminated by abortion.
    b. Publicity on "safe sex" to avoid AIDS has not been very effective.
    c. Most adolescents report that their first sexual experience was exciting.
    d. Adolescent sexual experiences determine adult sexual orientation.

13. Menopause occurs in women as a result of
    a. physiological causes that have not been identified.
    b. atrophy of ovarian tissue.
    c. decrease in sexual activity.
    d. reduction in estrogen production.

14. During menopause, a women is most likely to experience
    a. a lack of emotional control.
    b. a sharp decline in sexual desire.
    c. depression.
    d. hot flashes.

15. Research has shown that the *least* important variable in mate selection is
    a. proximity.
    b. physical attractiveness.
    c. complementarity.
    d. similarity of backgrounds.

16. Marital happiness is lowest for both men and women
    a. when their children are infants.
    b. when their children are young adolescents.
    c. just before their children leave home.
    d. just after their children leave home.

17. Research has shown that there is a positive correlation between job satisfaction and
    a. age.
    b. sex.
    c. intelligence.
    d. marital satisfaction.

18. The most important factor in the increasing proportion of people over 65 years of age in the United States is
    a. better diet and more exercise.
    b. genetic engineering.
    c. a high standard of living.
    d. medical technology.

19. People over 70 years of age are most likely to show a decline in tasks that assess
    a. short-term memory.
    b. perceptual-motor speed.
    c. vocabulary.
    d. verbal reasoning.

20. Investigators have found that levels of happiness and contentment are highest among
    a. adolescents.
    b. young adults.
    c. middle-aged adults.
    d. the elderly.

21. Grandparents are most likely to enjoy a visit from a grandchild if the grandchild is a(n) _____ and the visit is relatively _____.
    a. adolescent; short
    b. adolescent; long
    c. preschooler; short
    d. preschooler; long

22. The decline in cognitive abilities that occurs as a result of disease, alcoholism, or strokes is called
    a. dementia.
    b. paranoia.
    c. dissonance.
    d. senility.

23. The symptoms of Alzheimer's disease include
    a. memory loss.
    b. confusion and disorientation.
    c. personality changes.
    d. all of the above.

24. Which of the following is the correct order for the stages of dying proposed by Kübler-Ross?
    a. anger, denial, depression, bargaining, acceptance
    b. anger, depression, bargaining, denial, acceptance
    c. denial, anger, bargaining, depression, acceptance
    d. denial, depression, anger, bargaining, acceptance

25. Investigators have found that many people facing death experience Kübler-Ross's stage of
    a. anger.
    b. denial.
    c. bargaining.
    d. depression.

Multiple-Choice Test II

For the multiple-choice items, choose the best of the answers provided. Check your work with the answers at the back of your study guide, and be sure you understand why the keyed answers are correct.

1. There is disagreement among psychologists concerning whether G. Stanley Hall was accurate in his characterization of adolescence as a period of
   a. storm and stress.
   b. raging hormones and sexual preoccupation.
   c. trying and testing.
   d. self-absorption and self-consciousness.

2. As a stage of life, adolescence is best described as
   a. stormy and stressful.
   b. culturally defined.
   c. the final stage of childhood.
   d. the initial stage of adulthood.

3. The "growth spurt" in males occurs _____ than in females and proceeds at a _____ rate.
   a. earlier; faster
   b. earlier; slower
   c. later; faster
   d. later; slower

4. During Piaget's stage of moral realism, children think that the severity of punishment should be determined by
   a. the motive of the wrong-doer.
   b. the magnitude of the offense.
   c. the importance of the rule that was violated.
   d. the extent to which the behavior negatively affected another person.

5. Level III moral reasoning in Kohlberg's theory differs from earlier levels in its emphasis on
   a. conformity.
   b. motivation.
   c. retribution.
   d. conscience.

6. Carol Gilligan suggests that the morality of females emphasizes _____, and that the morality of males emphasizes _____.
   a. caring; justice
   b. conformity; conscience
   c. compassion; pragmatism
   d. emotion; reasoning

7. The stages in Erikson's theory of personality development are based on
   a. sexual orientation.
   b. prepotent motives.
   c. dominant conflicts.
   d. social norms.

8. Anita has changed majors several times and plans to travel and investigate other cultures before she makes definite plans for her future. James Marcia would assign Anita the identity status of
   a. postponement.
   b. moratorium.
   c. confusion.
   d. foreclosure.

9. Peers are likely to be more influential than parents in determining
   a. political beliefs.
   b. vocational choices.
   c. hair styles.
   d. all of the above.

10. The text suggests that the high rate of abortion among teenagers in the United States is largely attributable to
    a. lack of information.
    b. peer pressure.
    c. influence of the media.
    d. parental permissiveness.

11. Most experts would agree with Freud and Erikson in defining adulthood in terms of
    a. age and physical maturity.
    b. income and independence.
    c. conformity and compassion.
    d. work and love.

12. A 60-year-old person is most likely to experience a decline in
    a. abstract thinking.
    b. metacognitive skills.
    c. recall memory.
    d. associative learning.

13. Statistics show that 95 percent of Americans
    a. have had sexual intercourse before they graduate from high school.
    b. will spend their last years in a rest home.
    c. have been married at least once by the time they are 35 years old.
    d. eat too much salty and fatty food.

14. The filter theory of mate selection proposes that the first step in the process concerns
    a. physical attractiveness.
    b. proximity.
    c. complementarity.
    d. similarity.

15. Research has shown that income and job security are likely to be most important to a(n)
    a. bus driver.
    b. computer programmer.
    c. electrician.
    d. airline pilot.

16. The tests devised by Kuder and by Strong and Campbell provide profiles that could be helpful to you in choosing a
    a. college.
    b. lifestyle.
    c. mate.
    d. job.

17. People over 65 years of age are *less* likely than younger people to suffer from
    a. colds and influenza.
    b. broken bones.
    c. kidney dysfunction.
    d. high blood pressure.

18. The "myth" that intelligence declines steadily after the age of 50 is a result of
    a. research methodology.
    b. random sampling.
    c. use of invalid and/or unreliable tests.
    d. misinterpretation of data.

19. The greatest threat to happiness during old age is
    a. separation from old friends.
    b. reduced income.
    c. chronic illness.
    d. loneliness.

20. The term "senility" has been rejected by psychologists because it
    a. does not adequately describe the cognitive deterioration that occurs with age.
    b. became associated with changes that occur as a result of illness.
    c. implies that intellectual impairment is a natural consequence of age.
    d. was used to refer to both physical and mental deterioration.

21. The most common cause of dementia in the elderly is
    a. the process of aging.
    b. Alzheimer's disease.
    c. strokes.
    d. chronic alcoholism.

22. The text notes that there is a significant decrease in levels of _____ in the brains of Alzheimer's patients who have died.
    a. proteins
    b. acetylcholine
    c. hemoglobin
    d. glia

23. Kübler-Ross claims that a person who has just received a diagnosis of AIDS is most likely to say
    a. "What did I do to deserve this?"
    b. "I'd like to kill the person that infected me!"
    c. "I'm not afraid to die, but I hate to suffer."
    d. "There must be some mistake."

24. The stages of dying proposed by Kübler-Ross include all of the following *except*
    a. resolution.
    b. depression.
    c. bargaining.
    d. anger.

25. Psychologists have been most critical of Kübler-Ross's
    a. assumptions.
    b. lack of compassion.
    c. sampling.
    d. methodology.

Chapter 11

INTELLIGENCE

Learning Objectives

After studying this chapter, you should be able to:

1. Define intelligence.

2. Distinguish between intelligence and performance.

3. Discuss the historical development of intelligence testing, including the work of Galton, Binet, Terman, and Wechsler.

4. Define the concepts of mental age (MA) and chronological age (CA) and describe the subsequent development of the intelligence quotient (IQ).

5. Differentiate between a verbal IQ and a performance IQ, and discuss how they combine to create a full-scale IQ score.

6. Describe the key features of the WAIS and the WISC intelligence tests.

7. Compare the three criteria of intelligence tests: standardization, reliability, and validity.

8. Differentiate between aptitude tests and achievement tests.

9. Differentiate between the concepts of competence and performance.

10. Compare and contrast Spearman's g factor of intelligence with Thurstone's notions of seven primary mental abilities.

11. Discuss Sternberg's triarchic theory of intelligence and contrast it with Gardner's multiple intelligences.

12. Describe the stability of IQ scores across the lifespan.

13. Describe the characteristics of mentally retarded people.

14. Differentiate between organic and psychosocial mental retardation.

15. Describe the key findings in Terman's longitudinal study of intellectually gifted people.

16. Describe the relative contributions of heredity and environment to intelligence.

17. Describe the interpretation and application of the heritability ratio.

18. Critically examine the evidence suggesting inherent intellectual differences between races.

19. Discuss the various uses and abuses of IQ tests, citing alternative procedures for the assessment of intelligence.

Working with Names and Terms

From the alphabetized list below, choose the name or term that answers the question, using each name and term only once. Answers are at the back of your study guide.

componential
concurrent validity
Down, Langdon
experiential
factor analysis
Galton, Sir Francis
Gardner, Howard
g-factor
Goddard, Henry
heritability
Intelligence Quotient
Jensen, Arthur
longitudinal
percentile
predictive validity
psychosocial
reliability
Simon, Théophile
Spearman, Charles
split-half reliability
standardization
Sternberg, Robert
Terman, Lewis
Thurstone, Louis

_____ 1. What criterion for psychological tests involves administration of potential items for the test to a sample that is representative of the population for which the test is intended?

_____ 2. Which of the components of intelligence proposed by Robert Sternberg is most important for artists and inventors?

_____ 3. Who first described the physical symptoms of a well-known type of organic mental retardation?

_____ 4. What was Lewis Terman calculating when he divided "mental age" by "chronological age"?

_____ 5. Who tried to measure intelligence and failed because he did not emphasize measurement of cognitive skills?

_____ 6. Whose factor analysis led him to the conclusion that there is a core component that permeates all aspects of intelligence?

_____ 7. What criterion for psychological tests is met by a test that produces scores that are stable over time?

_____ 8. Who proposed the triarchic theory of intelligence?

_____ 9. Whose monograph in a scholarly journal fueled the controversy concerning the cause of racial differences in intelligence?

_____ 10. Who claimed that the concept of intelligence should be democratized by including factors that critics refer to as "talents"?

_____ 11. What type of score is most appropriate for describing the performance of an adult on an intelligence test?

_____ 12. What early twentieth-century psychologist was responsible for a major misuse of intelligence testing in the screening of immigrants?

_____ 13. Which of the components of intelligence proposed by Sternberg is most closely related to students' grade point averages?

_____ 14. What statistical procedure has been used to identify the components of intelligence?

_____ 15. What term has traditionally been used to refer to the central or dominant component in intelligence?

_____ 16. What is being assessed when scores on a new group intelligence test are correlated with scores made by the same individuals on the WISC?

_____ 17. What index is based on family resemblance studies and adoption studies?

_____ 18. What criterion for psychological tests is especially important when an intelligence test is used for employee selection?

_____ 19. Who adapted an intelligence test written for French children to be used by English-speaking children and did a longitudinal study of intellectually gifted children?

_____ 20. What is being assessed when a correlation is calculated between the scores on odd-numbered items and the scores on even-numbered items of a test?

_____ 21. Whose use of factor analysis led him to conclude that there are seven primary mental abilities?

_____ 22. What term is used to describe retardation that is apparently the result of economic, familial, and educational deprivation?

_____ 23. Who assisted Alfred Binet in construction of the first acceptable intelligence test?

_____ 24. What type of research design is appropriate for a study on the stability of IQ scores over time?

Essay Questions

Suggested answers for the essay questions are included at the back of your study guide.

1. The Kaplans are very hopeful that little Susie will have an IQ score high enough to qualify for a school for gifted children. What can the Kaplans do to maximize little Susie's score on an intelligence test?

2. Generate and discuss three hypotheses to explain why the average IQ score of black children is lower than the average IQ score for white children.

3. According to Robert Sternberg, the three types of intelligence are componential, experiential, and contextual. Describe each of these types of intelligence and identify occupations that take advantage of each type of intelligence.

4. Reliability and validity are usually very high for instruments that measure physical properties, like yardsticks for measuring distance and scales for measuring weight. Why can't psychological measurement, as in intelligence testing, achieve the same high levels of reliability and validity?

Multiple-Choice Test I

For the multiple-choice items, choose the best of the answers provided. Check your work with the answers at the back of your study guide, and be sure you understand why the keyed answers are correct.

1. Which of the following best summarized the public perception of intelligence, according to the text?
    a. Intelligence is what rich people have lots of.
    b. Intelligence is mostly irrelevant in the real world.
    c. Intelligence is what you get by going to school.
    d. Intelligence is in the eyes of the beholder.

2. Which of the following questions is most likely to have been asked by one of Sir Francis Galton's examiners?
    a. What is the meaning of "equivocate"?
    b. How did the archeologist know that the coin dated 137 B.C. was fake?
    c. Which of those two tones was louder?
    d. What is the cube root of 64?

3. The primary reason why Galton's intelligence test was a failure is because it lacked
    a. standardization.
    b. identifiable factors.
    c. reliability.
    d. validity.

4. The intelligence test developed by Binet and Simon was for the purpose of
    a. selecting candidates for the officer-training school of the French navy.
    b. selecting civil service employees for the French postal service.
    c. awarding scholarships to the Sorbonne and other faculties of the University of Paris.
    d. identifying retarded children for the Ministry of Education.

5. Who would be most likely to be classified as profoundly retarded if the method suggested by William Stern and used by Lewis Terman were used to describe his or her performance on the Stanford-Binet test?
    a. a mildly retarded child
    b. an adolescent who doesn't speak English very well
    c. a full professor at a prestigious university
    d. a child who lives in an inner-city ghetto

6. David Wechsler's primary objection to the Stanford-Binet was that it
    a. failed to produce scores for different aspects of intelligence.
    b. produced IQ scores, which are meaningless for adults.
    c. was designed to be individually administered.
    d. favored males who are white and live in cities.

7. What are the two major scales of the Wechsler intelligence tests?
   a. WAIS and WISC
   b. verbal and performance
   c. componential and experiential
   d. linguistic and quantitative

8. In the process of standardization, test developers
   a. choose items for the final version of the test.
   b. establish norms.
   c. provide guidelines for administering and scoring the test.
   d. do all of the above.

9. Which of the following best describes the type of sample that should be used to standardize a revised version of the WAIS?
   a. segmented
   b. homogenous
   c. representative
   d. integrated

10. Every day for a week, Henry reads the distance from home to work on his odometer. If he gets 15.3 miles on each reading, he can conclude that his odometer has
    a. test-retest reliability.
    b. split-half reliability.
    c. predictive validity.
    d. concurrent validity.

11. The split-half method is appropriate for measuring the reliability of
    a. a multiple-choice test.
    b. a bathroom scale.
    c. an alarm clock.
    d. any of the above.

12. Henry asks Harriet, who has a car that is much newer and more expensive than his, to measure the distance from his home to his workplace so he can check the _____ of his odometer.
    a. split-half reliability
    b. test-retest reliability
    c. predictive validity
    d. concurrent validity

13. Group intelligence tests are often preferred to individually administered tests because they are more
    a. thoroughly standardized.
    b. efficient.
    c. reliable.
    d. valid.

14. A student's competence in a college class is *least* likely to be reflected in her test score if she
    a. fails to study the night before the test.
    b. loses her book a week before the test.
    c. gets very anxious when she takes tests.
    d. studies the wrong chapters.

15. How would the g-factor proposed by Charles Spearman be supported by data from scores on the WAIS?
    a. There would be very high correlations among the subtests.
    b. There would be very low correlations among the subtests.
    c. Verbal IQ scores would be highly correlated with socioeconomic status.
    d. Performance IQ scores would be highly correlated with socioeconomic status.

16. Thurstone used the term _____ to refer to verbal comprehension, numerical skills, word fluency, spatial visualization, reasoning, and perceptual skills.
    a. prime factors
    b. core components
    c. primary mental abilities
    d. seminal skills

17. The primary difference between Sternberg's and Gardner's approach to intelligence and the approaches of earlier investigators is that Sternberg and Gardner
    a. treated intelligence as a unidimensional trait.
    b. treated intelligence as a multidimensional trait.
    c. emphasized the outcomes of intelligent behavior.
    d. emphasized the processes involved in intelligent behavior.

18. All of the following are abilities described by Sternberg in his triarchic theory *except*
    a. contextual.
    b. analytical.
    c. componential.
    d. experiential.

19. Howard Gardner is critical of the factorial approach to studying intelligence because
    a. factor analysis can be manipulated to support the hypotheses of the analyst.
    b. the results of factor analysis can be interpreted differently by different investigators.
    c. factor analysis does not capture the breadth and scope of human intelligence.
    d. factor analysis identifies factors that are tangential or irrelevant to intelligent behavior.

20. The majority of mentally retarded people are _____ retarded.
    a. mildly
    b. moderately
    c. severely
    d. profoundly

21. Down syndrome results from
    a. birth trauma.
    b. toxicity during the second trimester of pregnancy.
    c. inheritance of two recessive genes for the disorder.
    d. having an extra chromosome.

22. What statistical procedure is used in family resemblance and adoption studies to assess the relative importance of heredity and environment in the determination of intelligence?
    a. factor analysis
    b. correlation
    c. analysis of variance
    d. chi square

23. The index of heritability
    a. implies that intelligence is stable over time.
    b. can be applied both to individuals and to groups.
    c. can be applied equally to all ethnic and socioeconomic groups.
    d. should not be used for any of the above.

24. What was demonstrated by Henry Goddard's use of intelligence tests to screen people who were attempting to immigrate to the United States?
    a. Immigrants are ambitious people and have higher-than-average IQs.
    b. Language and cultural differences influence IQ scores.
    c. Intelligence is negatively correlated with pigmentation of the skin.
    d. Performance factors have little or no effect on the scores of highly motivated test-takers.

25. The text observes that the use of intelligence tests is especially controversial when
    a. they are used as a diagnostic tool by clinical psychologists.
    b. they are used in conjunction with other information to select children for remedial help.
    c. the test-giver is acting on behalf of someone other than the examinee.
    d. the predictive validity of the test is high.

Multiple-Choice Test II

For the multiple-choice items, choose the best of the answers provided. Check your work with the answers at the back of your study guide, and be sure you understand why the keyed answers are correct.

1. Wechsler's definition of intelligence includes all of the following *except*
    a. to evaluate critically.
    b. to deal effectively with the environment.
    c. to think rationally.
    d. to act purposefully.

2. The text suggests that an acceptable definition of "intelligence" should be
    a. analytical and logical.
    b. broad and general.
    c. definitive and specific.
    d. dynamic and culturally neutral.

3. The idea that intelligence is inherited is most strongly emphasized in the writing of
    a. David Wechsler.   c. David McClelland.
    b. Alfred Binet.   d. Sir Francis Galton.

4. When the test developed by Binet and Simon was used to assign children to special classes in the Paris school system, how did they define "retarded"?
   a. The child has an MA substantially higher than his or her CA.
   b. The child has a CA substantially higher than his or her MA.
   c. The child has an IQ of less than 85.
   d. The child has an IQ of less than 70.

5. The average and most frequently made score on intelligence tests is an IQ of _____ or a percentile score of _____.
   a. 1.00; 50
   b. 1.00; 100
   c. 100; 50
   d. 100; 100

6. Wechsler's work with poorly educated adults resulted in his inclusion of the _____ scale in his tests.
   a. experiential
   b. performance
   c. comprehension
   d. perceptual-motor

7. What is the most important change that was made in the 1986 revision of the Stanford-Binet Intelligence Test?
   a. A table was provided to convert percentile scores to IQ scores.
   b. Questions were added so that the test can be used with children as young as three years.
   c. The questions were grouped into categories.
   d. The questions were arranged in order of difficulty.

8. A new group-administered intelligence test was constructed and standardized. Psychologists and educators soon noticed that the majority of the scores were below the 50th percentile and that students and clients scored lower on the new test than they did on the Stanford-Binet or the Wechsler tests. What is the most logical explanation for this?
   a. The standardization sample was not representative.
   b. People's intelligence is decreasing for some unidentified reason.
   c. The reliability of the test is low.
   d. The test-takers are from a population in which intelligence is not normally distributed.

9. When Allison gets on and off her bathroom scale three times to see if she gets the same weight each time, she is assessing the _____ of her scale.
   a. concurrent validity
   b. predictive validity
   c. split-half reliability
   d. test-retest reliability

10. Professor Marks is quite accurate in measuring the heights of students' foreheads, even females with bangs and bald-headed males. He has had a lot of practice because this is the way he estimates intelligence. It is most accurate to say of his method that it has _____ reliability and _____ validity.
    a. some; some
    b. some; no
    c. no; no
    d. no; some

11. If a personnel manager uses a standardized test in employee selection, she would be most interested in the _____ of the test.
    a. concurrent validity
    b. predictive validity
    c. test-retest reliability
    d. split-half reliability

12. Allison weighed herself with all her clothes on just before she left the doctor's office. She rushed home and weighed herself on her own bathroom scale to test the _____ of her scale.
    a. test-retest reliability
    b. split-half reliability
    c. concurrent validity
    d. predictive validity

13. Which of the following best describes the relationship between aptitude and achievement?
    a. There is little or no difference between them.
    b. The distinction between them is blurred.
    c. They are independent.
    d. They are negatively correlated.

14. Performance factors include such things as
    a. self-fulfilling prophecy.
    b. cultural bias.
    c. time limits.
    d. motivation.

15. Thurstone disagreed with Spearman concerning whether intelligence
    a. is a general ability or a group of specific abilities.
    b. can be reliably and validly measured.
    c. is determined by heredity or environment.
    d. is a general characteristic of humans or a culture-specific characteristic.

16. In his triarchic theory of intelligence, Robert Sternberg took the _____ approach.
    a. factor analytic
    b. evolutionary
    c. information processing
    d. unidimensional

17. The ability Sternberg describes in his triarchic theory that is most similar to the ability or abilities measured by traditional intelligence tests is _____ intelligence.
    a. componential
    b. contextual
    c. analytical
    d. experiential

18. In his theory of intelligence, Gardner included the type of ability a person would need to become
    a. a ballet dancer.
    b. a well-adjusted person.
    c. a pianist at a piano bar.
    d. any of the above.

19. Recent developments may make it possible to construct a reliable and valid measure of intelligence in infants by measuring their
    a. acuity and sensitivity.
    b. discrimination and motor skills.
    c. attention and memory.
    d. movements and verbalizations.

20. Children who are classified as psychosocially retarded are most likely to be _____ retarded.
    a. mildly
    b. moderately
    c. severely
    d. profoundly

21. What criticism did McClelland make of Terman's and Jensen's interpretations of Terman's longitudinal study of gifted children?
    a. The test used to classify the children as gifted has become outmoded and largely irrelevant to the current definition of intelligence.
    b. The success of the gifted children could be the result of favorable social and economic conditions of their families.
    c. Terman's operational definition of success was narrow and biased to support his own position.
    d. Analysis of the data concentrated on the males in the sample of gifted children.

22. Adoption studies suggest that the IQ scores of adopted children are
    a. more closely related to the foster mother than to the biological mother.
    b. more closely related to the biological mother than to the adoptive mother.
    c. unrelated to the IQs of the foster mothers.
    d. unrelated to the IQs of the biological mothers.

23. What criticism did Kamin and others make of Jensen's comparison in black and white Americans?
    a. Jensen based his argument on unreliable data.
    b. The heritability index Jensen used was arbitrary.
    c. Jensen used differences within groups to make a between-group comparison.
    d. Jensen's data was gotten from group-administered tests.

24. The army collected IQ data during World War I. What important variable was overlooked when conclusions were reached about the intelligence of immigrants from European countries?
    a. the linguistic competence of the soldiers
    b. the educational achievement of the soldiers
    c. how long the soldiers had lived in the United States
    d. the ages of the soldiers

25. Which of the following most accurately summarizes what the National Academy of Sciences said about the use of intelligence tests?
    a. They should be used only with the consent of the test-taker.
    b. They should not be used to make decisions concerning blacks or people for whom English is a second language.
    c. They should not be used unless there is convincing evidence that the test is culture fair.
    d. They should be used in conjunction with information from other sources.

Chapter 12

SOCIAL COGNITION

Learning Objectives

After studying this chapter, you should be able to:

1. Describe the area of study for social psychologists.

2. Distinguish between social cognition and social influence.

3. Define the term schema and describe its role in impression formation.

4. Describe how schemata are modified, distinguishing between assimilation and accommodation.

5. Define primacy and recency effects in impression formation.

6. Explain what is meant by attribution.

7. Distinguish between the covariation and discounting principles of attribution.

8. Compare and contrast the correspondence bias and the actor-observer bias.

9. Describe how parents and peers influence attitude development.

10. Define cognitive dissonance and explain how it affects attitude change.

11. Compare and contrast the cognitive dissonance, self-perception, and impression management theories of attitude change.

12. List the characteristics of communicators and messages that increase their persuasive powers.

13. Discriminate among stereotypes, prejudice, and discrimination.

14. Describe how people learn racial prejudices.

15. Explain what is meant by a self-fulfilling prophecy and describe how it works to maintain prejudice.

16. Define liking and loving.

17. List and describe the factors that influence attraction.

18. Explain the difference between romantic love, companionate love, and consummate love.

19. Discuss the rules of self-disclosure.

Working with Names and Terms

From the alphabetized list below, choose the name or term that answers the question, using each name or term only once. Answers are at the back of your study guide.

accommodation	internal
actor-observer bias	Janis, Irving
assimilation	Jourard, Sidney
cognitive dissonance	Kelley, Harold
consensus	McGuire, William
consummate	Newcomb, Theodore
distinctiveness	Pettigrew, Thomas
Elaboration Likelihood Model (ELM)	primacy effect
Feshbach, Seymour	proximity
Festinger, Leon	realistic conflict
Freedman, Jonathan	scripts
Heider, Fritz	self-perception

_____ 1. Who collaborated with Irving Janis in the first study on the effects of fear in attitude change?

_____ 2. Who first made the distinction between internal and external causes of behavior?

_____ 3. What phenomenon accounts for the disproportionate importance of first impressions on our attitudes toward other people?

_____ 4. Which of the variables specified by the covariation principle is addressed by: "Many other members of the class also made low grades on the test"?

_____   5. Who did a study showing that cognitive dissonance can influence children's attitudes toward the attractiveness of a toy?

_____   6. What process occurs when we completely revise or enlarge our schemata to deal with incongruent information?

_____   7. Who did the classic study on attitude change among students at Bennington College and demonstrated the importance of attitude similarity on liking?

_____   8. Who proposed the concept of "groupthink" and described the conditions under which it occurs?

_____   9. Who proposed the theory of cognitive dissonance?

_____ 10. Whose research on self-disclosure has shown that college students disclose more to their mothers than to their fathers, and has suggested that men's limited self-disclosure adds stress to their lives?

_____ 11. What principle of attraction refers to our tendency to like neighbors and co-workers?

_____ 12. Whose research demonstrated the influence of cultural attitudes on prejudice against blacks in South Africa and the United States?

_____ 13. What type of love is demonstrated by a couple who, after many years of marriage, are both best friends and passionate lovers?

_____ 14. What theory claims that there is a central route and a peripheral route to persuasion?

_____ 15. Who proposed the covariation principle to explain why people make either internal or external attributions?

_____ 16. Who demonstrated the effects of cognition on attitudes by showing that when high school students changed their attitudes about one proposition, their attitudes toward logically related propositions also changed?

_____ 17. What theory says that prejudice results when members of groups compete for scarce resources?

_____ 18. Which variable specified by the covariation principle has to do with whether or not a particular behavior is habitual in a specific situation?

_____ 19. What type of schemata is comprised of general knowledge about what happens in particular situations like "cashing a check at the bank"?

_____ 20. What type of attribution is being made when a person's behavior is attributed to selfishness, diligence, or kindness?

_____ 21. What theory proposed that our attitudes are consistent with our behavior because we infer our attitudes from our behavior?

_____ 22. What term is used to refer to our tendency to make internal attributions for the behavior of others and external attributions for our own behavior?

_____ 23. What process is occurring when we distort perception or memory of information that is inconsistent with our schemata?

_____ 24. What theory claims that we will experience psychological discomfort if our behavior is inconsistent with our beliefs about ourselves?

Essay Questions

Suggested answers for the essay questions are included at the back of your study guide.

1. Use variables discussed in the text to explain how your best friend became your best friend.

2. Explain why biblical scholars urged rabbis not to insist that people believe before praying, but to get them to pray first.

3. Discuss and give examples of the types of attribution errors people are likely to make in explaining their own behavior and the behavior of others.

4. A good friend who is in your chemistry class got a "D" on the midterm. Use the dimensions of the covariation principle (distinctiveness, consistency, and consensus) to determine whether you would attribute the low grade to an external or an internal cause.

5. Explain how we acquire stereotypes.

Multiple-Choice Test I

For the multiple-choice items, choose the best of the answers provided. Check your work with the answers at the back of your study guide, and be sure you understand why the keyed answers are correct.

1. In Asch's pioneering study on impression formation, he found that the dimension of _____ strongly influenced subjects' impressions of the person described.
   a. dependable/undependable
   b. warm/cold
   c. industrious/lazy
   d. intelligent/unintelligent

2. The study in which Kelley described a guest lecturer to economics students as either warm or cold showed that
   a. attitudes can be changed by cognitions.
   b. discounting occurs in impression formation.
   c. dissonant cognitions make people uncomfortable.
   d. perception and interpretation are influenced by expectations.

3. Assimilation and accommodation are methods people use to
   a. alter their schemata.
   b. make attributions.
   c. reduce cognitive dissonance.
   d. justify discrimination.

4. Cathy told her parents that Archibald, the man she intended to marry, is a college graduate and has a good job before she told them that he had a child by a previous marriage. Cathy had studied social psychology and knew about
   a. the discounting principle.
   b. cognitive dissonance.
   c. the primacy effect.
   d. impression management theory.

5. Margo made a low grade on a test. People who know her are likely to attribute her low grade to the difficulty of the test if distinctive is _____, consistency is low, and consensus is _____.
   a. low; low
   b. low; high
   c. high; low
   d. high; high

6. Kelly claims that we are unlikely to attribute behavior to an internal cause if there is an equally plausible external cause. He calls this
   a. the discounting principle.
   b. self-serving bias.
   c. sufficient external justification.
   d. impression management.

7. The tendency of people to attribute their own behavior to external causes and the behavior of others to internal causes is called
   a. correspondence bias.
   b. impression management.
   c. the fundamental attribution error.
   d. actor-observer bias.

8. The primary difference between attitudes and belief is that attitudes
   a. influence behavior.
   b. are less firmly held.
   c. involve evaluation.
   d. are products of social cognition.

9. How do parents influence the attitudes of their children?
   a. Parents provide information.
   b. Parents reinforce and punish children's attitudes.
   c. Children identify with their parents.
   d. All of the above are social influences in parent-child relationships.

10. If a woman perceives herself as honest, and she cheats on a test, Festinger's theory predicts that she will experience
    a. realistic conflict.
    b. compensatory attribution.
    c. cognitive dissonance.
    d. negative self-perception.

11. What was the dependent variable in the study that Jonathan Freedman did to demonstrate cognitive dissonance in children?
    a. willingness to "play another game"
    b. attractiveness of a toy
    c. resistance to temptation
    d. liking for the experimenter

12. The theory of cognitive dissonance tells us that a politician who considers herself to be honest would be *least* likely to be uncomfortable after accepting a bribe if
    a. the person who paid the bribe was a friend.
    b. the person who paid the bribe was a stranger.
    c. the amount of the bribe was small.
    d. the amount of the bribe was large.

13. Impression management theory claims that people are motivated to
    a. make self-disclosures.
    b. be consistent.
    c. avoid making self-disclosures.
    d. appear consistent.

14. Research has shown that all of the following are important attributes for an effective communicator *except*
    a. complementarity.
    b. similarity.
    c. credibility.
    d. attractiveness.

15. Research has shown that level of education of the audience is related to the persuasiveness of
    a. fear-inducing communications.
    b. peripheral messages.
    c. two-sided communications.
    d. attractive communicators.

16. Research suggests that a political speech made on a busy street corner might be more effective than the same speech made in an auditorium because of
    a. distractions.
    b. audience expectancies.
    c. familiar contextual cues.
    d. discounting.

17. Pettigrew's research showed that prejudice has its roots in
    a. cognitions.
    b. behavior.
    c. culture.
    d. personality.

18. Social identity theory can help us understand how prejudice is related to
    a. competition.
    b. self-concepts.
    c. cultural norms.
    d. personality traits.

19. The study of Hamilton and Gifford showed that our prejudices and stereotypes are disproportionately influenced by
    a. economic conditions.
    b. competitive situations.
    c. media portrayals.
    d. salient stimuli.

20. If teachers or employers expect that members of a minority group will perform poorly in school or at work, and the behavior of the teacher or employer has a negative effect on the performance of minority students or employees, _____ is likely to occur.
    a. realistic conflict
    b. self-fulfilling prophecy
    c. discounting
    d. external justification

21. We would expect couples who are celebrating their 40th or 50th wedding anniversary to have what social psychologists call _____ love for each other.
    a. companionate
    b. fulfilled
    c. platonic
    d. mature

22. In the experiment done by Aronson and his associates that investigated the effect of competence on liking, one of the independent variables was whether or not
    a. the subjects' competence was similar to the competence of the persons being evaluated.
    b. the person being evaluated committed a blunder.
    c. the person being evaluated was of the same ethnic group as the evaluator.
    d. the person being evaluated had a "foreign sounding" name.

23. Aronson's law of marital fidelity tells us that a happily married man will put greater value on a compliment from his _____, and that he will be hurt more by criticism from his _____.
    a. wife; wife
    b. wife; neighbor's wife
    c. neighbor's wife; wife
    d. neighbor's wife; neighbor's wife

24. In an experiment by Dutton and Aron, male subjects evaluated the attractiveness of a woman who interviewed them after they had crossed a bridge. The experiment suggests that people are most likely to fall in love
    a. after a disaster.
    b. in the springtime.
    c. in familiar surroundings.
    d. when they are bored.

25. According to the text, variables that influence the extent to which self-disclosure occurs include all of the following *except*
    a. reciprocity.
    b. trust.
    c. similarity.
    d. gender.

Multiple-Choice Test II

For the multiple-choice items, choose the best of the answers provided. Check your work with the answers at the back of your study guide, being sure you understand why the keyed answers are correct.

1. Our beliefs about a person, our general impression of the person, and our expectations for the person are all part of our _____ for the person.
   a. schema
   b. icon
   c. engram
   d. attribution

2. Which of the follow is an example of what social psychologists call a "script"?
   a. what to expect when you visit your grandparents
   b. what to do when you eat in a cafeteria
   c. how to find a book and check it out of the library
   d. All of the above are examples of scripts.

3. When a person behaves in an altruistic way, a prejudiced person of a different ethnic group concludes that the altruistic behavior was motivated by the desire to impress others. This is an example of
   a. consensus.
   b. self-disclosure.
   c. assimilation.
   d. accommodation.

4. Research suggests that people are likely to accommodate discrepant information if the information is
   a. highly incongruent.
   b. ambiguous.
   c. memorable.
   d. any of the above.

5. Margo made a low grade on a test. People who knew her are likely to attribute her low grade to an internal cause if distinctiveness is _____, consistency is high, and consensus is _____.
   a. low; low
   b. low; high
   c. high; low
   d. high; high

6. The fundamental attribution error is the tendency of people to
   a. overestimate the role of external causes in attribution.
   b. overestimate the role of internal causes in attribution.
   c. attribute their own behavior to internal causes and the behavior of others to external causes.
   d. attribute their own behavior to external causes and the behavior of others to internal causes.

7. The actor-observer bias says that we are *least* likely to attribute our own failure to
   a. lack of ability.
   b. extenuating circumstances.
   c. bad luck.
   d. the influence of other people.

8. Our attitudes are influenced by
   a. other people.
   b. our behavior.
   c. our cognitions.
   d. all of the above.

9. Freud and Erikson emphasized the importance of _____ in attitude formation.
   a. identification
   b. reinforcement
   c. cognitive processes
   d. egocentrism

10. The study Theodore Newcomb did at Bennington College demonstrated
    a. assimilation of incongruent information.
    b. the acquisition of prejudice and stereotypes.
    c. reduction of cognitive dissonance.
    d. the role of social influence on attitudes.

11. How could parents use the idea of "sufficient external justification" to get a child to enjoy studying?
    a. They could give the child a large reward for studying.
    b. They could give the child a small reward for studying.
    c. They could associate studying with pleasant stimuli.
    d. They could associate failure to study with unpleasant consequences.

12. Which of the following statements best illustrates Bem's self-perception theory?
    a. I will vote for her because I agree with her position on issues.
    b. I like him because he likes me.
    c. I think Volvos are good cars because I own one.
    d. I eat liver because I like it.

13. When a politician speaks, his neat appearance, the flag beside the podium, and the presence of local dignitaries on the stage are all aspects of the _____ described by the Elaboration Likelihood Model.
    a. secondary persuaders
    b. positive frame
    c. contextual support
    d. peripheral route

14. What aspect of persuasion utilizes the "central route"?
    a. the communicator
    b. the message
    c. the medium
    d. the context

15. Research has shown that the use of fear in persuasion works best when
    a. there are explicit directions for escaping or avoiding the danger.
    b. the audience is poorly educated.
    c. the communicator speaks from personal experience.
    d. the audience has been aroused by other stimuli, like an exciting film.

16. Goethals and Reckman did a study in which high-school students were persuaded to change their attitudes toward busing. What hypothesis was supported by the study?
    a. Newer attitudes are maintained by distorting memory of older attitudes.
    b. Situational factors contribute to persuasion.
    c. Attitude change is more likely to occur if members of the audience perceive that the communicator is similar to themselves.
    d. Two-sided communications are more effective than one-sided communications.

17. Realistic conflict theory suggests that prejudice is likely to be strongest
    a. after a disaster, like an earthquake or a tornado, has occurred.
    b. among people in higher socioeconomic groups.
    c. when the rate of unemployment is high.
    d. among older adults.

18. Research has shown that our schemata for other ethnic groups, compared to our schema for our own ethnic group, are
    a. less rigid and tentative.
    b. less sensitive and complex.
    c. less consistent and emotional.
    d. all of the above.

19. It has been proposed that teachers should not have access to children's IQ scores because this information may influence their expectations and treatment of their students. This proposition is supported by research on
    a. cognitive dissonance.
    b. balance theory.
    c. impression-management theory.
    d. self-fulfilling prophecy.

20. Rosenthal and his colleagues suggested that self-fulfilling prophecy occurs in the classroom because teachers do all of the following for children they expect to do well *except*
    a. give more detailed feedback.
    b. provide a warmer emotional climate.
    c. give more opportunity to ask questions and respond in class.
    d. give them the benefit of the doubt when assigning grades.

21. Elaine Walster and her colleagues did a study in which students were asked how much they liked a blind date. The results of the study showed that the most important variable in students' liking for their dates was
    a. attractiveness.
    b. complementarity.
    c. warmth of personality.
    d. common interests.

22. The study Aronson did on the role of reciprocity in liking showed that we tend to like people most if their attitude toward us is
    a. consistently positive.
    b. consistently negative.
    c. negative at first and then positive.
    d. positive at first and then negative.

23. In the study done be Theodore Newcomb at the University of Michigan, a strong predictor of how well students liked others in their dormitory was
    a. reciprocity.
    b. competence.
    c. attitude similarity.
    d. proximity of rooms.

24. In companionate love, passion is replaced by
    a. equity.
    b. familiarity.
    c. inertia.
    d. commitment.

25. A study by Cozby suggested that women have more intimate friendships than men because women
    a. have more in common with each other.
    b. are less competitive.
    c. are more self-disclosing.
    d. are more trusting.

Chapter 13

SOCIAL INFLUENCE

Learning Objectives

After studying this chapter, you should be able to:

1. Identify two key motives for conformity.

2. Identify which factors promoted and which decreased obedience in the Milgram experiments.

3. Compare and contrast the theoretical explanations for the foot-in-the-door, the door-in-the-face, and the lowballing techniques used in compliance situations.

4. Cite some of the problems with instinct theories of aggression.

5. Compare and contrast the frustration-aggression (displacement) and excitation transfer theories of aggression.

6. Discuss how social learning theory explains aggressive behavior.

7. Describe how theories of aggression help explain family violence.

8. Discuss the relative effects of both mild and explicit pornography on aggressive behavior.

9. Explain the current view on the relationship between viewing violence on television and later aggressive behavior.

10. Differentiate between a laboratory and a field study, and explain how each is used to study television and aggression.

11. Describe the impact of diffusion of responsibility on helping behavior in emergencies.

12. Explain the relationship between arousal and the reward/cost analysis of helping behavior.

13. Discuss the relationship between egoism and altruism.

14. Define risky shift and explain when it is likely to occur.

15. Compare and contrast risky shift with group polarization.

16. Define groupthink and list the factors that promote it.

17. Explain how a minority opinion can influence the majority opinion in a group.

18. Discuss the trait, situational, and transactional theories of leadership.

19. Describe two types of leadership behavior.

20. Define the different leadership styles, and describe the situation in which each style may be most effective.

Working with Names and Terms

From the alphabetized list below, choose the name or term that answers the question, using each name and term only once. Answers are at the back of your study guide.

aggression
Asch, Solomon
Darley, John
diffusion of responsibility
Dollard, John
door-in-the-face
excitation transfer
group polarization
groupthink
halo error
illusion of invulnerability
Janis, Irving
LeBon, Gustave
Lewin, Kurt
Lorenz, Konrad
lowballing
Milgrim, Stanley
scapegoat
Schachter, Stanley
socioemotional
trait
transactional
vicarious reinforcement
Wallach, Michael

_____ 1. What term is used to describe a leader who helps others express themselves, eases tensions, and demonstrates positive feelings for other group members?

_____ 2. Who did a famous experiment demonstrating that nonconformists tend to be rejected by their peers?

_____ 3. Who collaborated with Bibb Latané in research designed to understand why bystanders did not intervene to help Kitty Genovese?

_____ 4. What term is used to designate the target of displaced aggression?

_____ 5. Who introduced the term "groupthink" and investigated the conditions under which it occurs?

_____ 6. What method of obtaining compliance is demonstrated by the car salesman who, after the customer has agreed to buy at a designated price, tells the customer that the tax, freight, radio, leather seats, sun roof, tape deck, heater, and tinted windows are "extras"?

_____ 7. What type of behavior did Freud consider to be the result of the conflict between the pleasure drive and *thanatos*?

_____ 8. Who was the principal investigator in the study that compared the effectiveness of several leadership styles with 10-year-old boys at a summer camp?

_____ 9. Who did the classic study demonstrating conformity in responses to a simple judgment task?

_____ 10. What factor influences behavior in both compliance and bystander intervention?

_____ 11. What has occurred when a person feels rewarded for observing the behavior of a successful aggressive model?

_____ 12. What technique is being used by the student who asks his parents for $200 when he or she hopes to get $50?

_____ 13. What phenomenon has occurred when a group of supporters get together to discuss their candidate and come away from the meeting with a much stronger commitment to the candidate than they had before the meeting?

_____ 14. Who worked with Walter Kogan to develop the *Choice Dilemma Questionnaire* and to demonstrate the "risky shift" phenomenon?

_____ 15. What theory of leadership is demonstrated by the statement that "a good leader is intelligent, well-organized, dependable, and honest"?

_____ 16. What theory claims that the arousal resulting from fear can intensify feelings of romantic love?

_____ 17. To what did Irving Janis attribute the Bay of Pigs fiasco?

_____ 18. What is occurring when people perceive a potential leader's behavior as more consistent with their own leadership schema than it actually is?

_____ 19. Who investigated aggression, wrote a book on the subject, and concluded that aggression is innate in humans and other animals?

_____ 20. What theory of leadership assumes that both the characteristics of the person and the demands of the situation determine who will become a leader?

_____ 21. Who did the classic experiment demonstrating that people can be very cruel when cruelty is demanded by an authority figure?

_____ 22. What characteristic of groupthink follows from the fact that individual in the group perceive all the group members to be smart and talented?

_____ 23. Who wrote *The Crowd* and claimed that humans have an unconscious component of personality that contains base desires and instincts?

_____ 24. Who investigated the relationship between frustration and aggression and wrote a well-known book on the subject?

Essay Questions

Suggested answers for the essay questions are included at the back of your study guide.

1. Describe two situations in which displaced aggression and scapegoating might occur.

2. Sam is a 17-year-old male who lives in the inner city. He is a leader in a gang that is noted for its aggression and violence, and Sam is accurately described as an aggressive and violent person. To what do you attribute this behavior?

3. When Tamera got home from shopoping, she noticed that there was smoke coming from one of the windows of the house next door. She went into her own home and started putting away groceries. Why didn't she respond to the possibility that the neighbors' house was on fire?

4. Ronald Reagan was a very popular president. What leadership qualities did he have that contributed to his acceptance by the American people?

5. Give an example of how the foot-in-the-door technique, the door-in-the-face technique, and lowballing are used in selling goods and services or in soliciting time or money for a nonprofit organization.

Multiple-Choice Test I

For the multiple-choice items, choose the best of the answers provided. Check your work with the answers at the back of your study guide, and be sure you understand why the keyed answers are correct.

1. The subjects in Asch's classic experiment on conformity were told that the experimenter was studying
   a. cognitive consistency.
   b. social influence.
   c. psychophysical methods.
   d. visual discrimination.

2. In interviewing his subjects, Asch found that the main reason why subjects conformed in his study was that they
   a. didn't trust themselves to make accurate judgments.
   b. didn't want to hurt the feelings of the other judges.
   c. were worried about what others would think of them if they deviated.
   d. were not paying close attention to the stimuli.

3. Compliance differs from conformity in that in compliance
   a. social pressure to behave in a specific way is more subtle.
   b. there is a direct request for a specific behavior.
   c. there are rewards and punishments for agreement and deviance.
   d. the response is an action rather than an attitude.

4. Milgrim believed that a crucial factor in understanding events like the Holocaust and the Jonestown Massacre is
   a. group coherence.
   b. diffusion of responsibility.
   c. innate aggression.
   d. the illusion of anonymity.

5. The study in which housewives consented to have large signs put in their yards after having previously consented to a small sign demonstrated the _____ technique for obtaining compliance.
   a. bait and switch
   b. foot-in-the-door
   c. door-in-the-face
   d. lowballing

6. Recent research suggests that the best explanation for the success of the foot-in-the-door techniques is offered by
   a. self-perception theory.
   b. cognitive dissonance.
   c. transactional theory.
   d. situational theory.

7. Which of the following is *not* an example of aggression?
   a. Francis tried to set fire to the neighbors' house, but he burned his finger before he got a fire started.
   b. The president of the savings and loan encouraged the couple to make an investment he knew to be worthless.
   c. Helen intentionally exaggerated when she described how she had been harassed by her boss.
   d. Gloria almost fainted from the pain when the dentist pulled her wisdom tooth.

8. Konrad Lorenz claimed that aggression in humans is more dangerous than it is in most other animals because
   a. humans can kill others without risking their own lives in the process.
   b. humans have more intelligence and more intense emotions than other animals.
   c. humans do not have a built-in safety device to keep them from killing each other.
   d. animals other than humans only behave aggressively to protect themselves and to satisfy biological needs.

9. The text reports several studies that demonstrate the role of _____ in producing anger and frustration.
   a. aversive events
   b. perceived unfairness
   c. poverty
   d. negative reinforcement

10. A child is being reinforced for aggression when
    a. no one is watching and the child grabs her baby sister's cookie.
    b. parents commend the child for "fighting back."
    c. the child's destructive behavior in the grocery store is terminated by buying her a popsicle.
    d. any of the above occurs.

11. Psychologists who have studied spouse abuse have suggested that a major cause of the problem is
    a. reinforcement of the abusing spouse by the compliance of the abused spouse.
    b. imitation of abuse seen on TV or in films.
    c. personality disorder of the abusing spouse.
    d. personality disorder of either the abusing spouse or the abused spouse.

12. Studies of the effects of TV watching on children have shown that there is a _____ correlation between watching TV violence and violent behavior, and a _____ correlation between the amount of TV watching children do and their IQs and reading scores.
    a. positive; positive
    b. positive; negative
    c. negative; positive
    d. negative; negative

13. Darley and Latané did a study to determine how long it would take subjects to notice and report that "smoke" was pouring from a vent in the room where they were working. The results of the study showed that
    a. males reacted more quickly than females.
    b. females reacted more quickly than males.
    c. subjects reacted more quickly when they were alone in the room.
    d. subjects reacted more quickly when there were several people in the room.

14. Research has shown that people are likely to intervene in an emergency if they are
    a. over 30.
    b. well-educated.
    c. aroused.
    d. religious.

15. The text reports a study in which a subway rider collapses, apparently as a result of being either lame or drunk. What hypothesis was tested in the study?
    a. The number of potential helpers determines whether anyone will help.
    b. People are more likely to help if the situation is clearly an emergency.
    c. Infrequent subway riders are more likely to help than people who ride the subway regularly.
    d. People analyze the costs and benefits of helping before they intervene.

16. Gustave LeBon observed that people tend to behave irrationally and destructively when they are
    a. in a crowd.
    b. frightened.
    c. isolated from others.
    d. angry.

17. At their meeting, the gang decided to rob a bank instead of a liquor store. Their decision is an example of
    a. displaced aggression.
    b. egoistic bias.
    c. decision making under uncertainty.
    d. risky shift.

18. Most of the individual club members thought the club should spend $50 to $100 on refreshments for the open house. At their meeting they discussed the matter and voted not to serve refreshments. This is an example of
    a. groupthink.
    b. group polarization.
    c. collective egoism.
    d. risky shift.

19. What happened when Kogan and Walker compared individual responses with group responses to their "Choice Dilemma Questionnaire"?
    a. The responses of individuals were influenced by the leaders in the group condition.
    b. The responses of individuals were not influenced by the leaders in the group condition.
    c. The responses of groups were not significantly different from the mean of the responses of the individuals.
    d. The responses of groups were riskier than the mean of the responses of the individuals.

20. The authors of the text emphasize the importance of _____ in situations where groupthink occurs.
    a. group coherence
    b. stereotyping
    c. self-aggrandizement
    d. directive leadership

21. The Board of Directors of a large company is discussing the possibility of buying another company. This would be risky because they would have to borrow the money to make the purchase. Which of the following statement by a board member suggests that groupthink is occurring?
    a. "Our accountants are such conservative old fogies that they wouldn't advise buying if we had the cash in the bank."
    b. "If there is a recession, we might have difficulty paying the interest on the loan."
    c. "I think we should defer making a decision until we have carefully examined their annual reports for the past several years."
    d. "I want all of you to express the pros and cons from the perspective of both your own position in the company and the company as a whole."

22. If a minority is to have an impact on a group decision, all of the following are important guidelines for the minority *except*
    a. make yourself noticed.
    b. create tension in the group.
    c. challenge the integrity of group members.
    d. take a consistent and uncompromising stand.

23. The idea that a nation will choose a member of the military to lead it at a time when the threat of war is high is most consistent with the _____ theory of leadership.
    a. transactional
    b. situational
    c. trait
    d. functional

24. In his book *The Mask of Command*, John Keegan made the point that leaders must
    a. maintain their distance from the group without appearing cold and aloof.
    b. be sensitive to the concerns of subgroups and be able to adapt their manner and message to suit the situation.
    c. behave in such a way that they are perceived as fitting the leadership schemata of group members.
    d. be able to sense and express the desires and goals of the group.

25. In the study by Lewin and his colleagues on the effectiveness of leadership styles, the results showed that groups were most productive when the leadership was _____, and that the groups were happiest when the leadership was _____.
    a. democratic; democratic
    b. democratic; directive
    c. directive; democratic
    d. directive; directive

Multiple-Choice Test II

For the multiple-choice items, choose the best of the answers provided. Check your work with the answers at the back of your study guide, and be sure you understand why the keyed answers are correct.

1. The independent variable in Asch's original study on conformity was
   a. judgments made in isolation versus judgments made in groups.
   b. possible versus impossible judgments.
   c. number of confederates.
   d. unanimity of the confederates versus the presence of a dissenter.

2. The study in which Stanley Schachter had groups of subjects make recommendations for the treatment of Johnny Rocco demonstrated that
   a. nonconformists are rejected.
   b. group polarization can be extreme.
   c. prejudiced attitudes can be based on people's names.
   d. females are more conforming than males.

3. Subjects who participated in Milgrim's experiment on obedience to an authority figure were told that the experimenter was studying
   a. visual discrimination.
   b. classical conditioning.
   c. authoritarianism.
   d. learning.

4. Carla first asked the man in the apartment next door to help her decide how much paint she would need to paint her apartment. After he told her that two gallons should do it, she asked him if he would help her with the painting. Carla used the _____ technique to obtain compliance from the neighbor.
   a. bait and switch
   b. lowballing
   c. foot-in-the-door
   d. door-in-the-face

5. A solicitor for a charity calls and asks people to donate $100. When they refuse, the solicitor asks if they would give $50. The solicitor is using the _____ technique.
   a. foot-in-the-door
   b. door-in-the-face
   c. lowballing
   d. bait and switch

6. You are invited to a cocktail party in honor of some neighbors who are moving. After you have consented to come, the hostess tells you that all the guests are expected to contribute $25 to buy beverages and a gift for the guests of honor. The hostess used the _____ technique.
   a. door-in-the-face
   b. foot-in-the-door
   c. lowballing
   d. bait and switch

7. Thomas Hobbes, Sigmund Freud, and Konrad Lorenz agreed in the belief that
   a. there is a cause-and-effect relationship between frustration and aggression.
   b. the illusion of invulnerability promotes aggression and violence.
   c. prejudice provides targets for displaced aggression.
   d. aggression is instinctual in humans.

8. Displaced aggression may contribute to
   a. mistreatment of minorities.
   b. child and spouse abuse.
   c. random violence.
   d. all of the above.

9. After attending a stimulating rock concert, Joe and Judy felt aroused and decided that they must be in love. A social psychologist would be most likely to consider this a case of
   a. excitation transfer.
   b. the halo error.
   c. mindless compliance.
   d. actor-observer bias.

10. A child will imitate the aggressive behavior of _____, especially if the model is rewarded for aggression.
    a. peers
    b. cartoon characters
    c. siblings
    d. any of the above

11. In the study done by Donnerstein and Berkowitz on the relationship between pornography and violence, they found that men who had *not* been angered by the female confederate of the experimenter behaved aggressively toward her if they saw a film depicting
    a. erotic but nonviolent sex.
    b. violent sex enjoyed by the woman.
    c. violent sex in which the woman suffered.
    d. any of the above.

12. The murder of Kitty Genovese aroused the interest of psychologists in
    a. diffusion of responsibility.
    b. random violence.
    c. altruistic behavior.
    d. excitation transfer.

13. Darley and Latané did an experiment in which one of the participants in a discussion group appeared to be having an epileptic seizure. What was the dependent variable in the experiment?
    a. response time
    b. arousal level of the subjects
    c. severity of the seizure
    d. number of subjects in the discussions groups

14. People are most likely to come to the aid of a person in distress if the cost of helping is _____ and the cost of not helping is _____.
    a. high; high
    b. high; low
    c. low; high
    d. low; low

15. The belief that people come to the aid of another person because they are good and kind is expressed in _____ theory.
    a. empathy-altruism
    b. trait
    c. sociobiological
    d. transactional

16. Individual members of the Board of Directors were uncertain of how the new soft drink would be received, and thought it should be quietly introduced in selected areas of the country. When the board met, they decided to introduce the new soft drink nationwide with a costly advertising campaign. The board has made a(n)
    a. group transaction.
    b. risky shift.
    c. consensual choice.
    d. opinion reversal.

17. If you were responding to the "Choice Dilemma Questionnaire" of Kogan and Wallach, you would
    a. decide whether or not you would help another person in a variety of situations.
    b. choose between two leaders who are described in the questionnaire.
    c. use descriptions of leaders to rate them on how effective you think they would be.
    d. choose the odds for success that you would accept for a risky decision.

18. Research has shown that group polarization can result in
    a. risky shifts.
    b. shifts toward caution.
    c. intensification of existing attitudes.
    d. any of the above.

19. Irving Janis claims that groupthink is characterized by deterioration of all of the following *except*
    a. mental efficiency.
    b. reality testing.
    c. moral judgment.
    d. group cohesiveness.

20. The Board of Directors of a large company is discussing the possibility of buying another company. This would be risky because they would have to borrow the money to make the purchase. Which of the following statements by a board member suggests that groupthink is *not* occurring?
    a. "We're a winning team, and I'm sure we'll be able to do whatever we decide to do."
    b. "We should consult with our bankers and accountants before we make a decision."
    c. "Our stockholders are old ladies and people with no business sense. They need us to do their thinking for them."
    d. "It's not our fault their management has gotten the company in such a mess. They should regard us as saviors instead of raiders."

21. What steps were taken to avoid groupthink during the Cuban missile crisis?
    a. The power of the enemy was realistically assessed.
    b. The president attended all the decision-making sessions.
    c. An effort was made to increase the cohesiveness of the decision-making group.
    d. All of the above steps were taken to avoid groupthink.

22. If a minority within a group wants to have an impact, it is important that they
    a. be consistent in their position.
    b. refrain from creating tension in the group.
    c. have a compromising attitude.
    d. do all of the above.

23. In a large study of leadership, the results showed that the subjects expected leaders to
    a. be energetic and task oriented.
    b. be self-confident and to have high achievement motivation.
    c. initiate structure and show consideration for others.
    d. think critically, speak clearly, and act decisively.

24. Bales and Slater studied leadership in unstructured groups of college students. They found that
    a. task leaders emerged.
    b. socioemotional leaders emerged.
    c. both task leaders and socioemotional leaders emerged.
    d. leadership passed from person to person, and a single leader did not emerge in most of the groups.

25. In his study of the effectiveness of leadership styles, Fred Fiedler found that democratic leadership is more effective than directive leadership when the group situation is
    a. favorable.
    b. neither highly favorable nor highly unfavorable.
    c. unfavorable.
    d. any of the above.

Chapter 14

PERSONALITY

Learning Objectives

After studying this chapter, you should be able to:

1. Define personality.

2. Compare and contrast the four major perspectives on personality as outlined in this chapter.

3. Explain the main characteristics of the three structures of personality according to Freud.

4. Explain the stages of personality development according to the psychodynamic perspective.

5. Define ego-defense mechanisms and give examples of behavior-channeling defenses and both primary and secondary reality-distorting defenses.

6. Describe the authoritarian personality.

7. Describe how modern psychoanalytic theory has modified Freud's original concepts.

8. Identify Freud's unique contributions to psychology.

9. Define projective testing and describe the format and uses of two leading projective tests.

10. Differentiate between type and trait theories of personality.

11. Describe the major criticisms of the trait approach to personality.

12. Discuss whether people are consistent in their behavior across time and/or across situations.

13. Define personality inventories and explain the uses of tests like the MMPI, the CPI, and the 16 PF.

14. Describe how the MMPI was constructed, distinguishing between the clinical scales and the validity scales.

15. Outline the major assumptions of the behavioral approach to personality.

16. Compare B. F. Skinner's radical behaviorism with social learning theory.

17. Describe the relationship between the person and the environment as explained by social learning theorists and cognitive social learning theorists.

18. Describe the perspectives and behaviors associated with an internal and an external locus of control.

19. Describe the current research focus on gender differences in personality.

20. Describe Carl Rogers' theory of personality.

21. Outline Maslow's hierarchy theory of motivation.

22. Describe the characteristics of a self-actualized person.

Working with Names and Terms

From the alphabetized list below, choose the name or term that answers the question, using each name and term only once. Answers are at the back of your study guide.

Allport, Gordon	libido
authoritarian	Mischel, Walter
deficiency motives	MMPI
denial	Murray, Henry
Eysenck, Hans	projection
fully functioning	projective
functional analysis	Rogers, Carl
id	Rotter, Julian
introjection	secondary
Jung, Carl	self-actualizing
Kohut, Heinz	self-efficacy
latency	superego

Allporting   1. What trait theorist claimed that introversion *versus* extraversion and stability *versus* instability are the primary dimensions of personality?

_____ 2. Who did pioneering research on personality traits and suggested that traits differ in how pervasively they manifest themselves in an individual's behavior?

_____ 3. What personality test includes items that measure people's attempts to make themselves look good or to make it appear that they are in need of help?

_____ 4. What defense mechanism do people use to protest the ego from threatening perceptions of the external world?

_____ 5. Whose perspective on personality uses the terms "self-concept" and "conditions of worth"?

_____ 6. What term did Allport use to describe personality traits that only manifest themselves in particular situations or at particular times?

_____ 7. Who collaborated with Christina Morgan in developing the Thematic Apperception Test?

_____ 8. Who originated the terms "introversion" and "extraversion"?

_____ 9. How did Carl Rogers describe a person who is well-adjusted and who has a realistic and consistent self-concept?

_____ 10. How did Abraham Maslow characterize Eleanor Roosevelt, William James, and Albert Einstein?

_____ 11. What social psychologist was joined by Jerry Phares and Herbert Lefcourt in research on locus of control?

_____ 12. Who questioned the idea that personality traits are stable and proposed "person variables" to explain behavior?

_____ 13. What term did Freud use to describe what happens when a child incorporates the morals and values of a parent?

_____ 14. What term did Maslow use to describe the lower levels in his hierarchy of needs?

_____ 15. Which of Freud's stages of psychosexual development includes elementary-school-age children?

_____ 16. What term did Adorno and his colleagues use to describe the personalities of people who make high scores on the F-scale?

_____ 17. What structure of the personality includes the conscience and the ego-ideal?

_____ 18. What term did Albert Bandura use to refer to people's perception of their skills in particular activities?

_____ 19. What term did Freud use to refer to the energy the id produces to obtain pleasure?

_____ 20. What aspect of personality is governed by the pleasure principle and engages and primary-process thinking?

_____ 21. What term did B. F. Skinner use to refer to the process of identifying the discriminative stimuli and reinforcers that maintain a behavior?

_____ 22. What ego-defense mechanism is a person using when the person attributes his own unacceptable impulses and motives to others?

_____ 23. What kind of personality test requires a person to use his or her imagination in making responses?

_____ 24. What contemporary psychoanalytic theorist emphasizes the development and influence of the self?

Essay Questions

Suggested answers for the essay questions are included at the back of your study guide.

1. Tad was raised in a family whose religion prohibits use of alcoholic beverages. He is at a party where all the other guests are drinking and appear to be having a good time. Discuss the conflict Tad is experiencing using Freud's psychodynamic perspective.

2. What is an external locus of control, and how do people come to have an external locus of control?

3. Define projection, reaction formation, and rationalization in your own words, and give an example of each.

4. Discuss the strengths and weaknesses of trait theories of personality.

5. Use cognitive social-learning concepts to explain how a person becomes an extravert.

Multiple-Choice Test I

For the multiple-choice items, choose the best of the answers provided. Check your work with the answers at the back of your study guide, and be sure you understand why the keyed answers are correct.

1. The key word in the definition of personality is
    a. individual.
    b. interaction.
    c. stability.
    d. patterning.

2. J. B. Watson and B. F. Skinner were to the behavioral perspective on the study of personality as Carl Jung was to the _____ perspective.
    a. psychodynamic
    b. cognitive
    c. individualistic
    d. trait

3. A major difference between the humanistic perspective and the psychodynamic perspective is that the humanistic psychologists emphasize
    a. early childhood experience.
    b. free will and personal responsibility.
    c. innate predispositions.
    d. values and expectancies.

4. Which of the following statements is consistent with Freud's theories?
    a. Personality develops and changes over most of the life span.
    b. Some people function well because they are born with strong egos.
    c. When children are 5 or 6 years old, secondary-process thinking replaces primary-process thinking.
    d. The superego develops as the child deals with the Electra or Oedipus complex.

5. Which structure of the personality is completely unconscious?
    a. the id
    b. the ego
    c. the superego
    d. None of the above are completely unconscious.

6. Being either extremely sloppy or excessively neat is associated with fixation at the _____ stage; being either a spendthrift or a miser is associated with fixation at the _____ stage.
    a. oral; oral
    b. oral; anal
    c. anal; oral
    d. anal; anal

7. The ego-defense mechanisms do all of the following *except*
    a. block threatening perceptions.
    b. control the id and superego.
    c. resolve conflicts.
    d. reduce anxiety.

8. A person who channels energy generated by aggressive urges into becoming a football player is using the ego-defense mechanism called
   a. projection.
   b. sublimation.
   c. reaction formation.
   d. identification.

9. If an adolescent girl who is sexually attracted to her stepfather is critical of him and hostile toward him, she is likely to be using the ego-defense mechanism called
   a. reaction formation.
   b. projection.
   c. rationalization.
   d. denial.

10. According to Adorno and his colleagues, all of the following are characteristics of the authoritarian personality *except*
    a. inability to accept sexuality in themselves.
    b. strong interest in power and authority.
    c. use of harsh discipline with children.
    d. unconventional values.

11. Which of the following is *not* a common criticism of Freud's theories?
    a. He puts too much emphasis on sex and aggression.
    b. His theories are not internally consistent.
    c. His ideas cannot be adequately tested.
    d. His theories are based on observations of disturbed people.

12. Type theories differ from trait theories in that type theories
    a. use a limited number of psychological categories.
    b. focus on groups rather than on individuals.
    c. use dichotomies of traits.
    d. do all of the above.

13. In Jung's personality theory sensation, intuition, thinking, and feeling are called
    a. cognitive styles.
    b. modalities.
    c. functions.
    d. processes.

14. Following the lead of Raymond Cattell and Hans Eysenck, investigators used _____ to identify the "big five."
    a. factor analysis
    b. the MMPI
    c. self-ratings
    d. multidimensional scaling

15. If you took the MMPI, you would get scores on
    a. hypochondria, hysteria, and lying.
    b. extraversion, intelligence, and dominance.
    c. stability, agreeableness, and openness.
    d. defensiveness, flexibility, and self-control.

16. Which of the following personality tests does *not* measure personality traits?
    a. CPI
    b. 16 PF
    c. TAT
    d. MMPI

17. All of the following are associated with Bandura and the social-learning theorists *except*:
    a. Learning can occur from observing others and without reinforcement.
    b. Perceived self-efficacy is a determiner of how reciprocal interactions proceed.
    c. The self is the organizing core of personality and behavior.
    d. Learning of a behavior does not necessarily result in performance of the learned behavior.

18. It is most accurate to say that social learning theorists focus on
    a. external determinants of behavior.
    b. consistency and veridicality of the self-image.
    c. dimensions of personality that can be observed and measured.
    d. reciprocal interactions of the person and the environment.

19. Davis and Phares did a study in which "internals" were compared with "externals" in a situation where subjects were to try to influence another person. What was the dependent variable in the study?
    a. amount of information sought about the to-be-influenced person
    b. whether subjects expected outcomes to be dependent upon luck or upon skill
    c. the locus of control of the to-be-influenced person
    d. the confidence subjects expressed in their ability to influence another person

20. Research has consistently supported gender differences in
    a. dependency.
    b. aggressiveness.
    c. competence.
    d. emotionality.

21. Which of the following statements about gender differences is *not* supported by research?
    a. Women are more likely than men to overestimate their performance on a task.
    b. Men are more likely than women to emerge as leaders of groups.
    c. Women are more likely than men to be influenced by the attitudes and behavior of others.
    d. Men are more likely than women to be influenced by physical attractiveness in mate selection.

22. The expressed interests of the humanistic perspective include
    a. the developmental aspects of personality.
    b. the illusion of free will.
    c. the positive side of human nature.
    d. all of the above.

23. Carl Rogers thought that serious psychological problems could result from
    a. unconditional positive regard during childhood.
    b. acceptance of responsibility for one's own behavior.
    c. avoidance of barriers to self-actualization.
    d. inconsistency between the organism and the self-concept.

24. What category did Maslow use to include the needs for competence, achievement, and autonomy?
    a. esteem needs
    b. actualization needs
    c. competitive needs
    d. self needs

25. The characteristics Maslow attributed to self-actualized people included all of the following *except*
    a. spontaneity in actions and feelings.
    b. acceptance of self.
    c. devotion to church and state.
    d. intimate interpersonal relationships.

Multiple-Choice Test II

For the multiple-choice items, choose the best of the answers provided. Check your work with the answers at the back of your study guide, and be sure you understand why the keyed answers are correct.

1. As an academic area of investigation and theorizing, personality is best described as the study of
    a. personal styles.
    b. individual differences.
    c. human traits.
    d. self-perceptions.

2. Early behaviorists objected to the personality theories of both Freud and Jung because of their emphasis on _____ in determining behavior.
    a. personality traits
    b. acquired drives
    c. internal factors
    d. hedonistic goals

3. When you sit in class and daydream about what you're going to have for lunch, you are engaged in what Freud called
    a. primary-process thinking.
    b. sublimation.
    c. hedonistic preoccupation.
    d. goal-oriented fantasizing.

4. Sucking is to the oral stage as _____ is to the anal stage.
    a. manipulation
    b. gratification
    c. stimulation
    d. elimination

5. One of Freud's female patients reported being sexually abused by her father when she was a child. When Freud realized that the sexual abuse had been a creation of the patient's childhood fantasy, he began to develop the concept of
    a. unconscious motivation.
    b. secondary-process thinking.
    c. primary process thinking.
    d. the Electra and Oedipus complexes.

6. Partial resolution of the conflict generated by the Oedipus and Electra complexes is obtained by
   a. repressing threatening thoughts.
   b. projecting dangerous impulses onto siblings or friends.
   c. identifying with the same-sex parent.
   d. daydreaming and fantasizing.

7. Which of the following ego-defense mechanisms are the most adaptive?
   a. denial and rationalization
   b. regression and repression
   c. identification and sublimation
   d. projection and reaction formation

8. What defense mechanism is being used by the adolescent who tries to dress like, think like, and be like a celebrity for whom the adolescent has great admiration?
   a. sublimation
   c. projection
   c. identification
   d. displacement

9. When we attribute our failures and behaviors we are ashamed of to external causes, we may be using the defense mechanism called
   a. reaction formation.
   b. displacement.
   c. denial.
   d. rationalization.

10. Kohut believed that parents who do not mirror their children's behavior and efforts and who are not good models of behavior and self-acceptance for their children increase the likelihood of _____ in their children.
    a. narcissistic disorders
    b. defensive strategies
    c. oral and anal fixations
    d. anxiety neuroses

11. The value of projective tests like the Rorschach and the TAT for studying personality and diagnosing problems appears to depend most heavily upon
    a. the verbal fluency of the subject or client.
    b. the insight and experience of the examiner.
    c. the content validity of the tests.
    d. the openness and honesty of the subject or client.

12. Jung thought that the basic dimension of personality is
    a. inner-directed versus outer-directed.
    b. stable versus unstable.
    c. introversion versus extraversion.
    d. dominant versus submissive.

13. If a person is passive at home, passive at work, and passive in social situations, Allport would be most likely to say that for this person, passivity is a _____ trait.
    a. primary
    b. dominant
    c. dispositional
    d. cardinal

14. Of the "big five" traits, which did Eysenck consider to be basic?
    a. openness and conscientiousness.
    b. extraversion and agreeableness.
    c. openness and agreeableness.
    d. stability and extraversion.

15. What criticism have Mischel and other social learning theorists directed at trait theories?
    a. Traits are not always stable over time and situations.
    b. Trait theories do not explain how traits develop.
    c. Little or not attention is given to how traits interact.
    d. There is little empirical evidence to support the existence of traits.

16. What was the key concept in B. F. Skinner's radical behaviorism?
    a. Behavior is determined by minute-to-minute needs and motives.
    b. Behavior is determined by its consequences.
    c. Mental structures are shaped by internal forces.
    d. Mental structures are shaped by external forces.

17. Mischel claims that competencies, encoding strategies, expectations, values, and the self-regulatory system are important in person-environment interaction. He called these attributes
    a. cardinal traits.
    b. cognitive structures.
    c. individual styles.
    d. person variables.

18. Which of the following statements is most likely to have been made by a person with an external locus of control?
    a. It's not easy to change people's attitudes, but it can be done if you keep working at it.
    b. People who make a lot of money are smart; luck has nothing to do with it.
    c. It is futile for an individual to try to influence political institutions.
    d. People get high grades because they work for them.

19. Research suggests that a woman is more influential with men if she is _____, and more influential with other women if she is _____.
    a. tentative; tentative
    b. tentative; assertive
    c. assertive; tentative
    d. assertive; assertive

20. Sociobiologists propose that human evolution shaped men to be _____ in mating, and females to be _____ in mating.
    a. promiscuous; selective
    b. assertive; tentative
    c. hesitant; receptive
    d. quality-oriented; quantity-oriented

21. According to the text, which two perspectives on personality appear to be converging?
    a. behavioral and trait
    b. trait and psychodynamic
    c. psychodynamic and humanistic
    d. behavioral and humanistic

22. The goals of the humanistic approach include emphasizing
    a. people's unique perception of the world.
    b. free will and personal responsibility.
    c. the positive side of human nature.
    d. all of the above.

23. Kohut's concept of the self and his ideas about the importance of mirroring by the parents in childhood are most similar to the concepts and ideas of
    a. Henry Murray.
    b. Gordon Allport.
    c. Albert Bandura.
    d. Carl Rogers.

24. Which of the following did Maslow consider to be a growth need?
    a. the need for love and belongingness
    b. the need for self-esteem
    c. the need for self-actualization
    d. all of the above

25. Which of the following is true of the humanistic approach to understanding personality?
    a. It emphasizes the subjective reality of the individual.
    b. It takes an empirical approach.
    c. It defines terms and concepts objectively.
    d. It rejects Freud's idea of innate motives.

Chapter 15

HEALTH AND STRESS

Learning Objectives

After studying this chapter, you should be able to:

1. Define health psychology and stress.

2. Describe the Social Readjustment Rating Scale and what it is intended to measure.

3. Discuss how stress affects the immune system.

4. Explain the psychosomatic specificity hypothesis.

5. List the characteristics of the Type A personality.

6. Describe the role of subjective judgment in the perception of an event as stressful.

7. Describe the characteristics of stressful events.

8. Identify the two types of appraisal and discuss when they occur.

9. Describe the different types of disruptions that occur during stress.

10. Describe what happens physiologically during stress reactions.

11. Discuss the three stages of the general adaptation syndrome.

12. Discuss how defense mechanisms work to reduce stress.

13. Explain how cognitive reappraisal can be an effective coping strategy.

14. List the three types of arousal reduction and describe how they work to reduce the effects of stress.

15. Define anticipatory coping and describe how it works.

16. Discuss the role of social support in helping individuals to cope with stress.

Working with Names and Terms

From the alphabetized list below, choose the name or term that answers the question, using each name and term only once. Answers are at the back of your study guide.

antigens	Kobasa, Suzanne
approach-approach	Lazarus, Richard
arteriosclerosis	lymphocytes
avoidance-avoidance	posttraumatic stress disorder
Cannon, Walter	progressive relaxation
daily hassles	psychosomatic specificity
fight or flight	Riley, Vernon
General Adaptation Syndrome	risk factors
Graham, David	Rosenman, Ray
hardiness	sedatives
Holmes, Thomas	self-monitoring
intellectualization	Selye, Hans

_____ 1. What attribute is possessed by people who regard life events as challenges, who are involved in their environment, and who believe that they can determine their own fate?

_____ 2. What problem continued to make some Vietnam veterans miserable long after the war was over?

_____ 3. Who worked with Richard Rahe in developing the Social Readjustment Rating Scale?

_____ 4. What name is given to the stress-provoking events that frustrate us in our daily lives?

_____ 5. What leading stress researcher emphasized the importance of primary and secondary appraisal in determining perception of stress and coping with it?

_____ 6. What type of conflict was experienced by the donkey that starved to death between two bales of hay?

_____ 7. What does a person have if the person has hard, fatty plaques on the inside of the artery walls?

_____ 8. What class of drugs includes ethyl alcohol and barbiturates and is used to reduce psychological arousal and to induce sleep?

_____ 9. Whose research has supported the psychosomatic specificity hypothesis?

_____ 10. Whose pioneering research on rats showed a causal relationship between stress and impairment of the immune system?

_____ 11. What type of conflict confronted the prisoner when the judge asked him if he would rather be shot or hung?

_____ 12. Who described the effects of chronic stress in his General Adaptation Syndrome?

_____ 13. What hypothesis relates specific coping mechanisms to specific illnesses?

_____ 14. To what classification of cells do T-cells and B-cells belong?

_____ 15. What name is given collectively to things like high blood pressure, smoking, drinking excessively, failure to exercise, and having a Type A behavior pattern?

_____ 16. Who coined the term "homeostasis" and described the "fight or flight" response?

_____ 17. What defense mechanism allows people to divorce themselves from the emotional aspects of stressful situations?

_____ 18. What cardiologist worked with Meyer Friedman in describe the Type A behavior pattern?

_____ 19. Who studied a large group of business executives and described a trait called "hardiness"?

_____ 20. What general term is used to refer to foreign substances in the body, like viruses, bacteria, and cancer cells?

_____ 21. What term is used to designate the ability to recognize and control signs of a stress reaction?

_____ 22. What theory describes the stages experienced by people who are confronted with severe and chronic stress?

_____ 23. What response may have been more adaptive for humans who lived in caves than it is for humans who live in condos?

_____ 24. What is Pamela doing when she alternately tenses and relaxes each of the major muscles in her body?

Essay Questions

Suggested answers for the essay questions are included at the back of your study guide.

1. Getting a divorce is a major life change. Describe the stress-provoking aspects of the situation from the perspective of the husband. His ex-wife's name is Donna.

2. Write a short article discussing why doctors should be more concerned about the relationship between stress and illness.

3. Holmes and Rahe's list of stressful life events includes Christmas. How can Christmas be a stressful event?

4. Describe the psychosomatic specificity hypothesis and give an example that would support the hypothesis. Also, evaluate the hypothesis from the standpoint of your own experience.

Multiple-Choice Test I

For the multiple-choice questions, choose the best of the answers provided. Check your work with the answers at the back of your study guide, and be sure you understand why the keyed answers are correct.

1. The aims of health psychology include
   a. reduction of stress in the lives of individual members of society.
   b. use of psychological knowledge to identify factors responsible for health and illness.
   c. encouragement of medical professional to be aware of psychological factors in illness.
   d. making a distinction between psychosomatic illnesses and real illnesses.

2. During the years from 1900 to 1980, _____ have become increasingly important as conditions that result in death.
   a. risk factors
   b. infectious diseases
   c. stressful occupations
   d. substance abuse and addiction

3. Holmes and Rahe claimed that the 43 life events included in their rating scale are stressful because they
   a. threaten people's egos.
   b. occur without warning.
   c. require a change.
   d. disrupt psychological homeostasis.

4. From her research on business executives, Suzanne Kobasa found that some people can manage life stress without health consequences. She called this ability
   a. intellectualization.
   b. stress resistance.
   c. resiliency.
   d. hardiness.

5. Research has shown that better health and greater ability to cope with stress are associated with
   a. an optimistic disposition.
   b. economic security.
   c. physical attractiveness.
   d. religious beliefs.

6. Homeostasis is best defined as
   a. physiological consonance.
   b. internal equilibrium.
   c. acceptance of the inevitable.
   d. psychological stability.

7. Destroyers are to the navy as _____ are to the immune system.
   a. antigens
   b. T-cells
   c. zygotes
   d. plaques

8. The pioneering PNI research of Vernon Riley established a causal link between
   a. stress and impairment of the immune system.
   b. stress and cardiovascular disease.
   c. appraisal and coping strategies.
   d. specific coping strategies and specific diseases.

9. Which of the following statements is consistent with the psychosomatic specificity hypothesis?
   a. Acne is more common among adolescents who feel guilty about their sexual impulses.
   b. Type A behavior pattern predisposes people to coronary heart disease (CHD).
   c. People who repress their hostility are prone to ulcers.
   d. All of the above are consistent with the hypothesis.

10. If an illness is described as psychosomatic, it means that
    a. the person who is ill is a hypochondriac.
    b. there is no organic pathology to explain the pain the person experiences.
    c. psychological factors are a contributing cause of the illness.
    d. the illness cannot be effectively treated with medication or surgery.

11. Coronary heart disease (CHD) has been linked to all of the following *except*
    a. cigarette smoking.
    b. high-cholesterol diet.
    c. high-pressure employment.
    d. Type A behavior pattern.

12. Attempts to refine the Type A behavior pattern have suggested that the most important trait in susceptibility to CHD is
    a. hostility.
    b. ambition.
    c. impatience.
    d. competitiveness.

13. The components of stress include all of the following *except*
    a. the individual's personality.
    b. the stressful event.
    c. the appraisal of the event.
    d. the reaction to the event.

14. What term is used to describe frustrating practical problems like misplacing things, gaining weight, and finding that a new tire costs a lot more than you thought it would?
    a. habitual stressors
    b. daily hassles
    c. minor mishaps
    d. bugs

15. The text says that three important characteristics of stressful event are
    a. frequency, intensity, and validity.
    b. inevitability, perceptibility, and frustration.
    c. helplessness, overload, and conflict.
    d. predictability, intensity, and duration.

16. Helplessness is most closely related to
    a. Type A behavior pattern.
    b. instability
    c. aversive conditioning.
    d. having an external locus of control.

17. The lottery winner can choose to take the money as a lump sum or as an annuity. The winner's dilemma is a(n) _____ conflict.
    a. approach-avoidance
    b. double approach-avoidance
    c. approach-approach
    d. avoidance-avoidance

18. Richard Lazarus and his colleagues did a study in which subjects watched a film depicting gruesome industrial accidents. The study demonstrated the importance of _____ in determining people's reaction to potentially stressful events.
    a. primary appraisal
    b. secondary appraisal
    c. person variables
    d. situation variables

19. The most common emotional responses to stress are
    a. guilt and inadequacy.
    b. anxiety and depression.
    c. irritation and anger.
    d. conflict and confusion.

20. Cannon's work on the physiological symptoms of stress suggest that the body's reaction to stress is most adaptive for a person who is
    a. confronted by a bear.
    b. flying an airplane.
    c. taking an exam.
    d. conducting an orchestra.

21. The stages of Hans Selye's General Adaptation Syndrome are
    a. arousal, plateau, and resolution.
    b. alarm, resistance, and exhaustion.
    c. appraisal, activation, and action.
    d. perception, cognition, and behavior.

22. Defense mechanisms, reappraisal, and arousal reduction are
    a. primary stress reactions.
    b. secondary stress reactions.
    c. cognitive-focused coping methods.
    d. emotion-focused coping methods.

23. Although the Jews in Germany in the 1930s were confronted with evidence of hostility and persecution, many of them made no effort to leave the country. The most reasonable explanation for this is that they
    a. attributed their arousal to internal causes.
    b. were lacking in emotion-focused coping methods.
    c. used the mechanism of denial.
    d. did not seek social support.

24. In coping with stress, both exercise and relaxation are useful for
    a. reducing arousal.
    b. regaining cognitive control.
    c. facilitating secondary appraisal.
    d. channeling emotions.

25. Self-monitoring involves
    a. being aware of your repertoire of coping strategies.
    b. being able to recognize symptoms of stress reaction.
    c. keeping control of the emotional component of stress.
    d. making both primary and secondary appraisals.

Multiple-Choice Test II

For the multiple-choice questions, choose the best of the answers provided. Check your work with the answers at the back of your study guide, and be sure you understand why the keyed answers are correct.

1. Antigens include such things as
    a. epinephrine and norepinephrine.
    b. lymphocytes and leukocytes.
    c. viruses and cancer cells.
    d. T-cells and B-cells.

2. A psychoneuroimmunologist is most likely to be involved in
    a. treating people who have psychosomatic illnesses.
    b. studying the developmental aspect of the Type A behavior pattern.
    c. analyzing the symptoms reported by victims of posttraumatic stress disorder.
    d. doing research on the effect of stress on proliferation of cancer cells.

3. Research has shown that immunosuppressive effects occur when
    a. men become widowers.
    b. spouses separate.
    c. people lose their jobs.
    d. any of the above happens.

4. Which of the following is consistent with the psychosomatic specificity hypothesis?
    a. Asthma is used as a means of avoiding threatening situations.
    b. People who keep themselves in a high state of arousal may be suppressing their immune systems.
    c. People tend to have idiosyncratic physiological symptoms that appear whenever they are stressed.
    d. All of the above are consistent with the hypothesis.

5. When David Graham and his colleagues did a study to confirm the link between specific coping strategies and specific illnesses, what did they ask subjects to do?
   a. list 10 people they admire
   b. pick adjectives that describe them from a list of adjectives
   c. choose a cartoon from a set of cartoons
   d. respond to selected TAT pictures

6. According to the aims of health psychology, a health psychologist might
   a. design a program to help people quit smoking.
   b. conduct seminars to help people with Type A behavior pattern modify their behavior.
   c. study the relationship between loneliness and mortality.
   d. any of the above.

7. The effect of stress on mortality was dramatically demonstrated in
   a. children who were raised in foster homes.
   b. older men whose wives had died.
   c. women who are divorced after they are 50 years old.
   d. men who work in stressful occupations.

8. Events on the Social Readjustment Rating Scale of Holmes and Rahe include
   a. marriage.
   b. retirement.
   c. death of a close friend.
   d. all of the above.

9. All of the following are aspects of what Suzanne Kobasa called "hardiness" *except*
   a. having an external locus of control.
   b. being challenged rather than threatened by life events.
   c. having high self-efficacy in most situations.
   d. being involved in environmental events.

10. Research done since the original research of Holmes and Rahe suggests that life changes are stressful only if the change
    a. results in a lower standard of living.
    b. is permanent and irreversible.
    c. is negatively appraised by the individual.
    d. occurs in the absence of social support.

11. To describe Type A behavior pattern, Friedman and Rosenman used all the following adjectives *except*
    a. reflective.
    b. impatient.
    c. ambitious.
    d. hostile.

12. A study done in Finland suggests that a man is most likely to be vulnerable to coronary heart disease (CHD) if he
    a. takes on more responsibilities than he can manage.
    b. is frequently angry or irritable with co-workers.
    c. represses perceptions and impulses that are inconsistent with his self-image.
    d. feels that others do not recognize and appreciate his competence and conscientiousness.

13. The definition of stress includes all of the following *except*
    a. an environmental event is seen as a threat to important goals.
    b. the threat taxes one's ability to cope.
    c. psychological and physiological functioning is disrupted.
    d. the environmental event has not been anticipated.

14. The three types of stressful events describe in the text are
    a. personal, social, and occupational.
    b. frustration, conflict, and helplessness.
    c. life changes, daily hassles, and chronic stressors.
    d. primary, secondary, and residual.

15. Ellen Langer and Judith Rodin demonstrated the effects of _____ in nursing-home residents.
    a. frustration
    b. helplessness
    c. lack of social support
    d. lack of attention

16. The psychological experience that accompanies overload is
    a. cognitive confusion.
    b. emotional exhaustion.
    c. frustration.
    d. time pressure.

17. Marge wants the cashmere sweater, but it is very expensive. As Marge thinks about whether or not she should buy the sweater, she is experiencing a(n) _____ conflict.
    a. approach-approach
    b. avoidance-avoidance
    c. approach-avoidance
    d. double approach-avoidance

18. Richard Lazarus would say that potentially stressful situations we are accustomed to handling are less stressful for us than they might be for others because of our
    a. secondary appraisals.
    b. self-efficacy.
    c. self-perception.
    d. hardiness.

19. All Angelina can think about is what will happen to her plans if she makes low scores on the SAT. Psychologist use the term _____ to describe her thinking.
    a. compulsive
    b. obsessive
    c. neurotic
    d. psychotic

20. Cannon's work is to the functioning of internal organs as _____ work is to the structure of internal organs.
    a. Riley's
    b. Graham's
    c. Selye's
    d. Lazarus'

21. The text observes that for the treatment of posttraumatic stress disorder (PTSD), _____ is especially effective.
    a. hypnosis or meditation
    b. systematic desensitization
    c. drug therapy (sedatives)
    d. group therapy

22. The ability to use intellectualization to cope with stress would be most valuable for a(n)
    a. sociobiologist.
    b. astronaut.
    c. undertaker.
    d. private detective.

23. In a study by Langer and her associates, surgical patients were encouraged to think of hospitalization as a time to escape responsibilities and be pampered. What method of coping did the study demonstrate?
    a. cognitive reappraisal
    b. intellectualization
    c. emotion-focused
    d. arousal reduction

24. Anticipatory coping involves such things as
    a. learning what is involved in the surgical procedure you are contemplating.
    b. practicing speech you are going to give on your parents.
    c. studying for an exam.
    d. any of the above.

25. Bardow and Porritt did a study on two groups of men who were hospitalized after serious automobile accidents, The better health and adjustment of the experimental group after the hospitalization demonstrated the value of _____ in stressful situations.
    a. cognitive appraisal
    b. social support
    c. emotion-focused coping strategies
    d. progressive relaxation

Chapter 16

MAJOR PSYCHOLOGICAL DISORDERS

Learning Objectives

After studying this chapter, you should be able to:

1. Identify the four major criteria of abnormality and list the limitations of each.

2. Discuss the innovations introduced by the DSM-III-R, and describe the five axes used in diagnosis.

3. Discuss the advantages and disadvantages of diagnosis for psychological disorders.

4. Differentiate between the medical, psychodynamic, behavioral, cognitive, and humanistic perspectives on psychological disorders.

5. Define and differentiate among the following: anxiety, somatoform, and dissociative disorders.

6. Distinguish among the different types of anxiety disorders: panic disorders, phobias, generalized anxiety disorders, and obsessive-compulsive disorders.

7. Distinguish among the different types of somatoform disorders: hypochondriasis and conversion disorders.

8. Distinguish among the different types of dissociative disorders: psychogenic amnesia and multiple personality.

9. Describe the primary characteristics of mood disorders.

10. Define and distinguish among the mood disorders: major depressive episodes, manic episodes, and bipolar disorders.

11. Differentiate among the three explanations for mood disorders: biological, psychodynamic, and cognitive-behavioral.

12. Describe the symptoms of schizophrenia.

13. Discriminate among the types of schizophrenia: disorganized, paranoid, catatonic, and undifferentiated.

14. Explain the dopamine hypothesis, the brain atrophy model, and the diathesis-stress model of schizophrenia.

15. Describe the changes likely to accompany substance abuse.

16. Define alcoholism and trace the development of this disorder through its early, middle, and chronic phases.

17. Outline the significant predictors of initial use of mind-altering drugs and the continued use of drugs.

18. Distinguish among paranoid, histrionic, obsessive-compulsive, and antisocial personality disorders.

Working with Names and Terms

From the alphabetized list below, choose the name or term that answers the question, using each name and term only once. Answers are at the back of your study guide.

agoraphobia
anhedonia
anxiety
Beck, Aaron
biogenic amine
bipolar disorder
delusions
diathesis-stress
dissociative
dopamine
Freud, Sigmund
hallucination
histrionic
hypochondriasis
mood
multiaxial
obsessive-compulsive
Rosenhan, David
secondary gains
Seligman, Martin
Skinner, B. F.
Szasz, Thomas
tolerance
undifferentiated

_____ 1. What cognitive behaviorist investigated "learned helplessness" and suggested that it is causally linked to depression?

_____ 2. What hypothesis links norepinephrine and serotonin to depression and mania?

_____ 3. What psychologist with his associates demonstrated that when a person is labeled schizophrenic, interpretations of the person's behavior are influenced by the diagnosis?

_____ 4. Which personality disorder is associated with impulsiveness, poorly formulated ideas, and exaggerated and colorful behavior?

_____ 5. What hypothesis suggests interaction of biological and psychological factors in explaining mental disorders?

_____ 6. What name is given to the disorder that frequently results in a person's being fearful of leaving home or of being alone?

_____ 7. What description of the DSM-III-R calls attention to the fact that diagnoses require evaluation on five dimensions?

_____ 8. Who claimed that psychological disorders result from unconscious conflicts?

_____ 9. To what classification of disorders do phobic disorder and panic disorder belong?

_____ 10. Who described the "cognitive triad" and related distorted and pessimistic thinking to depression?

_____ 11. Who claimed that both normal and abnormal behavior are functions of situational cues?

_____ 12. What personality disorder is portrayed by a person who is a perfectionist that pays extraordinary attention to details and who finds it difficult to make decisions?

_____ 13. What diagnosis is assigned to a person who alternates between euphoria and depression?

_____ 14. What is occurring when an alcoholic experiences the sensation of being covered with spiders?

_____ 15. What term did Freud use to refer to benefits, like attention and sympathy, that reward illness?

_____ 16. What condition makes it necessary for substance abusers to use increasingly larger doses to produce the same effect?

_____ 17. What diagnosis is given to a schizophrenic whose symptoms are borrowed from several diagnostic categories?

_____ 18. To what classification of disorders do psychogenic amnesia and multiple personality belong?

_____ 19. In what disorder is the individual likely to have a home pharmacy and a long list of doctors?

_____ 20. What is being experienced by the schizophrenic who tells her therapist that she is E.T.'s mother and that she has come to earth to look for him?

_____ 21. To what classification of disorders do depressive disorder and bipolar disorder belong?

_____ 22. Who accused mental-health professionals of being "social engineers" when they decide which behaviors and beliefs are socially appropriate?

_____ 23. What neurotransmitter appears to be implicated in schizophrenic behavior?

_____ 24. What term is used to describe the condition in which a person has lost the ability to experience pleasure?

Essay Questions

Suggested answers for the essay questions are included at the back of your study guide.

1. Abnormality is defined in terms of statistical deviation, social deviation, maladaptive behavior, and personal distress. Give an example of how each of these criteria is applicable to a particular disorder and one reason why the criterion is inadequate.

2. Choose any two of the disorders described in the text and discuss how symptoms of the disorder are manifested in "normal" people.

3. Choose any disorder that is described in the text and imagine that you have just recovered from an acute episode of the disorder. Describe your experience as you would in a letter to a friend.

4. Generate as many hypotheses as you can to explain why depression is diagnosed more frequently in women than in men.

Multiple-Choice Test I

For the multiple-choice questions, choose the best of the answers provided. Check your work with the answers at the back of your study guide, and be sure you understand why the keyed answers are correct.

1. Diagnosis of retardation in children who score below 68 on the Wechsler Intelligence Test of Children is based on the _____ criterion of abnormality.
   a. statistical
   b. social deviance
   c. maladaptive behavior
   d. personal distress

2. Use of the criterion of personal distress to define abnormality could be used to diagnose all of the following *except*
   a. mania.
   b. generalized anxiety.
   c. agoraphobia.
   d. depression.

3. All of the following would appear on complete multiaxial diagnoses of hypothetical patients *except*
   a. agoraphobia.
   b. mother had multiple phobias.
   c. extremely poor vision.
   d. spouse died six months ago.

4. Diagnoses are important in research investigating mental disorders because they frequently
   a. direct the design of the research.
   b. enable researchers to use statistical tests.
   c. define the independent variable.
   d. define the dependent variable.

5. The medical perspective is reflected in use of the term
   a. maladjustive functioning.
   b. psychological disorder.
   c. behavioral disorder.
   d. mental illness.

6. B. F. Skinner's most vehement criticism of Freud's psychodynamic theory concerned Freud's
   a. failure to consider childhood experiences as determiners of adult behavior.
   b. effort to localize functions in the brain.
   c. disregard for the influence of cognitive processes on behavior.
   d. emphasis on internal causes of behavior.

7. In explaining abnormal behavior, psychologists who take the cognitive perspective are most likely to emphasize
   a. interpretations people make of environmental events.
   b. personality traits that are stable over time.
   c. motives that have no adaptive value.
   d. emotional responses that are inappropriate and maladaptive.

8. Panic disorder, phobia, and generalized anxiety are most appropriately defined as abnormal based on the criterion of
   a. statistical frequency.
   b. social deviance.
   c. maladaptive behavior.
   d. personal distress.

9. What disorder involves massive arousal of the sympathetic nervous system?
   a. phobic disorder
   b. somatoform disorder
   c. panic disorder
   d. conversion disorder

10. The most famous literary example of psychological disorder is portrayed by Lady Macbeth's repeated attempts to wash the blood from her hands. The DSM-III-R would classify her problem as
    a. obsessive-compulsive disorder.
    b. conversion disorder.
    c. psychogenic amnesia.
    d. phobic disorder.

11. Elmer keeps a chart on which he records his temperature, weight, blood-sugar level, and the results of measurements he takes on his urine every morning. He also puts a gold star on his chart when he has a normal bowel movement. Elmer's behavior suggests that he might have
    a. hypochondriasis.
    b. phobic disorder.
    c. obsessive-compulsive disorder.
    d. conversion disorder.

12. People who suffer from the rare condition called _____ disorder are extraordinarily susceptible to hypnotism.
    a. psychogenic amnesia
    b. conversion
    c. multiple-personality
    d. agoraphobic

13. Pressure of speech, flight of ideas, and grandiose delusions are symptomatic of
    a. conversion hysteria.
    b. catatonic schizophrenia.
    c. histrionic personality disorder.
    d. the manic phase of bipolar disorder.

14. Suicide occurs most frequently among
    a. middle-aged black females.
    b. young white females.
    c. older white males.
    d. young black males.

15. The biogenic amine hypothesis claims that depression occurs when the level of norepinephrine is _____ and the level of serotonin is _____ at synapses in the brain.
    a. low; low
    b. low; high
    c. high; low
    d. high; high

16. Mourning for the death of a loved one was used as a model of clinical depression by
    a. Sigmund Freud.
    b. Walter Mischel
    c. Martin Seligman.
    d. Aaron Beck.

17. Learned helplessness, a negative view of the self and the world, and internal attributions for personal failures are explanations offered by the _____ perspective to explain _____ disorder.
    a. cognitive-behavioral; generalized anxiety
    b. cognitive-behavioral; depressive
    c. humanistic; generalized anxiety
    d. humanistic; depressive

18. Schizophrenia is characterized by disorganization of
    a. thought.
    b. perception.
    c. emotions.
    d. all of the above.

19. Hallucinations are symptoms of disorganized
    a. thought.
    b. perception.
    c. emotion.
    d. behavior.

20. Blunted affect is a _____ symptom of schizophrenia; anhedonia is a _____ symptom.
    a. negative; negative
    b. negative; positive
    c. positive; negative
    d. positive; positive

21. Antipsychotic drugs _____ the activity of dopamine in the brain and reduce the _____ symptoms of schizophrenia.
    a. increase; positive
    b. increase; negative
    c. decrease; positive
    d. decrease; negative

22. "High risk studies" are investigating environmental factors that increase the likelihood of schizophrenia. The subjects in these studies are
    a. predisposed children living with adoptive parents.
    b. children who have a schizophrenic mother.
    c. fraternal twins, one of whom is schizophrenic.
    d. identical twins, one of whom is schizophrenic.

23. Delusions are symptoms seen in people who are victims of
    a. substance abuse.
    b. schizophrenia.
    c. bipolar disorder.
    d. all of the above.

24. The symptoms of personality disorders are _____, and people who have the disorders are best described as _____.
    a. enduring; inflexible
    b. enduring; flexible
    c. episodic; inflexible
    d. episodic; inflexible

25. All of the following are descriptive of people with antisocial personality disorder *except*
    a. fearless.
    b. lack of social skills.
    c. lack of conscience.
    d. stimulus seeking.

Multiple-Choice Test II

For the multiple-choice questions, choose the best of the answers provided. Check your work with the answers at the back of your study guide, and be sure you understand why the keyed answera are correct.

1. All of the following are used to define abnormal behavior *except*
    a. statistical frequency.
    b. personal distress.
    c. inappropriate arousal.
    d. maladaptive behavior.

2. The most frequent criticism of social deviance as a criterion for abnormality is that it
    a. suggests that highly creative people are abnormal.
    b. discriminate against minority groups.
    c. forces mental health professionals to define social norms.
    d. implies that abnormality is culturally relative.

3. The primary advantage that the DSM-III-R has over DSM-I and DSM-II is that it appears to have increased the _____ of diagnoses.
    a. precision
    b. reliability
    c. flexibility
    d. validity

4. The study in which David Rosenhan and his colleagues were admitted to mental hospitals because they complained of hearing voices demonstrated a problem that can result from using
    a. The DSM-III-R for diagnoses.
    b. subjective diagnostic criteria.
    c. diagnostic categories as labels.
    d. paraprofessionals as diagnosticians.

5. Which perspective puts the greatest emphasis on early childhood experience in explaining abnormal behavior?
    a. psychodynamic
    b. humanistic
    c. behavioral
    d. cognitive

6. The behavioral approach to understanding behavior has been criticized for all of the following *except*
    a. self-imposed limitations.
    b. too few concepts.
    c. failure to recognize the importance of cognitive processes.
    d. lack of supporting research.

7. The humanistic perspective of Carl Rogers suggests that one of the sources of psychological disorders is that the person
    a. uses emotion-focused coping methods.
    b. has become egocentric and inner-directed.
    c. is overly dependent upon the positive regard of others.
    d. has not found a role that is consistent with motives and goals.

8. The anxiety disorders include all of the following *except* _____ disorder.
   a. obsessive-compulsive
   b. conversion
   c. panic
   d. phobic

9. In the introduction to the chapter on psychological disorders, the text describes a housewife who avoids supermarkets, department stores, and other crowded places. The most likely diagnosis for the woman is
   a. agoraphobia.
   b. conversion disorder.
   c. generalized anxiety.
   d. paranoid personality disorder.

10. In panic disorder, the symptoms are acute and episodic; in _____ disorder, the symptoms are similar but chronic.
    a. depressive
    b. generalized anxiety
    c. conversion
    d. phobic

11. A patient with conversion disorder is most likely to
    a. be unable to recognize his wife.
    b. think she is dying of cancer.
    c. wake up one morning with a paralyzed arm.
    d. make grossly inaccurate interpretations of the behavior of others.

12. The symptoms of depression include all of the following *except*
    a. low self-esteem and feelings of worthlessness.
    b. grandiose delusions and auditory hallucinations.
    c. loss of interest in work and recreation.
    d. fatigue and insomnia.

13. People who are diagnosed as having bipolar disorder have
    a. manic episodes.
    b. depressive episodes.
    c. both manic and depressive episodes.
    d. either manic or depressive episodes.

14. The rumination-distraction hypothesis tells us that
    a. characteristic coping styles determine how anxiety disorders will be manifested.
    b. women are more likely than men to attempt suicide.
    c. depressed people either think too much or too little about their problems.
    d. men and women react differently to depression.

15. The text presents evidence that there may be a genetically transmitted vulnerability to _____ disorders.
    a. dissociative
    b. anxiety
    c. somatoform
    d. mood

16. The attribution theory of depression says that depressed people tend to make attributions for their own failures that are
    a. internal, stable, and global.
    b. internal, unstable, and specific.
    c. external, stable, and global.
    d. external, unstable, and specific.

17. The term used to express the idea that depressed people have more accurate self-perceptions than nondepressed people is
    a. deficiency of defenses.
    b. depressive realism.
    c. realistic self-monitoring.
    d. cognitive vulnerability.

18. The positive symptoms of schizophrenia include all of the following *except*
    a. disjointed speech and thought.
    b. delusions.
    c. blunted affect.
    d. hallucinations.

19. "Derailment" is a symptom of _____ that entails _____.
    a. depression; loss of identity
    b. depression; incoherent speech
    c. schizophrenia; loss of identity
    d. schizophrenia; incoherent speech

20. All of the following are types of schizophrenia *except*
    a. anhedonic.
    b. paranoid.
    c. catatonic.
    d. disorganized.

21. In some schizophrenics, brain atrophy has resulted in enlarged _____, most frequently in the _____ lobes.
    a. auricles; occipital
    b. auricles; temporal
    c. ventricles; occipital
    d. ventricles; temporal

22. The symptom of organic mental disorder that is characterized by disturbance of attention and other cognitive functions is
    a. somathesis.
    b. delirium.
    c. anoxia.
    d. hysteria.

23. Surveys of college seniors in 1969, 1978, and 1989 showed a decrease in the use of all of the following *except*
    a. heroin.
    b. alcohol.
    c. amphetamines.
    d. marijuana.

24. Mistrust, suspicion, hostility, and manipulation are manifested in the behavior of people diagnosed as having _____ personality disorder.
    a. paranoid
    b. schizoid
    c. histrionic
    d. obsessive-compulsive

25. Research suggests that antisocial personality disorder is best explained by
    a. chaotic family environments.
    b. genetic transmission.
    c. the autonomic-reactivity hypothesis.
    d. the diathesis-stress hypothesis.

Chapter 17

TREATMENT OF PSYCHOLOGICAL DISORDERS

Learning Objectives

After studying this chapter, you should be able to:

1. Contrast moral treatment with the earlier methods of dealing with psychological disorders.

2. List and discuss the six key concepts of classical psychoanalysis.

3. Explain the difference between classical psychoanalysis and psychoanalytic psychotherapy.

4. Describe three key differences in the approaches and techniques of psychoanalysis and behavioral therapy.

5. Outline six methods of behavior therapy.

6. Explain how the principles of operant conditioning are used in behavior therapy.

7. Discuss the three essential qualities of a client-centered therapist.

8. Compare and contrast the assumptions of psychoanalytic, behavior, and humanistic therapies.

9. Discuss the advantages of group therapy compared to individual psychotherapy.

10. Explain how self-help groups and family therapy differ from other forms of group therapy.

11. Explain why it is difficult to answer the question, "How effective is psychotherapy?"

12. Discuss the advantages of a multimodal approach to therapy.

13. Describe the power of the patient's expectation of success in the effectiveness of therapy.

14. Discuss the differences between psychotherapy and medical treatments.

15. Identify and describe the effects of antianxiety drugs, antipsychotic drugs, antidepressant drugs, and lithium.

16. Describe the goals of the deinstitutionalization of people with psychological disorders.

17. Describe the limitations of the deinstitutionalization of people with psychological disorders.

Working with Names and Terms

From the alphabetized list below, choose the name or term that answers the question, using each name and term only once. Answers are at the back of your study guide.

anxiety hierarchy	Gestalt
Beck, Aaron	lithium
benzodiazepines	manifest content
biofeedback	Pinel, Philippe
Breuer, Joseph	psychiatrist
Charcot, Pierre	psychoanalyst
congruence	Rogers, Carl
conversion disorder	spontaneous remission
deinstitutionalization	tardive dyskinesia
depressive	token economy
Ellis, Albert	transference
free association	Wolpe, Joseph

_____ 1. What cognitive psychologist originated rational-emotive therapy?

_____ 2. What condition is a side effect of antipsychotic drugs?

_____ 3. What type of mental health professional has attended an institute to learn to use the treatment techniques originated by Freud?

_____ 4. Which of Carl Rogers' qualifications for therapists specifies that therapists should be genuine and honest in relationships with clients?

_____ 5. What name is given to the process of substituting community care for confinement in a mental hospital?

_____ 6. From whom did Freud get the idea of using hypnosis in psychotherapy?

_____ 7. Who is notable in the history of psychology because he instituted humane practices in the treatment of people with psychological disorders?

_____ 8. What essential component of systematic desensitization requires the therapist and the patient to order the things the patient fears?

_____ 9. What pioneering behavior therapist originated systematic desensitization?

_____ 10. What aspect of a dream are you disclosing when you tell a friend about your dream?

_____ 11. Who claimed that therapists should be accepting, empathetic, and genuine?

_____ 12. What type of therapy is most frequently used to treat stress-related problems like headaches and high blood pressure?

_____ 13. Who attributed depression to the "cognitive triad"?

_____ 14. What term is used to describe the situation in which the symptoms of a psychological disorder disappear without any type of treatment?

_____ 15. What type of mental health professional is an M.D. who specializes in the treatment of mental disorders?

_____ 16. What has happened when a patient tells his therapist that she "nags and criticizes, just like my mother used to do"?

_____ 17. To what class of drugs do Valium. Lithium, and Xanox belong?

_____ 18. What colleague worked with Freud for several years in the development of classical psychoanalysis?

_____ 19. What is the best medicine for the mania experienced by people with bipolar disorder?

_____ 20. What is the modern name for the disorder Freud called "hysteria"?

171

_____ 21. What humanistic therapy tries to put people in touch with their feelings and has clients act out their dreams?

_____ 22. What process is a patient of a psychoanalyst demonstrating when she talks about anything that comes to mind?

_____ 23. For what disorder is electroconvulsive therapy most effective?

_____ 24. What system is being used in a mental institution when an inmate gets a poker chip for brushing his teeth and two poker chips for filling water glasses in the dining room?

Essay Questions

Suggested answers for the essay questions are included at the back of your study guide.

1. Describe how a cognitive-behavioral therapist would treat a person who is chronically depressed.

2. A peer counseling centers at a university decided to use Roger's client-centered therapy to treat students who came to the center for help. Why do you think this type of therapy was chosen?

3. Imagine that you have become increasingly depressed for several months, and are functioning poorly as a result. What criteria would you use in choosing a therapist?

4. Compare the role of the therapist in psychoanalytic therapy, cognitive-behavioral therapy, and client-centered therapy.

Multiple-Choice Test I

For the multiple-choice test, choose the best of the answers provided. Check your work with the answers at the back of your study guide, and be sure you understand why the keyed answers are correct.

1. Philippe Pinel is associated with
   a. prefrontal lobotomies.
   b. discovery of the benefits of lithium carbonate.
   c. electroconvulsive therapy.
   (d) moral treatment.

2. Classical psychoanalysis includes all of the following *except*
   (a) confrontation.   c. working through.
   b. transference.   d. free association.

3. According to Freud, the unconscious meaning of a dream is its _____ content, and the aspects of the dream we remember are the _____ content.
    a. latent; manifest
    b. manifest; latent
    c. structural; functional
    d. functional; structural

4. The patient "forgot" an appointment, and at the next session he kept changing the subject. In classical psychoanalysis, the patient's behavior is called
    a. resistance.
    b. incongruence.
    c. reaction formation.
    d. manifestation.

5. What is the classical psychoanalyst doing when she asks the patient, "Do you think the queen who has appeared in several of your dreams could be your mother"?
    a. cathecting
    b. transferring
    c. interpreting
    d. probing

6. Compared to Freud, neo-Freudians like Adler, Horney, and Erikson put more emphasis on the influence of
    a. early childhood experiences.
    b. society and culture.
    c. the power of the id.
    d. all of the above.

7. A behavior therapist would be most likely to describe the problem of an alcoholic as
    a. escaping from reality.
    b. lack of self-control.
    c. stimulus-seeking behavior.
    d. drinking too much.

8. Learning progressive relaxation and constructing an anxiety hierarchy are two essential steps in
    a. systematic desensitization.
    b. biofeedback therapy.
    c. Gestalt therapy.
    d. client-centered therapy.

9. *In vivo* desensitization would be most difficult to do with a person whose problem is fear of
    a. open spaces.
    b. mice.
    c. thunder and lightening.
    d. high places.

10. When his blood pressure goes up, the loudness of the tone increases; and when his blood pressure goes down, the loudness of the tone decreases. He is experiencing
    a. systematic desensitization.
    b. autonomic programming.
    c. aversive therapy.
    d. biofeedback therapy.

11. Before taking her first airplane trip, a "catastrophiser" might say:
    a. "If the plane is hijacked, I'll probably get shot."
    b. "Wouldn't it be terrible if the pilot had a heart attack."
    c. "I can just see us crashing into a mountain."
    d. The "catastrophiser" might say any of the above.

12. The primary goal of rational-emotive therapy is to
    a. reduce emotional involvement.
    b. improve interpersonal skills.
    c. change irrational beliefs.
    d. increase self-esteem.

13. The token economies that are set up in institutions like prisons and homes for the mentally retarded apply the principles of
    a. classical conditioning.
    b. response substitution.
    c. positive reinforcement.
    d. stimulus substitution.

14. The process in which behavior-modification techniques are used to teach a person a new skill is called
    a. hierarchial learning.
    b. componential conditioning.
    c. behavioral integration.
    d. shaping.

15. A student who wanted to lose weight kept a record of what she ate, when she ate it, the people who ate with her, and the mood she was in when she ate. She was doing this as part of a
    a. self-control procedure.
    b. stimulus-substitution program.
    c. Gestalt exercise.
    d. behavioral contract.

16. The steps in self-control procedures include all of the following *except*
    a. identifying motives.
    b. analyzing the situation.
    c. managing discriminative stimuli.
    d. managing consequences.

17. Gestalt therapy takes the _____ approach to the treatment of mental disorders.
    a. psychodynamic
    b. cognitive
    c. humanistic
    d. behavioral

18. What term did Carl Rogers use to express the belief that therapists must wholeheartedly accept their clients?
    a. acceptance of the human condition
    b. unconditional positive regard
    c. agape
    d. congruence

19. The technique in which a client-centered therapist summarizes the content and feeling of a client's message is called
    a. interpretation.
    b. confirmation.
    c. reflection.
    d. mirroring.

20. Encounter groups were devised by _____ psychologists for the purpose of _____.
    a. cognitive; social insight
    b. cognitive; personal growth
    c. humanistic; social insight
    d. humanistic; personal growth

21. Terms like "enmeshed" and "disengaged" are used in _____ family therapy.
    a. structural
    b. systematic
    c. experiential
    d. interactive

22. A major problem in evaluating the effectiveness of psychotherapy is
    a. locating people who are willing to be subjects.
    b. getting therapists who are willing to participate.
    c. choosing a dependent variable or variables.
    d. choosing an independent variable or variables.

23. Benzodiazepines are most likely to be prescribed for
    a. somatoform disorders.
    b. anxiety disorders.
    c. mood disorders.
    d. schizophrenia.

24. Fluxetine (Prozac) and tricyclic drugs are used to treat
    a. mania.
    b. depression.
    c. schizophrenia.
    d. anxiety disorders.

25. Community mental-health centers offer all of the following *except*
    a. crisis intervention.
    b. shelter for the homeless mentally ill.
    c. counseling and psychotherapy.
    d. day care programs for severely disturbed patients.

Multiple-Choice Test II

For the multiple-choice test, choose the best of the answers provided. Check your work with the answers at the back of your study guide, and be sure you understand why the keyed answers are correct.

1. Freud and Breuer determined that the cause of hysteria was
   a. a week ego.
   b. unconscious hostility turned against the self.
   c. traumatic events in childhood.
   d. failure to resolve the Oedipus/Electra complex.

2. Freud used the phrases "the fundamental rule of psychoanalysis" to refer to _____, and "the royal road to the unconscious" to refer to _____.
   a. resistance; transference
   b. resistance; dream analysis
   c. free association; transference
   d. free association; dream analysis

3. In the dream of Freud's patient, Little Hans, the giraffes were an aspect of the _____ content of the dream.
   a. latent
   b. manifest
   c. structural
   d. functional

175

4. In the terminology of classical psychoanalysis, Melvin is demonstrating transference when he
   a. responds to the therapist as if the therapist were his father.
   b. allows the therapist to participate in his fantasies.
   c. brings unconscious material into conscious awareness.
   d. translates unconscious impulses into symbolic representations in his dreams.

5. In classical psychoanalysis, the process that follows insight by the patient is called
   a. metamorphosis.
   b. readaptation.
   c. working through.
   d. integration.

6. Behavior therapy assumes that psychological disorders are the result of
   a. faulty learning.
   b. misdirected thinking.
   c. lack of self-control.
   d. unresolved conflicts.

7. Wolpe's systematic desensitization is an application of the principles of
   a. classical conditioning.
   b. operant conditioning.
   c. stimulus substitution.
   d. discrimination learning.

8. "You are in an elevator and the door closes. The elevator starts up. The other passengers are all standing quietly and facing the door. When the elevator stops at the third floor, you want to get off, but you are determined to go up, up, up, to the top floor." The therapist would be most likely to say this to a person undergoing
   a. client-centered therapy.
   b. experiential therapy.
   c. Gestalt therapy.
   d. systematic desensitization.

9. Desensitization procedures are most effective for the treatment of _____ disorder.
   a. obsessive-compulsive
   b. phobic
   c. panic
   d. generalized anxiety

10. Diana decided it would be a good idea to take assertion training before she
    a. shops for a wedding dress.
    b. tells her boss that he is assigning her too much work.
    c. signs up for the statistics class.
    d. decides whether or not to have her face lifted.

11. Albert Ellis claims that one of the causes of psychological causes is the belief that
    a. others must like you and approve of your attitudes and behavior.
    b. anything can be accomplished with enough hard work and persistence.
    c. failures are caused by external factors, like bad luck and the influence of others.
    d. it is important not to appear to be too competent or too successful.

12. The cognitive therapy developed by Aaron Beck and his colleagues was designed to treat
    a. somatoform disorders.
    b. generalized anxiety.
    c. depression.
    d. phobias.

13. The fee for admission to a movie is 10 poker chips in the mental hospital that has
    a. socialization training.
    b. a work-for-pay program.
    c. community simulation.
    d. a token economy.

14. The method called "reinforcement of alternative behavior" would be most appropriate in the case of a child who
    a. refuses to learn to walk.
    b. eats applesauce with her fingers.
    c. steals money from other children.
    d. wets himself when he is upset.

15. The first step in self-control procedures is
    a. analyzing the situation.
    b. identifying reinforcers.
    c. making a contract.
    d. managing discriminative stimuli.

16. The goals of humanistic therapy for helping clients include all of the following except
    a. getting in touch with his or her true self.
    b. removing blocks to self-actualization.
    c. identifying and correcting problem behaviors.
    d. promoting continued growth.

17. The primary goal of Gestalt therapy is to
    a. help clients accept their weaknesses and failures.
    b. teach clients to relate to others.
    c. put clients in touch with their true feelings.
    d. improve clients' self-esteem.

18. According to Carl Rogers, all of the following are attributes of a good client-centered therapist except
    a. empathy.
    b. congruence.
    c. unconditional positive regard.
    d. authority.

19. When a client describes his therapist as "real, genuine, and openly herself," the client is referring to what Carl Rogers called
    a. openness.
    b. congruence.
    c. consonance.
    d. empathy.

20. "Experiential" and "structural" are two types of
    a. family therapy.
    b. support groups.
    c. encounter groups.
    d. humanistic therapy.

21. A study in which the subjects were 86 women who had metastatic breast cancer demonstrated the positive effects of _____ in perception of pain and longevity.
    a. encounter groups
    b. client-centered therapy
    c. family therapy
    d. support groups

22. If patients *believe* that their psychotherapy is effective treatment for their problem, _____ may occur.
    a. spontaneous remission
    b. symptom substitution
    c. the placebo effect
    d. evaluation bias

23. Antipsychotic drugs, like chlorpromazine, work because they
    a. facilitate the reuptake of dopamine.
    b. reduce the supply of dopamine at synapses.
    c. function as inhibitory neurotransmitters.
    d. attach to dopamine receptors.

24. Lithium is unlike other medications used to treat psychological disorders because
    a. it prevents future episodes of mania and depression.
    b. it has few side effects.
    c. it is not a drug in the conventional sense of the term.
    d. of all of the above.

25. Electroconvulsive therapy has been very successful in
    a. forestalling future episodes of depression.
    b. preventing suicide.
    c. reducing symptoms of schizophrenia.
    d. doing all of the above.

Appendix

METHODS AND STATISTICS IN PSYCHOLOGY

Learning Objectives

After studying the appendix, you should be able to:

1. Describe the two methods whose use justifies causal inference from the results of true experiments, and explain how these two methods are used in research.

2. Explain how experimental research differs from correlational research in the manner in which data are collected.

3. Give an example of a correlation that could result from the third variable problem and a correlation that illustrates the directionality problem.

4. Discuss reasons why researchers do correlational research.

5. Define "empiricism" and contrast it with other ways of acquiring knowledge.

6. Explain how a psychologist would use descriptive and inferential statistics in analyzing data from experimental research.

7. Explain how one would construct a frequency distribution and a graphical representation of the frequency distribution.

8. Describe a skewed, a bimodal, and a normal distribution, and explain why the normal distribution is considered the most important.

9. Name three measures of central tendency, explain how each is calculated, and describe circumstances in which each measure is appropriate.

10. Define "variability" and name two measures used to describe it.

11. Describe the relationship between the standard deviation and z-scores, and explain why z-scores are useful.

12. Give an example of a pair of variables that would produce a positive correlation and an example of a pair of variables that would produce a negative correlation.

13. Explain how one would construct a scatter plot and how scatter plots represent the magnitude and direction of correlations.

14. Identify "pearson *r*" and state the limits within which its values fall.

15. Explain why psychologists use inferential statistics, and relate their use to the concepts of random assignment, replicability, measurement error, and chance fluctuations.

Working with Names and Terms

From the alphabetized list below, choose the name or term that answers the question, using each name and term only once. Answers are at the back of your study guide.

bimodal
confounding
descriptive statistics
directionality
empiricism
independent variable
inferential statistics
mean
measurement
median
negative correlation
normal

organismic
Pearson *r*
random assignment
range
scatter plot
skewed
spurious
standard deviation
statistically significant
third variable
variability
z-scores

_____ 1. What term is used to describe correlations that do not result from a direct causal connection between the variables?

_____ 2. What statistic is used to determine the direction and strength of the relationship between two variables?

_____ 3. What does a researcher have after she plots a point on a graph for each pair of scores in her data?

_____ 4. What characteristic of a distribution of scores is described by the standard deviation?

_____ 5. What was used that resulted in the highest score in the class on the final exam being 2.34?

_____ 6. What problem is illustrated by the example of training children to improve their eye movement patterns as a result of a positive correlation between reading ability and eye movement patterns?

_____ 7. What procedure would an experimenter use to avoid having all the subjects with good memories in the same group?

_____ 8. What term is used to refer to methods that condense and summarize raw data?

_____ 9. What is the basic idea that underlies all methods of research used in psychology?

_____ 10. What relationship between variables is the researcher hoping to show if he is delighted when the statistic he has calculated has a value of -.82?

_____ 11. What causes differences between the scores of the control group and the experimental group in a true experiment?

_____ 12. What type of distribution is likely to result when measurements come from two distinct groups?

_____ 13. What term is used to refer to the process of applying a rule to assign numbers to observable events?

_____ 14. What type of distributions will be produced by the annual income of families living in the United States, scores on a very difficult test, and the number of teeth in the mouths of Miss Cooney's sixth-grade class?

_____ 15. What term is used to refer to methods used to determine the conclusions that can be drawn from a set of data?

_____ 16. What statistic is used to calculate the average annual rainfall in Needles, California?

_____ 17. What term is used to describe an experimental result that is unlikely to have occurred by chance?

_____ 18. What term is used to describe frequency distributions that are unimodal and symmetric?

_____ 19. Which measure of central tendency would be most appropriate for describing the average age of people who ride the merry-go-round at Disneyland?

_____ 20. What measure of variability is rarely used in science because it is crude and ignores patterns of dispersion?

_____ 21. What term is used to describe an uncontrolled variable that influences the dependent variable in an experiment?

_____ 22. What problem is illustrated by the study showing that in Taiwan there is a positive correlation between use of contraception and the number of small appliances in the home?

_____ 23. What statistic is symbolized by s and the Greek letter, σ?

_____ 24. What term is used to describe variables that cannot be used as independent variables in true experiments because they reflect properties of the subjects being studied?

Essay Questions

Suggested answers for the essay questions are included at the back of your study guide.

1. A dentist noticed that cavities were rare in children he examined during the annual health fair at the schools in Aullville. He reported his observation to a researcher at the state university dental school. How will the researcher investigate the dentist's claim? If it is true that the children of Aullville have an unusually small number of cavities, how will the researcher proceed to look for an explanation?

2. Describe both the "third variable problem" and the "directionality problem" and give an example of each.

3. Why do psychologists do correlational research in spite of the restriction on causal inference from correlational data?

4. Research has shown that the performance of females on memory tasks is somewhat superior to the performance of males. If you were going to do an experiment on memory, how could you keep sex differences from biasing your results?

Multiple-Choice Test I

For the multiple-choice items, choose the best of the answers provided. Check your work with the answers at the back of your study guide, and be sure you understand why the keyed answers are correct.

1. The unique strength of the experiment as a method of investigation is that it allows researchers to
   a. replicate results.
   b. make causal inferences.
   c. predict behavior.
   d. test hypotheses.

2. The primary purpose of random assignment is to
   a. avoid systematic bias in assigning subjects to groups.
   b. minimize errors of measurement.
   c. insure that results will be statistically significant.
   d. exclude the possibility of replication.

3. The probability that random assignment will produce equivalent groups increases as _____ increases.
   a. reliability of measurement
   b. validity of measurement
   c. number of subjects
   d. number of groups

4. A farmer wants to compare the effectiveness of a new fertilizer with the fertilizer he is currently using on his tomato plants. The results of the experiment he is planning will be confounded if he
   a. uses the same variety of tomatoes in both groups.
   b. waters the tomatoes too frequently.
   c. plants one group of tomatoes on the south side of the house and the other group on the north side of the house.
   d. does not use a dependent variable that includes both the size and the number of tomatoes produced by his "subjects."

5. A coin was tossed to determine which of the mother rat's two pups would be assigned to the experimental group. This is an example of
   a. covariation.
   b. matched random assignment.
   c. genetic confounding.
   d. the single-blind procedure.

6. The key concepts of experiments include all of the following *except*
   a. manipulation.
   b. random assignment.
   c. control.
   d. replication.

7. If you were to read that bald-headed men have a higher median annual income that men with more hair, you shouldn't shave your head to increase your income because the relationship between these two variables is probably an example of
   a. the directionality problem.
   b. the third variable problem.
   c. selective sampling.
   d. misleading advertising.

8. Correlations that occur because two unrelated variables are both related to a third variable are best described as
   a. spurious.
   b. nonsignificant.
   c. regressive.
   d. fortuitous.

9. A researcher would be likely to do correlational research rather than experimental research if she were interested in studying
   a. effects of abuse during childhood.
   b. reactions to disasters, such as riots or earthquakes.
   c. behavioral differences between religious and nonreligious people.
   d. any of the above.

10. Which of the following would preclude the use of correlation for making a prediction?
    a. The causal relationship is bidirectional.
    b. One of the variables is an organismic variable.
    c. The correlation coefficient is negative.
    d. None of the above preclude the use of a correlation to make a prediction.

11. A researcher is most likely to use a tabular frequency distribution when he
    a. has several hundred raw scores.
    b. is doing correlational research.
    c. expects the distribution of scores to be skewed.
    d. intends to use the median as the measure of central tendency.

12. A normal distribution would be most likely to occur in the frequency polygon for
    a. annual salaries of employees of the Mobil Oil Company.
    b. IQ scores of children classified as retarded.
    c. scores of a college class on a very difficult test.
    d. blood pressure of elementary school children.

13. If boys are significantly more aggressive than girls, one would expect the frequency distribution of the scores of elementary school children on a measure of aggressiveness to be
    a. leptokurtic.   c. skewed.
    b. bimodal.   d. symmetric.

14. One of the reasons why normal distributions are considered to be the most important distributions is because they make it possible to
    a. use either the median or the mean as a measure of central tendency.
    b. calculate powerful inferential statistics.
    c. differentiate between normal and abnormal behavior.
    d. convert raw scores to z-scores.

15. When data are normally distributed, psychologists are most likely to use the _____ as a measure of central tendency. When distributions are severely skewed, the _____ is a more appropriate measure of central tendency.
    a. mean; median   c. median; mean
    b. median; mode   d. mode; median

16. If the median of a distribution of scores is greater than the mean and smaller than the mode, the distribution is
    a. spurious.   c. skewed.
    b. restricted.   d. confounded.

17. Before using the formula in the text to calculate the standard deviation of a distribution of scores, one would need to calculate
    a. the mean.   c. the median.
    c. the mode.   d. all of the above.

18. In a normal distribution of test scores, the z-scores for 68.26% of the test-takers will fall between
    a. −.50 and +.50.
    b. −1.00 and +1.00.
    c. 0 and +1.00.
    d. 0 and +2.00.

19. If your score on a test is below the mean, you should hope that the standard deviation is _____; if your score on a test is above the mean, you should hope that the standard deviation is _____.
    a. large; large
    b. large; small
    c. small; large
    d. small; large

20. If Jim's z-score on the final exam in Introductory Sanskrit is +2.16, his grade on the test will probably be
    a. A.
    b. B.
    c. C.
    d. D or F.

21. One would be most likely to obtain a positive correlation between
    a. temperature and sale of soft drinks.
    b. miles per gallon of gasoline and weight of automobiles.
    c. average daily temperature of cities and their distance from the equator.
    d. malnutrition of children and income level of their parents.

22. Neurons in the brain do not regenerate or replace themselves, but they do deteriorate and disintegrate. The correlation between age and number of brain cells is _____, and the slope of the points on a scatter plot of the data will be _____.
    a. positive; upward
    b. positive; downward
    c. negative; upward
    d. negative; downward

23. A developmental psychologist who studies the entire life span should *not* use the Pearson *r* to assess the relationship between age and reaction time because
    a. it makes no sense to convert ages to z-scores.
    b. the distribution of reaction times is likely to be skewed.
    c. the relationship between the variables is not linear.
    d. age is measured in years, and reaction time is measured in milliseconds.

24. Differences between means of groups in experiments can result from
    a. measurement error.
    b. nonequivalent groups.
    c. effects of the independent variable.
    d. all of the above.

25. When a researcher says that the result of her study was significant at the .05 level, it means
    a. that random assignment produced equivalent groups.
    b. that there was little or measurement error.
    c. that the result was unlikely to have occurred by chance.
    d. all of the above.

Multiple-Choice Test II

For the multiple-choice items, choose the best of the answers provided. Check your work with the answers at the back of your study guide, and be sure you understand why the keyed answers are correct.

1. The two methods that make it possible to claim that manipulation of the independent variable caused differences among subjects on the dependent variable are
   a. experimental control and random assignment.
   b. peer review and replication.
   c. description and inference.
   d. empiricism and quantification.

2. In experiments, random assignment is used to
   a. manipulate the independent variable.
   b. construct frequency polygons.
   c. determine whether results are significant.
   d. assign subjects to groups.

3. When an experimenter repeats the experiment of another researcher in all its essential details, _____ has occurred.
   a. verification
   b. amplification
   c. reproduction
   d. replication

4. Two psychology majors designed and executed an experiment comparing interviewing styles. One of the students ran the subjects in the "friendly interviewer" condition, and the other student ran the subjects in the "detached interviewer" condition. In commenting on their project, the professor is most likely to have observed that
   a. "interviewing styles" is an organismic variable.
   b. there is a confounding variable in the study.
   c. they should have used the Pearson r to analyze their data.
   d. they used too many subjects in their study.

5. An experimenter thinks that the results of the experiment he is designing could be influenced by the mathematical ability, motivation, and cooperativeness of the high school students who will serve as subjects in his experiment. What should he do?
   a. He should use screening tests to select subjects.
   b. He should randomly assign subjects to groups.
   c. He should choose a dependent variable that is not sensitive to individual differences.
   d. He should use only subjects who volunteer to participate in his experiment.

6. Which of the following results justifies causal inference?
   a. Children had fewer cavities in the city that adds fluorine to the drinking water.
   b. Smokers do not live as long as nonsmokers.
   c. Students who attend private schools make higher SAT scores than students who attend public schools.
   d. None of the above justifies causal inference.

7. Assume that the following pairs of variables are correlated. Which is most likely to be an example of the third variable problem?
   a. number of phone booths and number of rapes reported in American cities
   b. malnutrition in childhood and IQ scores in adolescence
   c. annual income and number of years of formal education
   d. the price liquor stores charge for Old Gutruster and the numbers of liters of Old Gutruster they sell.

8. People who favor the "nature" view emphasize the influence of IQ scores on academic achievement; those who favor the "nurture" view emphasize the influence of academic achievement on IQ scores. This disagreement is an example of the _____ problem that occurs in interpreting correlations.
   a. variability
   b. statistical
   c. reciprocity
   d. directionality

9. Which of the following is the *least* compelling argument for doing correlational studies?
   a. Correlational studies are naturalistic.
   b. Correlational studies can be used for preliminary investigations.
   c. Correlations can be used to make predictions.
   d. Correlational studies can be used when it is difficult or impossible to randomly assign subjects to groups.

10. Organismic variables include such things as
    a. sexual orientation.
    b. socioeconomic class.
    c. race.
    d. all of the above.

11. Scientists believe that knowledge is obtained through observation. This belief is called
    a. epistemology.
    b. empiricism.
    c. teleology.
    d. rationalism.

12. In correlational research, the raw data are
    a. pairs of scores.
    b. numbers between −1.00 and +1.00.
    c. scores on the dependent variable.
    d. z-scores.

13. In a frequency distribution of heights of adult males in the United States, professional basketball players could be described as
    a. modal cases.
    b. anchors.
    c. skewers.
    d. outliers.

14. One would be most likely to use a grouped frequency distribution to represent
    a. the IQ scores of pupils in Ms. Clair's first-grade class.
    b. the scores a subject makes on subtests of the MMPI.
    c. the SAT scores of high school seniors in the Los Angeles School District.
    d. the behavior of a schizophrenic during an acute episode.

15. By mistake, Professor Riley gave the students in his introductory psychology class the test he had prepared for his statistics class. The distribution of scores on the test is most likely to be
    a. leptokurtic.
    b. skewed.
    c. bimodal.
    d. symmetric.

16. If the lowest score in a distribution of scores were changed from 102 to 53, it would change the value of
    a. the mean.
    b. the median.
    c. the mode.
    d. all of the above.

17. If the scores on a standardized test are normally distributed, the _____ will be equal.
    a. mean and median
    b. mean and mode
    c. mode and median
    d. mean, median, and mode

18. If scores on an intelligence test are normally distributed with a mean of 100 and a standard deviation of 15, 2.5% of the scores will be above
    a. 110.
    b. 120.
    c. 130.
    d. 140.

19. The mean for each of the midterms in Early Morning Bird Calls was 62. Harold got 50 on all four midterms. He is is most likely to have gotten an "F" rather than a "D" on the midterm that had a standard deviation of
    a. 5.
    b. 7.
    c. 10.
    d. 12.

20. Margo's z-scores on all the tests she took in Basket Weaving were 0. She probably got a(n) _____ in the course.
    a. A
    b. B
    c. C
    d. D or F

21. One would be most likely to obtain a negative correlation between
    a. gasoline consumption and the weights of automobiles.
    b. age and salary of public school teachers.
    c. the enrollment of universities and the number of courses offered.
    d. average daily temperature of cities and their distance from the equator.

22. If a scatter plot looks like a star map of the MIlky Way, the correlation between the variables was most likely to be
    a. 0.
    b. −.25.
    c. −.50.
    d. −.75.

23. If the correlation between the number of lectures students attended during the term and their final grades was +.67, one would expect that the correlation between the number of lectures *not* attended during the term and final grades would be
    a. 0.
    b. −.67.
    c. within one standard deviation of +.67.
    d. within two standard deviations of +.67.

24. Pearson *r cannot* produce a correlation coefficient of
    a. 0.
    b. −.21.
    c. 3.16.
    d. any of the above.

25. Researchers use inferential statistics to determine
    a. whether the results of an experiment can be generalized.
    b. whether the results of an experiment can be replicated.
    c. whether the results of an experiment are likely to result from factors like measurement error or nonequivalent groups.
    d. all of the above.

Chapter 1: WELCOME TO PSYCHOLOGY

Answers for Working with Names and Terms

1. random assignment
2. cognitive
3. double-blind
4. behavioral
5. catharsis
6. Hall
7. Neisser
8. conditioned reflex
9. confounded
10. neuroscience
11. case study
12. Maslow
13. multimethod approach
14. operational definition
15. humanistic
16. independent
17. statistical analysis
18. law of effect
19. introspection
20. psychodynamic
21. correlational
22. dependent
23. James
24. Sperry

Answers for Essay Questions

1. Freud's psychodynamic theory portrays humans as self-centered and irrational. The instinctual drives Freud saw as the motivators of human behavior emphasize sexual gratification and aggression. Satisfaction of these drives often results in behavior that is selfish and sinful. Because the drives are unconscious, people frequently do not understand their motives and behave in irrational ways as they attempt to satisfy or control these drives.

    Behaviorists like Watson thought that human behavior is determined by the conditioning and learning is produced by forces outside the self and that people are neither inherently good or bad nor inherently rational or irrational. We are what our conditioning produces.

    Humanists like Rogers and Maslow objected to the idea that human behavior is determined either by instinctual drives or by environmental forces. They believed that humans are free to make choices and that we are capable of taking responsibility for the choices we make. They also believed that humans are inherently good and rational, and that we have an innate motive for self-actualization.

2. Naturalistic observation has the advantage of external validity because organisms behave as if they were not being observed. It also has the advantage of suggesting hypotheses to be tested using other research methods. A disadvantage of naturalistic observation it that the observer may have to wait a long time to see the behavior in which he or she is interested.

    The survey method has the advantage of allowing investigators to collect large quantities of data for relatively small effort. However, the value of the data is questionable for several reasons. Respondents may have faulty memories or may misrepresent themselves in their answers. The multiple-choice format does not allow people to qualify their answers, and self-selection of the sample occurs if people can choose whether or not to participate in the survey.

    The case history method has the advantage of providing in-depth understanding of individuals, but it has the disadvantage of lacking generalizability. Also, case histories may reflect the biases of the interviewer.

The correlational method enables researchers to assess relationships between variables, and thus can furnish valuable preliminary data on a question or hypothesis. The primary disadvantage of the correlational method is that it does not provide data upon which causal inferences can be made.

The experimental method has the advantage of providing controls that enable investigators to identify causal relationships. One of the disadvantages of experimentation is that the artificiality of the experimental situation diminishes the external validity of studies. Unexpected effects of the independent variable can also be a problem in experimentation.

3. The independent variable in the study is "caffeine versus no caffeine." "Caffeine" could be operationally defined as 500 milligrams of coffee made by adding 45 grams of Taster's Choice freeze-dried coffee to one liter of water. "No caffeine" could be operationally defined as the same quantity of decaffeinated coffee made with the same recipe.

    The dependent variable is "performance on a problem-solving task." The dependent variable could be operationally defined by scores (number correct) on an anagram test, a math test, or a series-completion test.

4. The Liebert and Baron experiment tested the hypothesis that observation of violence on TV will increase aggressive behavior in children. The goal of *description* is fulfilled by the experiment--by describing how the independent variable was manipulated and the effect the manipulation had on the dependent variable. *Explanation* in the study is the attribution of the higher incidence of aggressive behavior in the experimental group to the children's watching violence on TV. *Prediction* involves generalization from the experimental situation to the real-life consequences of children's watching violence on TV. *Application* might be informing parents of the effects of TV violence or social pressure on TV producers and programmers to reduce the incidence of violence in TV shows, especially shows that are viewed by children.

Answers for Multiple-Choice Test I

1. c	6. c	11. d	16. a	21. d
2. a	7. c	12. d	17. b	22. d
3. d	8. a	13. a	18. d	23. a
4. c	9. b	14. b	19. d	24. c
5. d	10. c	15. d	20. b	25. d

Answers for Multiple-Choice Test II

1. d	6. a	11. c	16. a	21. b
2. d	7. d	12. d	17. d	22. a
3. a	8. b	13. b	18. a	23. b
4. d	9. b	14. d	19. a	24. a
5. c	10. a	15. b	20. d	25. b

Chapter 2: BRAIN AND BEHAVIOR

Answers for Working with Names and Terms

1. somatic
2. endocrine
3. all-or-none response
4. sodium ions
5. endorphins
6. convolutions
7. corpus callosum
8. Gall
9. brain graft
10. thalamus
11. synapse
12. Penfield
13. dendrite
14. Fechner
15. spinal reflex
16. visual agnosia
17. soma
18. amygdala
19. hormones
20. hippocampus
21. aphasia
22. limbic system
23. Berger
24. somatosensory cortex

Answers for Essay Questions

1. Pressure-sensitive sensory receptors and heat-sensitive receptors are activated as the warm chunk of meatball lands in my lap. Neural impulses travel on sensory neurons to the spinal cord and up through the central core of the brain to the thalamus. The thalamus directs the excitatory potential to the somatosensory cortex. Association areas of the cortex interpret the message as "warm thing in lap" and communicate with the motor cortex. The motor cortex sends impulses to the cerebellum which coordinates neural signals in motor neurons that enable me to use my arm and hand to pick up the meatball.

2. Neurotransmitters are chemical substances that communicate neural information across the gaps or synapses between the axon terminals of one neuron and the receptor sites on the dendrites of another neuron. Neurotransmitters are stored in synaptic vesicles, and are released when an action potential moves down the axon. Neurotransmitters can either excite an impulse in another neuron or inhibit the neuron from firing.
    One type of neurotransmitter, endorphins, inhibits pain signals. Neuroscientists believe that neurotransmitters are involved in regulation of processes like blood pressure, body temperature, and hunger. It appears that they are involved in complex processes like learning and memory, in emotions like fear and anxiety, and in addiction to psychoactive drugs. There is also evidence that dopamine plays a role in schizophrenia and that norepinephrine plays a role in affective disorders.

3. A number of areas of psychology interest me, but I think neuroscience is the most exciting at the present time because of important problems waiting for solutions, new tools to be used in research, and new technologies to be explored.
    Neurotransmitter functions are an example of a problems looking for solutions. Science is just beginning to understand that they may have profound effects on behavior, but how they do this is currently not well understood.
    Brain-scan equipment is an example of a new tool. The potential of this equipment for localizing functions in the brain is an exciting challenge. Brain grafting is an example of a new technology that has been successfully used to treat Parkinson's

disease and could be used to treat other disease that cause damage or deterioration in areas of the brain.

4. The methods that have been used to identify functions of specific areas of the brain are recording of electrical activity, imaging techniques, electrical stimulation, and effects of injuries, tumors, and diseases.

   Recording of electrical activity by an electroencephalograph can be used by researchers to determine what part or parts of the brain show increased activity when subjects are engaged in specific tasks.

   Imaging techniques can also display the level of activity in various parts of the brain by monitoring glucose consumptions. These techniques make it possible to detect the presence of pathology deep in the brain, and this pathology can be related to behavior changes seen in the patient.

   Penfield used electrical stimulation of the brain during surgery and was able to observe responses that occurred when various areas were stimulated, Olds and Milner used electrical stimulation to study "pleasure centers" in the hypothalamus.

   Localization of functions in the brain can be studied in animals by observing the behavioral changes that occur as a result of removal of brain tissue, In humans, injury or disease in a particular part of the brain may affect particular behaviors. for example, Phineas Gage showed changes in personality after injury to his frontal lobes.

5. As the neural impulse reaches the axon terminals, synaptic vesicles rupture and neurotransmitter molecules cross the synapse to receptor sites on the dendrites of surrounding neurons. If the neurotransmitter has an excitatory effect, the receiving neuron is depolarized as sodium ions pass through the semipermeable cell membrane and upset the delicate balance between the electrical charges inside and outside the membrane. The action potential set up by the depolarization moves from the dendrites through the soma and to the axon of the neuron. It travels down the axon to the axon terminals, rupturing the synaptic vesicles of the neuron, and the process is repeated as the impulse is passed to the next neuron or neurons.

Answers for Multiple-Choice Test I

1. d	6. c	11. b	16. a	21. d
2. c	7. d	12. c	17. a	22. a
3. c	8. a	13. a	18. b	23. a
4. d	9. c	14. d	19. b	24. b
5. c	10. c	15. d	20. d	25. d

Answers for Multiple-Choice Test II

1. a	6. c	11. a	16. a	21. a
2. b	7. d	12. a	17. d	22. c
3. d	8. d	13. d	18. c	23. c
4. c	9. b	14. b	19. a	24. c
5. a	10. d	15. a	20. d	25. c

Chapter 3: *SENSATION AND PERCEPTION*

Answers for Working with Names and Terms

1. signal detection
2. binocular disparity
3. papillae
4. transduction
5. closure
6. rods
7. attention
8. Weber
9. oval window
10. olfactory mucosa
11. aerial haze
12. ossicles
13. Wald
14. cornea
15. shape constancy
16. dichromat
17. Helmholtz
18. fovea
19. Hering
20. kinesthesis
21. Wundt
22. amplitude
23. cones
24. complementary

Answers for Essay Questions

1. One reason people might disagree in their reports of the incident is that they may have been attending to different aspects of the situation, or some people may have started watching the combatants and listening to them sooner than others and thus had better understanding of the problem.

    Differences in reports could also result from differences in perceptual set, which is the tendency of people to see what they expect to see. Perceptual set might, for example, affect people's reports on who struck the first blow. The perceptual context might affect people's reports because they could have different expectations concerning what might happen in a dingy bar compared to an elegant restaurant.

    The perceptual sets people have are determined by such things as their motives and their life experiences. For example, if a person favored one of the combatants, this might be reflected in the person's perception and interpretation of the argument and fight. Past experience might result in a person's being influenced by other fights he or she has seen or by attributions made on the basis of the race, clothing, or haircut of the combatants.

2. The artist will use some of the same cues we use in monocular vision. One of these is relative size--the farther away an object is, the smaller the retinal image of the object will be. In her painting, the artist can use this cue by making the cows in the foreground of the picture larger than those that are to appear farther away.

    The artist will use interposition. Objects in the picture will be partially covered by objects on the same line of sight that are to appear closer to the viewer.

    If there is a road, a stream, or fences in the picture, the artist will use linear perspective. Although the sides of the road and the stream and the fences on opposite sides of a field are actually parallel, the artist will portray them as converging as they move from the foreground to the background of the picture.

    The artist can also use aerial haze to achieve the illusion of depth. Objects that are to be seen as nearer will be more clearly delineated than objects that are to appear to be more distant, and more detail will be observable on objects that are to appear nearer to the viewer.

3. I do not think we would be better off if our senses were more sensitive than they are. Thinking about increased sensitivity of the various senses is, in fact, frightening. If we could see better than we can, we might see germs crawling around on the lips of the person we thought we wanted to kiss. Hearing each other's stomachs and intestines digesting food wouldn't be very romantic either. And maybe our ability to smell each other would make things even worse.

   If our sense of taste were more sensitive, we might find that our favorite foods have all kinds of subtle flavors we hadn't noticed before and don't particularly like. We might find that nothing is very appetizing, particularly because we can see little things crawling around on our food too. And we might feel those little things crawling around on our bodies if our pressure sensitivity were increased.

4. The hamburger is in a bun which I sense as round, light brown on the outside and white on the inside. The meat is also round, but not as big as the bun and dark brown with black stripes on it. The odor of the hamburger is difficult to describe--it has a meaty smell and also a charcoal smell. When I take a bite, I can taste salt. There are other taste sensations that are probably a mixture of the four basic tastes (sweet, sour, bitter, and salty). I can feel the bite of hamburger in my mouth. The meat is warmer than the bun and heavier, but when I get it chewed it is mixed together and is just a warm lump in my mouth until I swallow it.

   The orange soda is in a paper cup, so I can only see the top of it. It looks like a round orange circle with cubes of transparent stuff in it. Actually, I only think I see a round stimulus, because both the surface of the soda and the hamburger make elliptical images on my retina. The soda has a pleasant fruity odor and when I smell it, little bubbles cause a tickling sensation on my nose. I can taste both sweet and sour when I take a drink, and the soda in my mouth feels cold. The carbonation of the soda evidently causes variations in pressure that I find pleasant. I can feel the weight of the soda as it moves around in my mouth.

Answers for Multiple-Choice Test I

1. c	6. d	11. d	16. c	21. d
2. d	7. b	12. a	17. d	22. b
3. a	8. a	13. b	18. a	23. c
4. a	9. c	14. b	19. b	24. b
5. c	10. c	15. a	20. c	25. d

Answers for Multiple-Choice Test II

1. a	6. d	11. b	16. d	21. c
2. a	7. c	12. d	17. c	22. d
3. d	8. a	13. c	18. a	23. a
4. c	9. c	14. b	19. a	24. a
5. b	10. b	15. d	20. b	25. c

Chapter 4: *MOTIVATION AND EMOTION*

Answers for Working with Names and Terms

1. Darwin
2. Murray
3. testosterone
4. fitness
5. incentive
6. Plutchik
7. extrinsic
8. Kinsey
9. homeostasis
10. Schachter
11. James
12. set point
13. Johnson
14. ventromedial
15. opponent-process
16. Hull
17. Wilson
18. Maslow
19. sexually dimorphic
20. fixed-action pattern
21. refractory phase
22. autonomic
23. sociobiological
24. anterior

Answers for Essay Questions

1. Sexual behavior is physiologically motivated in all animals, but there are many other stimuli that motivate sexual behavior in humans. These stimuli include such things as sights, sounds, odors, and fantasies created by the mind.
    Reproduction is the sole purpose of sexual behavior in animals other than human. In humans, sexual behavior provides pleasure and a means of expressing emotions, like love and intimacy, or in some cases, emotions like hatred and aggression.
    Physiological arousal may be less directed in humans than it is in other animals. For example, arousal from other stimulation may be interpreted as sexual arousal, or sexual arousal may be interpreted as love.

2. Do you criticize people who are overweight or obese because you perceive them as lacking in will power? Actually, many of these people have made heroic efforts to lose weight and have succeeded, then discovered that the only way to keep from regaining the lost weight is to tolerate perpetual hunger.
    Science has several theories that might help us understand the problem of obesity. One theory is that the hypothalamus plays a role in hunger and satiation. A problem in the lateral hypothalamus could result in a person's being more likely than others to experience hunger when the body does not need food; a problem in the ventromedial hypothalamus could result in delay or attenuation of signals to stop eating. Failure of a "stop eating" signal could also occur if the body produces an insufficient supply of a hormone called cholecystokinin (CCK}.
    Adoption studies in Denmark supported the idea that obesity is hereditary. The mechanism through which genetics could operate include number of fat cells, set point, or metabolic rate. Some scientists believe that humans are born with a fixed number of fat cells, and that when we lose weight these cells shrink, but continue to cause hunger until they are "filled."
    Set-point theory claims that people have a genetically determined weight, and that hunger and metabolic efficiency are determined by a person's weight relative to the person's set point.
    People differ in the rate at which they metabolize nutrients. People with a high metabolic rate can eat as much as they want without gaining weight, whereas people

with a low metabolic rate need far less food to maintain a constant body weight. It may be that no one has enough will power to stay thin if the person's genes are stacked against him or her.

3. The text classifies work motives as rational-economic motives, social motives, and self-actualization motives.

   Rational economic motives are satisfied by extrinsic rewards like pay, pension and medical benefits, and opportunities for advancement. A good job satisfies the physiological and safety needs of Maslow's hierarchy.

   Social motives refer to relationships with co-workers and supervisors. In a good workplace, there is a spirit of geniality and cooperation, and individuals feel that they are valued members of the group. A good job helps fulfill Maslow's needs for acceptance, affiliation, approval, and recognition.

   Self-actualization motives refer to the ability of the job to provide a context in which an employee can develop his or her potential. A good job would include a variety of tasks and responsibilities that enable the employee to explore and express his or her abilities. This type of need is related to Maslow's need for achievement and to the higher levels of the hierarchy.

4. The facial feedback hypothesis suggests that if we smile, even "when we're feeling blue," our subjective state will move toward happiness.

   Darwin considered facial expressions to be a means of communicating with others, and a smile communicates friendship and pleasure at seeing the recipient of the smile. The smile usually stimulates a response: the recipient smiles back and gives a friendly greeting. We are thus reinforced for smiling and feel a little better about ourselves. After a smile is returned a few times, the forced smile may become a real smile.

   It is difficult or impossible to experience a positive and a negative emotion simultaneously; so, if we are smiling, it is difficult to be sad, angry, or fearful. A smile helps to dissipate negative emotions.

Answers for Multiple-Choice Test I

1. d	6. a	11. c	16. c	21. a
2. a	7. a	12. c	17. d	22. c
3. b	8. b	13. a	18. a	23. b
4. b	9. d	14. b	19. d	24. a
5. c	10. d	15. b	20. d	25. c

Answers for Multiple-Choice Test II

1. c	6. c	11. d	16. b	21. c
2. d	7. c	12. b	17. d	22. b
3. a	8. b	13. a	18. a	23. c
4. a	9. a	14. c	19. a	24. b
5. b	10. c	15. a	20. d	25. d

Chapter 5: *STATES OF CONSCIOUSNESS*

Answers for Working with Names and Terms

1. hallucinogens
2. Mesmer
3. mindfulness
4. narcolepsy
5. analgesics
6. activation-synthesis
7. sleep apnea
8. circadian rhythm
9. anesthesia
10. psychoactive
11. introspection
12. dissociated
13. James
14. latent content
15. state
16. confabulation
17. amnesia
18. Benson
19. sleep spindles
20. dichotic listening
21. depersonalization
22. Hofman
23. delta
24. hypermnesia

Answers for Essay Questions

1. Consciousness includes the external stimuli and internal mental events we are aware of at any given time. It is what is momentarily the object of our attention. The memory storage of consciousness has a capacity just large enough to allow us to experience continuity of consciousness. William James referred to this aspect of mental life as the "stream of consciousness."

   Preconscious processes include all the knowledge and skills we have accumulated that are not currently the focus of attention. They also include automatic behaviors like walking or driving a car. We need a lot of memory capacity for preconscious processes because of the vast amount of information and number of action patterns we have available.

   Unconscious processes include the regulation of bodily processes. They also include "mental work" that proceeds below the level of conscious awareness. Sometimes, after working on a problem and being unable to solve it, the solution just happens. This is thought to be a result of unconscious processing.

   Freud thought that the unconscious stores thoughts, memories, and impulses related to sex and aggression. He thought people repressed self-knowledge and motives that are primitive and socially unacceptable. He also thought the unconscious represents a large proportion of our memory.

2. Freud thought dreams are wish fulfillments--that during sleep, material from the unconscious is transformed and expressed in dreams. He thought psychoanalysis could get a glimpse into a person's unconscious by interpreting the latent content of a person's dreams.

   The activation-synthesis hypothesis is a neuropsychological theory which claims that the pons activates the cortex in a random manner during sleep and that dreams are the efforts of the cortex to add meaning to this random neural activity.

   Neither of these theories can be scientifically tested, so support for either of them comes from the study of one's own dreams and others' reports of their dreams. Considering how we forget dreams, this is a very questionable source of data. Freud's theory seems a bit far-fetched to me, but I prefer it to the activation-synthesis hypothesis because I think dreams are too coherent to be the product of random activation. Also, I have noted in my own dreams that there are certain themes that occur over and over, and I think Freud's theory explains these recurring themes better than the theory of Hobson and McCarley.

3. Preferences for drugs could be determined by personality. For example, people who feel lethargic much of the time and who don't have much energy could prefer stimulants that make them feel more energetic. On the other hand, people who have high arousal levels and feel stressed much of the time might prefer sedatives that "calm them down." Both stimulants and sedatives probably increase the self-image of users during the periods when the drugs are having an effect.

    It may be that people who use psychedelics are curious and adventuresome and want to explore changes in mental processes that psychedelic drugs can produce.

    At the physiological level, drug preferences could be related to neurotransmitter functions or processes in the brain. For example, drugs used to treat depression alter people's mood by altering neurotransmitter activity.

4. It seems reasonable to use hypnosis for memory enhancement in criminal investigations when hypnosis might help to identify a suspect or assist in solving a crime. Hypnosis is justifiable as an investigative tool. The example of the man's remembering the license number under hypnosis when the children were kidnapped is an example of a situation in which hypnosis was useful and justifiable.

    Miscarriage of justice would be likely to occur if testimony gotten under hypnosis were permitted in courts. There could, for example, be subtle hypnotic suggestions made by an interrogator that could lead a witness to believe and testify to an event that did not occur. Also, when people recall an event under hypnosis, they are likely to confabulate--adding material to what they witnessed to make their report of the incident coherent.

Answers for Multiple-Choice Test I

1. b	6. d	11. b	16. b	21. b
2. a	7. c	12. c	17. b	22. b
3. c	8. a	13. d	18. c	23. a
4. d	9. d	14. d	19. a	24. a
5. c	10. a	15. a	20. d	25. c

Answers for Multiple-Choice Test II

1. d	6. a	11. d	16. c	21. c
2. c	7. b	12. a	17. d	22. b
3. a	8. d	13. c	18. d	23. d
4. c	9. d	14. b	19. b	24. d
5. b	10. b	15. a	20. a	25. a

Chapter 6: CONDITIONING AND LEARNING

Answers for Working with Names and Terms

1. reflexive
2. conditioned reinforcers
3. Garcia
4. variable ratio
5. generalization
6. discriminative stimulus
7. instinctual drift
8. insight
9. shaping
10. Tolman
11. instrumental cond.
12. extinction
13. Bernstein
14. chaining
15. associative
16. Hollis
17. fixed interval
18. observational
19. operant conditioning
20. preparedness
21. negative punishment
22. Mowrer
23. learned helplessness
24. negative reinforcement

Answers for Essay Questions

1. When Little Allison was bitten by the dog, the pain and distress of being bitten was the unconditioned stimulus (US). The unconditioned response (UR) was fear. Because the sight of the dog was paired with pain and distress, it became a conditioned stimulus (CS) for fear, and the fear is the conditioned response (CR).

    Although the conditioned stimulus is the particular collie dog that belongs to the neighbors, stimulus generalization could occur and little Allison will respond with fear to all large dog, or all dogs, or even other animals that resemble the neighbors' collie in some way.

2. Within moments of the time Margo first encounters her new roommate, she notices many things about her--whether she is thin or overweight, the color and style of her hair, her facial expression, the color of her skin, aspects of her voice, the way she walks and stands and moves her arms, whether she makes eye contact with Margo, and the clothing she is wearing. People tend to have classically conditioned emotional responses to all these things that can be positive or negative and conscious or unconscious. These emotional responses are learned by associating attributes of people with pleasant or unpleasant experiences. For example, Margo and her mother are very close, so if the new roommate has a voice that resembles the voice of Margo's mother, Margo will have a positive emotional response toward the roommate. But the way the new roommate walks may be associated in Margo's mind with being conceited, and this aspect of the roommate will elicit a negative emotional response. Margo's overall impression of the roommate will be determined by the total of the positive and negative emotions elicited by the roommate.

3. Punishment can have a number of adverse reaction, so in raising your child, it is best to use it sparingly and wisely.

    One of the problems with punishment is that it can lead to withdrawal and inhibition of the child. Punishment also triggers strong negative emotions, like anger or fear in a child, and these emotions can become classically conditioned to the person who administers the punishment or to the environment in which the punishment was given.

When adults use punishment, they are setting an example of the use of aggression to manipulate the child's behavior. The child who sees that adults get their own way through the use of punishment may follow the example set by the adults.

Punishment should only be used in situation in which a behavior puts the child at risk, like running into the street or eating the leaves of a plant. If punishment is to be effective, it must be immediate and intense enough to be memorable. It should also be administered on a continuous schedule--the child is invariably punished for the undesirable behavior. It is important that the child be made aware of an alternative behavior that is acceptable. For example, the child should know that he is to tell Mommy if his ball goes in the street and that people only eat leaves that Mommy gets from the refrigerator and puts on a plate.

4. Some parents misuse reinforcement in dealing with their children because they are inconsistent or because reinforcement and punishment are not contingent on the child's behavior. However, parents who are careful to be consistent and to use reinforcement wisely can also misuse it inadvertently.

One way in which parents can misuse reinforcement is to overuse it for some behaviors. For example, it is desirable for a child to eat well and to keep his or her room neat and tidy, but it is also possible for parents to praise these behaviors to the point where the child is in danger of becoming compulsive.

Well-meaning parents are probably most likely to misuse reinforcement when they are unaware of what they are reinforcing. For example, when a parent reinforces a child for brushing his teeth, the parent may be reinforcing eating tooth paste, or when the parent reinforces the child for drinking her milk, the child may be simultaneously wetting her pants. At any time, children can be doing more than one thing and thinking about something else, so parents are likely to reinforce behaviors or thoughts they did not intend to reinforce, even if they are careful.

Answers for Multiple-Choice Test I

1. d	6. c	11. b	16. c	21. b
2. b	7. c	12. b	17. d	22. c
3. c	8. d	13. c	18. a	23. d
4. b	9. d	14. a	19. d	24. a
5. d	10. a	15. b	20. d	25. c

Answers for Multiple-Choice Test II

1. b	6. a	11. a	16. d	21. a
2. a	7. c	12. c	17. b	22. b
3. a	8. b	13. b	18. a	23. d
4. c	9. b	14. b	19. d	24. d
5. c	10. d	15. a	20. c	25. c

Chapter 7: *HUMAN MEMORY*

Answers for Working with Names and Terms

1. Ebbinghaus
2. Bahrick
3. method of loci
4. Bartlett
5. Loftus
6. chunking
7. schema
8. short-term
9. acetylcholine
10. encoding failure
11. Miller
12. elaborative
13. flashbulb memory
14. engram
15. Lashley
16. Paivio
17. Sperling
18. maintenance
19. episodic
20. anterograde amnesia
21. procedural
22. retrieval failure
23. proactive interference
24. vasopressin

Answers For Essay Questions

1. The student uses visual sensory memory to input the material from the printed page. Her eyes move in a series of fixations as she reads the text. Sensory memory records her fixations briefly, but does not interpret the visual stimuli.
    The letter shapes and spaces become meaningful when they are transferred to short-term memory. Short-term memory processes the information. Elaborative rehearsal occurs if the student thinks about meaning and relates the information to her existing schemata. The student can scan the words, but if she does not attend to what she reads, there will be nothing in long-term memory when test time comes.
    The extent to which the information in the text is processed and organized during reading will determine how well the student retains what she reads. For maximum retention, the new information must be stored in long-term memory with retrieval cues that will assist the reader in recalling the information.

2. Procedural memory stores programs for performing a variety of motor tasks including walking, swimming, driving a car, shaving, writing, and eating. We are largely unaware of the content of procedural memory because the programs it contains are so well learned that we run them automatically.
    Semantic memory contains all the information we have about the world. Our vocabulary, our knowledge of history, geography, and math are all stored in semantic memory. It resembles a combination dictionary and encyclopedia in some respect, but it also includes information like the names of friends and telephone numbers.
    Episodic memory is autobiographical--it is like a diary in that it stores the sequence of events that occur in our lives.

3. The encoding failure hypothesis claims that Kester cannot remember the name of the teacher because he never stored the name in his long-term memory. Children do not use teacher's first names, so Kester may have heard the name only a few times, and when he did, he did not attend to it and rehearse it for long-term storage.
    Interference theory claims that other memories he stored before or after learning the name of his third-grade teacher have blocked access to the teacher's name. The interference is most like to be retroactive because he has heard and learned many

first names since he was in the third grade.

Decay theory attributes Kester's forgetting the name to the passage of time. He has not thought about the teacher for a long time, and her first name has just faded from his memory.

Retrieval failure suggests that the name is still stored in Kester's long-term memory, but that he cannot find a cue that would enable him to locate it. He can visualize the classroom and see the teacher at her desk, but the name does not come to memory, perhaps because he never heard the teacher's first name in this context.

4. Retrieval failure suggests that memories cannot be recalled because retrieval cues for the memories are not available. For older people, many of the retrieval cues that might have brought back memories are gone; places they went when they were younger are no longer there, and people who might cue memories have died or moved away. Also, for older people, cues lose their distinctiveness because many memories may be attached to the same cue.

Interference occurs when a particular memory is blocked by a similar memory that was stored before (proactive interference) or after (retroactive interference) the target memory. Young people probably experience more retroactive interference, but because they have stored so many memories, older people are likely to have more of a problem with proactive interference. The new information that was acquired last week or last month is similar to information acquired over the years, and these older memories tend to block retrieval of newer memories.

5. You are probably thinking about something else as you read, so a lot of the information from your texts is not being processed in your short-term memory for storage in your long-term memory. You need to do something that will keep your attention focussed on your text and help you organize what you read so the information will be stored in such a way that you can retrieve it at test time. You might try outlining what you read or writing answers to the learning objectives if your text includes them.

Answers for Multiple-Choice Test I

1. d	6. a	11. d	16. c	21. b
2. c	7. d	12. b	17. a	22. b
3. b	8. d	13. b	18. d	23. c
4. a	9. c	14. a	19. b	24. d
5. b	10. d	15. b	20. c	25. a

Answers for Multiple-Choice Test II

1. b	6. c	11. c	16. d	21. d
2. a	7. b	12. d	17. a	22. d
3. a	8. a	13. c	18. c	23. a
4. c	9. a	14. c	19. c	24. a
5. d	10. b	15. a	20. a	25. b

Chapter 8: *THINKING AND LANGUAGE*

Answers for Working with Names and Terms

1. Whorf
2. mean length utterance
3. functional fixedness
4. morpheme
5. anchoring
6. Chomsky
7. displacement
8. availability
9. Rosch
10. Collins
11. algorithm
12. framing
13. confirmation bias
14. Tversky
15. semantics
16. deductive
17. subgoal analysis
18. connotative
19. utility
20. heuristics
21. generativity
22. inductive
23. von Frisch
24. Simon

Answers for Essay Questions

1. Functional fixedness is lack of the ability to think of unusual uses for common objects. Lack of ability to think of anything to do with a wire coat hanger except for hanging clothes is an example of functional fixedness. A more flexible and creative person could think of other uses for a coat hanger, such as a stick for roasting wieners or as a tool for recovering an object that has gotten under the refrigerator or freezer.

   Mental set is the tendency to use the same familiar method for problem solving, even though there is a more efficient method of arriving at a solution. The text uses a set of Luchins' water jar problems to illustrate mental set. The formula that is used to solve the first six problems can also be used to solve the last two, but mental set often prevents people from seeing that there is an easier method for solving for the last two problems. People who use computers frequently have mental sets. They continue to perform operations in the accustomed way even though there are faster and more efficient way to perform the operations.

2. The representativeness heuristic involves making generalizations from stereotypes in decision making. A presidential candidate will want to identify himself with stereotypes that have positive emotional connotations, like "he was raised on a small farm," "he served in the military," or "he goes to church." The candidate attempts to identify his opponent with stereotypes that have negative connotation, like "he smoked pot when he was in college," "he belongs to the American Civil Liberties Union" or "he is soft on criminals."

   The availability heuristic is the tendency of people to be influenced by information that has been frequently repeated, has been acquired recently, or is salient for some other reason. If the presidential candidate has some damaging information about the opponent, it is to his advantage to release it only a few days before the election so it will be "fresh" in voter's memories and the opponent will not be able to defend himself. Also, the candidate should repeat information that is favorable to him frequently and should look for opportunities to do things that are noteworthy or dramatic and that will make a strong impression. He might, for example, have himself photographed distributing food in a disaster area.

3. Use of an algorithm would involve trying all the permutations of the six letters until one of the arrangements forms a word. There are 720 permutation of the six letters, so it could take a long time to find a word.

    To use a heuristic, one would use knowledge about English spelling to eliminate rare or impossible letter combinations and try common letter combinations. For example, English words do not begin with RP or RS and PS is rare. Words are more likely to begin with a consonant or consonant pair, like SP or PR. After the initial consonant or consonant pair, there will be a vowel, so one would try combinations like PRA, PRI, SPI, SPA, or SPE. From PRA, one is likely to discover that PRAISE is a solution. From SPI one might discover that SPIREA is a solution. (Spirea is a flowering shrub that is familiar in some parts of the country.

4. Children will learn the names of particular animals first, like dog and cat. Then, if the child has picture books, farm animals and zoo animals will be introduced, and the child will get the idea that a creature can be both a dog and an animal or a giraffe and an animal. The child is likely to acquire a set of attributes for animals that includes things like has four legs, has a tail, and has babies. There is probably a delay before the child includes birds, fish, insects, and reptiles in his or her animal schema, and another delay before humans are added.

5. One advantage that oral language has given humans is displacement. We can speak of things that happened in the past or may happen in the future, and of things that happened in other places and to other people. One of the advantages of this is that it enables us to pass information from generation to generation and to talk about the experiences of people who have visited other places.

    Another advantage language gives humans is its use as a set of symbols for thought and memory storage.

    Language provides social advantages. Because people can communicate, they can establish societies with rules and responsibilities. Language can also be used by the group to plan a strategy for a hunting expedition and to instruct the young.

Answers for Multiple-Choice Test I

1. d	6. c	11. b	16. c	21. b
2. c	7. b	12. a	17. a	22. c
3. a	8. a	13. c	18. d	23. a
4. c	9. d	14. d	19. d	24. b
5. b	10. d	15. b	20. a	25. a

Answers for Multiple-Choice Test II

1. c	6. c	11. b	16. c	21. d
2. c	7. d	12. a	17. c	22. d
3. b	8. a	13. d	18. b	23. b
4. a	9. d	14. d	19. a	24. a
5. d	10. c	15. a	20. a	25. d

Chapter 9: INFANCY AND CHILDHOOD

Answers for Working with Names and Terms

1. sensorimotor
2. sociobiology
3. reversibility
4. Gesell
5. gender constancy
6. Harlow
7. dominant
8. nature
9. longitudinal
10. gender schema
11. Freud
12. fetus
13. visual cliff
14. critical period
15. Kohlberg
16. preoperational
17. object permanence
18. cross-sectional
19. genes
20. teratogen
21. Baumrind
22. continuity
23. placenta
24. zygote

Answers for Essay Questions

1. The primary reason why it is difficult to collect data from infants and young children is that they cannot produce or comprehend language. It is thus difficult for investigators to identify a response that can be used as a dependent variable.

    Developmental psychologists have resolved the problem by measuring responses that are in the repertoire of infants and young children. Physiological responses have been used; for example, changes in heart rate have been used to determine that infants can detect changes in the frequency of auditory stimuli. Sucking and "looking at" have also been used as dependent variables.

    The visual cliff is a good example of how ingenuity has been used to study depth perception in young organisms. The dependent variable in studies using the visual cliff concern the subjects' willingness to cross the "deep side" of the apparatus.

2. In cross-sectional studies, children of different ages are studied at the same time. An advantage of this method is that investigators can collect data quickly. One problem with the method is that samples of subjects must be comparable on attributes other than age. For example, an investigator should not use 4-year-old children from a suburban nursery school and 6-year-old children from an inner-city elementary school.

    If an investigator wanted to study the effects of a disaster (earthquake, riot, flood) on children of different ages, the investigators would have no choice but to use the cross-sectional method.

    In longitudinal studies, the same group of children is studied at intervals over a long period of time. An advantage of this method is that the developmental process can be observed in individual children. The investigator does not have to be concerned about group differences. The major disadvantage of the method is that it is costly and time consuming, and that subjects may be lost. Another disadvantage is that the sample being studied may show "cohort effects" that occur because of social conditions at the time they are growing up. Cohort effects could result from growing up during a war or depression or when certain child-rearing practices are advocated.

    It is necessary to use the longitudinal method to study stability and change over time. If a developmental psychologist wants to study the stability of intelligence, she would need to retest the same children periodically for a number of years.

3. Psychologists test conservation of number by asking children if the number of coins changes as the coins are moved farther apart. Conservation of quantity is studied by pouring liquid from a tall, narrow container into a short, wide container.

   One of the precursors a child would need is an extension of the concept of object permanence that allows the child to understand that quantity is a constant attribute that does not magically change when the shape is transformed. Piaget referred to the idea of constancy over transformations as reversibility. In the case of conservation, reversibility means that liquid can be poured from one container to another and back to the original container. This is a concrete and reversible operation.

   Children also need to be able to integrate two or more dimensions of objects. Children who cannot conserve focus only on the height or width of the containers, failing to integrate the two dimensions for a concept of quantity.

4. One of the enduring controversies is continuity versus discontinuity. This controversy concerns whether development, primarily cognitive development, occurs in a gradual way or whether there are identifiable stages in development. Continuity theorists claim that children master conservation as they slowly accumulate knowledge about the world. Piaget, a discontinuity theorist, claims that conservation is evidence of a qualitatively different way of thinking.

   Another of the enduring controversies is stability versus change. The controversy concerns whether patterns of growth, personality traits, and cognitive abilities remain relatively constant from infancy and early childhood through adulthood. Using the trait "energetic" as an example, the stability view claims that if a child is active and energetic early in life, the child will become an active and energetic adult. The change view claims that attributes seen in childhood do not predict adult attributes.

   The third controversy is nature versus nurture, or heredity versus environment. This controversy has been especially heated concerning whether intelligence is primarily determined by genetics or by environmental influences.

Answers for Multiple-Choice Test I

1. d	6. c	11. c	16. c	21. a
2. a	7. b	12. b	17. b	22. d
3. b	8. d	13. d	18. d	23. c
4. a	9. d	14. a	19. d	24. b
5. c	10. a	15. c	20. b	25. b

Answers for Multiple-Choice Test II

1. c	6. b	11. d	16. a	21. b
2. b	7. d	12. b	17. b	22. d
3. a	8. c	13. d	18. d	23. c
4. c	9. a	14. c	19. c	24. c
5. d	10. b	15. c	20. a	25. a

Chapter 10: ADOLESCENCE, ADULTHOOD, AND AGING

Answers for Working with Names and Terms

1. longitudinal
2. Gilligan
3. metacognitive skills
4. role confusion
5. intimacy
6. Piaget
7. Kübler-Ross
8. Neugarten
9. foreclosure
10. Erikson
11. empty nest
12. Hall
13. Kalish
14. Freud
15. secondary sex characteristics
16. filtering
17. moral realism
18. Marcia
19. self-accepted principles
20. dementia
21. cross-sectional
22. decrement model
23. Kohlberg
24. Alzheimer

Answers for Essay Questions

1. Many adolescents are physically adult and their cognitive skills are at their peak, yet they are likely to be treated as "big kids" because their lack of experience precludes their taking an adult role and living independently of their families. They frequently resent adult supervision and may act out their resentment in antisocial behavior.

    Adolescents are exposed to many material objects they would like to possess--electronic gadgets, fashionable clothes, cars. Their earning power is small, so some adolescents may turn to crime to get the things they want. The chance of an adolescent engaging in criminal behavior is increased if peers have made this choice.

    Some adolescents are motivated to "prove" that they are grown up. Risk-taking behaviors like fast driving, drug use, and criminal behavior are perceived by them as proof of adulthood. Adolescents also tend to think they are invulnerable: "I won't have an accident," "I won't get hooked on drugs," "I won't get caught stealing."

    Some adolescents feel hopeless about the future. They do not believe that they can succeed in the larger society, so they identify with peers and adults who adopt crime as a way of life.

2. The most important aspect of developing an identity is to know yourself--to be able to realistically assess talents and weaknesses, assets, and handicaps.

    Another criterion that is important to identity is to have plans and goals for the future that are consistent with a realistic self-image.

    A strong identity manifests itself in relationships with other people. It is demonstrated in the ability to sustain friendships without being overly susceptible to pressure for conformity. It is demonstrated in having a good relationship with parents, and in not expecting them to be more than human. It is demonstrated in gender identity, in feeling secure in one's sexuality and sexual role.

    Identity is demonstrated in thoughtful consideration of social, political, and religious values and behavior that is consistent with one's values.

    Erikson claimed that each life stage builds upon earlier stages and looks forward to later stages. Thus, the adolescent who is likely to form a strong and realistic identity is likely to have a sense of trust in self and his or her world, to feel capable of self-direction, to be able to take the initiative, and to feel that industriousness will be rewarded. Looking to the future, the adolescent contemplates the intimacy of marriage and the ability to be a productive member of society.

3. It seems reasonable to identify the transition from childhood to adulthood as a distinct stage that begins and ends with puberty. Adolescence, as it is currently defined, begins with the onset of puberty and ends at the age of 18 or 19 years, when a person is assumed to have become an adult. This extends the stage of adolescence several years beyond reaching physical maturity for most young people, and I think this expansion of the transition period is culturally, rather than biologically, defined.

The extension of adolescence seems to depend upon cultural definitions of "adult." In primitive societies, a young person who could hunt, sow and reap, or bear and rear children is an adult. In industrialized nations, a young person must have years of schooling and training before he or she can fulfill an adult role in society, so we have extended the period of adolescence as the requirement of adult responsibilities have become more complex.

4. In interviews and questionnaires, people are asked to respond to or comment on a series of questions or statements. There is no guarantee that subjects' responses will give an accurate account of their attitudes or behavior. Reasons for this include failure of memory for past events and lying to make oneself "look good."

Survey data can also show sampling bias. The answers the investigator gets are likely to depend upon the sample he or she chooses, and the cooperation gotten from the sample. In many surveys, the participants are those who consent to be interviewed or who fill out and return a questionnaire.

Correlational data has limited value because it does not necessarily indicate a causal relationship between variables. For example, if an investigator found a negative correlation between drug use and self-esteem in adolescents, it could result from low self-esteem being a causal factor in drug use, in drug use being a causal factor in self-esteem, or it could result from the effects of some third variable.

Answers for Multiple-Choice Test I

1. b	6. d	11. a	16. c	21. c
2. c	7. c	12. b	17. a	22. a
3. a	8. b	13. d	18. d	23. d
4. a	9. a	14. d	19. b	24. c
5. d	10. b	15. c	20. d	25. b

Answers for Multiple-Choice Test II

1. a	6. a	11. d	16. d	21. b
2. b	7. c	12. c	17. a	22. b
3. c	8. b	13. c	18. a	23. d
4. b	9. c	14. b	19. c	24. a
5. d	10. a	15. a	20. c	25. d

Chapter 11: INTELLIGENCE

Answers for Working with Names and Terms

1. standardization
2. experiential
3. Down
4. IQ
5. Galton
6. Spearman
7. reliability
8. Sternberg
9. Jensen
10. Gardner
11. percentile
12. Goddard
13. componential
14. factor analysis
15. g-factor
16. concurrent validity
17. heritability
18. predictive validity
19. Terman
20. split-half reliability
21. Thurstone
22. psychosocial
23. Simon
24. longitudinal

Answers for Essay Questions

1. Things the Kaplans can do to maximize Susie's IQ score can be classified as general strategy and specific tactics.
    The general strategy involves all the activities and stimulation that are believed to increase cognitive skills in children, These include reading to Susie, talking with her, asking her questions, encouraging creative play, providing a variety of experiences, and reinforcing both effort and accomplishment at cognitive skills.
    The specific tactics involve finding out what kind of items are likely to be on an intelligence test for children and providing practice on the tasks she will be asked to perform. There are toys, games, puzzles, and workbooks available that closely resemble materials used in intelligence tests.
    It would be a good idea for the Kaplan's to have Susie privately tested before she is tested by the school for gifted children. This will give Susie experience in the testing situations and will identify skills on which Susie is weak.
    Children enjoy activities that are intellectually challenging, provided they are not too difficult. The Kaplans are ambitious parents and they should be careful to move at Susie's speed and to make intellectual activities satisfying, rather than frustrating, for her.

2. Three hypotheses concerning IQ differences between blacks and whites involve genetics, environmental factors, and the content and administration of tests.
    There could be genetic differences in what evolution has produced in blacks and whites because of differences that existed in adaptation to the African and the European environments in which the races evolved.
    The environmental disadvantage of blacks began with slavery. They did not know the language of their masters and frequently did not share a common African language. Discrimination continues to depress the economic status of blacks, and a disproportionate number of blacks grow up in conditions of poverty where they are likely to be intellectually disadvantaged. Poverty also affects medical care and nutrition, both of the mother during pregnancy and the child after birth. Environmental deprivation begins in the womb.

Cultural bias in testing may not be so much a matter of bias in individual test items as it is in the whole situation of being tested and in differences in the knowledge and skills valued and emphasized in black and white cultures.

3. Componential intelligence includes such things as problem-solving ability, verbal fluency, and numerical skills. It is closely related to what tests like the Stanford-Binet and the Wechsler tests measure. People with high componential intelligence should be good scholars, engineers, teachers, accountants, or attorneys.

   Experiential intelligence is the ability to perceive novel and creative solutions to problems. Artists, musicians, and writers probably have high experiential intelligence. Scientists who are outstanding in research design, inventors, and creative people in advertising may also have high experiential intelligence.

   Contextual intelligence involves being adept at dealing with the environment, at understanding the social order, and at influencing other people. Salesmen and politicians need this kind of intelligence.

4. Reliability refers to consistency of measurement. A perfectly reliable instrument would produce the same "score" each time it was used to measure an object, providing the object itself does not change. Reliability of psychological tests is reduced because humans do change over time as a result of development, learning, and temporary states of mind and body. Also, the attributes of people that are measured by psychological tests are more complex and not as precisely defined as attributes measured by yardsticks and scales. This further reduces the reliability of psychological tests.

   Validity is the ability of a measuring instrument to measure what it claims to measure. The validity of physical measurement is rarely questioned. Validity of psychological tests is estimated by comparing scores with scores on tests that are suppose to measure the same thing or by the ability of the test to predict performance or behavior. The instruments or measures used to establish the validity of psychological test are themselves imperfect.

Answers for Multiple-Choice Test I

1. d	6. a	11. a	16. c	21. d
2. c	7. b	12. d	17. d	22. b
3. d	8. d	13. b	18. b	23. d
4. d	9. c	14. c	19. c	24. b
5. c	10. a	15. a	20. a	25. c

Answers for Multiple-Choice Test II

1. a	6. b	11. b	16. c	21. b
2. b	7. c	12. c	17. a	22. b
3. d	8. a	13. b	18. d	23. c
4. b	9. d	14. d	19. c	24. c
5. c	10. b	15. a	20. a	25. d

Chapter 12: *SOCIAL COGNITION*

Answers for Working with Names and Terms

1. Feshbach
2. Heider
3. primacy effect
4. consensus
5. Freedman
6. accommodation
7. Newcomb
8. Janis
9. Festinger
10. Jourard
11. proximity
12. Pettigrew
13. consummate
14. ELM
15. Kelley
16. McGuire
17. realistic conflict
18. distinctiveness
19. scripts
20. internal
21. self-perception
22. actor-observer bias
23. assimilation
24. cognitive dissonance

Answers for Essay Questions

1. My best friend and I went to the same high school and got to know each other when we both worked on a committee. Proximity made it possible for us to become friends. I admired him because he did such a great job at the meetings. He became the informal leader of the committee because he could get us organized and accomplishing things and still keep everyone happy. You could say that I was impressed by his competence.

    As we got to know each other better, we found that we have a lot in common and agree about most everything. We like the same movies and both like to go to a place that serves chili dogs after we see a movie. Also, we both have fairly conservative views about politics and other things, which makes us different from most of the students at our high school. There was an increase in reciprocal liking as we spent time together, and we share private personal confidences because we trust each other.

2. One of the ways in which beliefs and attitudes are changed is by behavior. Self-perception theory suggests that if a person sees himself praying, then the person assumes someone (God) is listening.

    The theory of cognitive dissonance explains the scholars' advice to the rabbis by observing that after the nonbeliever prays, she has the dissonant cognitions: "I do not believe in God." "I prayed to God." To reduce the discomfort associated with the inconsistent cognitions, the person will tend to change the cognition concerning belief in God.

3. The fundamental attribution error, or correspondence bias, is the tendency to overestimate the importance of internal factors and underestimate the importance of internal factor is explaining the cause of the behavior of others. For example, if a clerk doesn't give a customer enough change, the customer is likely to attribute the error to dishonesty or stupidity rather than to an external cause like one of the items purchased being marked incorrectly.

    Actor-observer bias is the tendency to attribute our own behavior to external or dispositional causes and the behavior of others to internal or situational causes. When a student makes a low grade on a test, the student is likely to attribute the grade to the difficulty or unfairness of the test. If another person makes a low grade, it is more likely to be attributed to lack of ability or failure to study.

4. In this situation, distinctiveness refers to whether getting a "D" on a chemistry test is usual or unusual for my friend. If it is unusual, then distinctiveness is high. Consistency is high if my friend usually gets low grades on tests in other classes, and consensus is high if many people in the class got a low grade on the test.

   I would attribute my friend's low grade to the difficulty of the test if distinctiveness is high (a low grade on a chemistry test is unusual for her), consistency is low (she rarely makes a low grade in any of her classes), and consensus is high (many students in the class made a low grade on the test).

   I would attribute my friend's low grade to an internal cause, like lack of ability or poor study habits if distinctiveness is low (she often makes low grades on chemistry tests), consistency is high (she often makes low grades in other classes), and consensus is low (very few students made a low score on the chemistry test).

5. Operant learning plays a role in the acquisition of stereotypes. Children can acquire stereotypes if parents reinforce criticism or prejudiced behavior toward a group with explicit or tacit approval. When a person has an unpleasant encounter or relationship with a person of another group, escape or avoidance learning may occur.

   Observational learning is also an important factor in the acquisition of stereotypes. We observe the things people we admire or identify with say or do and imitate their behavior and adopt their attitudes.

   Cognitive processes are involved in the development of stereotypes. We can interpret the behavior of people who are different from the self positively or negative, and we can reason about the attributes of other groups based on our perceptions and interpretations. After a positive or negative stereotype develops, people tend to assimilate information that justifies their beliefs about the group.

Answers for Multiple-Choice Test I

1. b	6. a	11. b	16. a	21. a
2. d	7. d	12. d	17. c	22. b
3. a	8. c	13. d	18. b	23. c
4. c	9. d	14. a	19. d	24. a
5. b	10. c	15. c	20. b	25. c

Answers for Multiple-Choice Test II

1. a	6. b	11. b	16. a	21. a
2. d	7. a	12. c	17. c	22. c
3. c	8. d	13. d	18. b	23. c
4. c	9. a	14. b	19. d	24. d
5. a	10. d	15. a	20. d	25. c

Chapter 13: *SOCIAL INFLUENCE*

Answers for Working with Names and Terms

1. socioemotional
2. Schachter
3. Darley
4. scapegoat
5. Janis
6. lowballing
7. aggression
8. Lewin
9. Asch
10. diff. of responsibility
11. vicarious reinforcement
12. door-in-the-face
13. group polarization
14. Wallach
15. trait
16. excitation transfer
17. groupthink
18. halo error
19. Lorenz
20. transactional
21. Milgrim
22. illusion of invulnerability
23. LeBon
24. Dollard

Answers for Essay Questions

1. It has been suggested that the treatment of the Jews in Germany in the 1930s and 1940s was displaced aggression. The German people were frustrated and angry because the economic situation was very bad. The Nazis directed the anger and aggression that resulted from the frustration toward the Jews by blaming them for the economic condition of the country.

   The foreman at work is perceived as critical and unreasonable, and one of his employees became very angry when the foreman made him redo a task. The employee did not express his anger to the foreman because he feared retaliation. When he went home, he punished his son severely for a trivial misbehavior.

2. If aggression is genetically transmitted, Sam could be inherently more aggressive than most other people.

   Sam's aggression and violence could result from the frustration he experiences in his life situation. He lives with his mother and siblings in a tiny apartment, he does not have money to buy the things he sees on TV, and school is frustrating because he never learned to read very well.

   Sam has learned to be aggressive and violent through operant conditioning. He learned early that he could get his own way with his siblings at home and peers at school by hitting them if they failed to do what he told them to do.

   Observational learning has also played a role in Sam's violence and aggression. When he was a little boy, his father beat him when he displeased his father. He has seen lots of violence and aggression on TV and in the movies. He has also observed that violent and aggressive males in his neighborhood are the ones with the flashy clothes and sporty cars.

3. Tamera may have failed to define the situation as an emergency. She could not actually see the flames, so the smoke coming from the kitchen window could be from something burning on the stove.

   Tamera could have gone to the neighbor's house to see if anyone was home and to investigate the cause of the smoke. But she didn't want to get involved. If someone was at home, maybe the person would think she is nosey.

Tamera could have called the fire department, but there is a man working in the yard next door and lots of cars passing on the street. If there is really a fire, someone has probably already called the fire department.

4. President Reagan probably fit the leadership schema of most Americans very well. He was perceived as good, sincere, and capable. After he was shot, he was also perceived to be courageous. His acting ability helped him play the leadership role well in public appearances and photo opportunities.

   President Reagan "initiated structure" in his leadership because he was consistent in his conservative ideology and in his support of legislation that supported it.

   Ronald Reagan was perceived as "showing consideration." Although he was certainly not a champion of the poor and minorities, he presented a public image of being a caring person. Also, when he spoke, he made people feel good about themselves and proud to be Americans.

5. The foot-in-the-door technique is used by businesses that sell products or services for the home. They advertise "free demonstrations" or "free estimates." The demonstration or estimate is given by a salesperson, and once the person gets into a home, he or she will try very hard to sell the product or service.

   The door-in-the face technique could be used by real estate salespeople. The salesperson first takes the potential buyer to see houses that are grossly overpriced, both for the property and the buyers' budget. When the potential buyers are shown a house that is realistically priced and within their budget, they are likely to think they have found a bargain and the salesperson will have made a sale.

   Car salespeople use the low-balling technique. The buyer finds a car he or she likes and a price is agreed upon. Only after the buyer has agreed to a price is he or she informed that the radio, the white-walled tires, the air-conditioner, the heater, the air bags, the leather upholstery, are all extras that will be added to the agreed-upon price.

Answers for Multiple-Choice Test I

1. d	6. a	11. a	16. a	21. a
2. c	7. d	12. b	17. d	22. c
3. b	8. c	13. c	18. b	23. b
4. b	9. a	14. c	19. d	24. c
5. b	10. d	15. d	20. a	25. a

Answers for Multiple-Choice Test II

1. a	6. c	11. b	16. b	21. a
2. a	7. d	12. c	17. d	22. a
3. d	8. d	13. a	18. d	23. c
4. c	9. a	14. c	19. d	24. c
5. b	10. d	15. a	20. b	25. b

Chapter 14: *PERSONALITY*

Answers for Working with Names and Terms

1. Eysenck
2. Allport
3. MMPI
4. denial
5. Rogers
6. secondary
7. Murray
8. Jung
9. fully functioning
10. self-actualized
11. Rotter
12. Mischel
13. introjection
14. deficiency
15. latency
16. authoritarian
17. superego
18. self-efficacy
19. libido
20. id
21. behavior analysis
22. projection
23. projective
24. Kohut

Answers for Essay Questions

1. Tad's id is urging him to have a drink and join in the fun. His superego was developed by identification with his parent's values, and his conscience is saying "no." External reality is represented by the others at the party and there is real or imagined social pressure to conform to the behavior of other.

    Tad's ego is weighing the costs and payoffs of having a drink. If he takes a drink, he will probably have more fun and won't have to worry about being rejected by the other guests. If he doesn't take a drink, he can avoid the guilt that will be his superego's revenge. His ego is pragmatic and will probably consider the probability that his parents or mother members of the church finding out about his behavior.

    If his ego defers to the id and external reality, it will try to alleviate feeling of guilt by using rationalization, projection, or some other defense mechanism.

2. An external locus of control is the belief that what happens in one's life is determined by external forces, like other people, circumstances, and fate or luck.

    Inconsistent use of reinforcement and punishment by parents contributes to development of an external locus of control. In this situation, the child cannot associate his or her behavior with consistent and dependable consequences.

    Social conditions in which a person's efforts are unrewarded also contribute to development of an external locus of control. Luck or fate, rather than the person's own initiative, are perceived to be in control of the person's destiny.

    An eternal locus of control could also be learned by observation. If the adults the child observes and imitates do not feel that they are in control of their own lives, the child is likely to adopt this feeling of hopelessness.

3. Projection is an ego-defense mechanism in which a person attributes his or her own motives or emotions to another person. A student who is very tempted to cheat on exams compensates by being scrupulously honest. The student projects his temptation to cheat onto other students and is likely to believe that "almost everyone in my classes cheats on exams."

    Reaction formation is an ego-defense mechanism in which a person behaves in a manner that is the opposite of the way he or she would unconsciously like to behave.

A mother who rejects her child may be overprotective, or a person who is attracted to violent pornography may be a member of a group that protests its availability.

Rationalization is an ego-defense mechanism in which people attribute their failures or shortcomings to causes that relieve them of responsibility for their own behavior. A person says "I didn't write or call because I was so busy" or "I failed the exam because the proctor stood over me and made me nervous."

4. One of the strength of trait theories is that the manner in which personality is defined makes it possible to describe and measure personality. Another strength of these theories is that they are more closely related to the way people think about personality than other theories.

    One of the weaknesses of trait theories is that they do not explain how people acquire personality traits or why they acquire some traits and not others. Another weakness is that they do not explain how traits interact to produce a consistent and stable personality. Trait theories also ignore environmental variables that affect behavior in specific situations.

5. Cognitive social-learning theory emphasizes learning through both operant conditioning and observational learning. Operant conditioning occurs when a person becomes extraverted because he or she is reinforced for behaviors associated with extraversion. Observational learning plays a role in becoming an extravert if the people one chooses to imitate and "be like" are friendly and outgoing.

    In his cognitive social-learning theory, Walter Mischel emphasizes cognition and person variables, like competencies, expectancies, values, encoding systems, and self-regulatory systems. According to Mischel, an extravert is a person who has good social skills and who values these skills in self and others, who evaluates others on traits associated with extraversion, and who prefers extrinsic rewards to intrinsic rewards. Michele seems to be telling us that a person who is an extravert perceives self, others, and events from a perspective that is consistent with being a friendly, outgoing person.

Answers for Multiple-Choice Test I

1. a	6. d	11. b	16. c	21. a
2. d	7. c	12. d	17. c	22. c
3. b	8. b	13. c	18. d	23. d
4. d	9. a	14. a	19. a	24. a
5. a	10. d	15. a	20. b	25. c

Answers for Multiple-Choice Test II

1. b	6. c	11. b	16. b	21. a
2. c	7. c	12. c	17. d	22. d
3. a	8. c	13. d	18. c	23. d
4. d	9. d	14. d	19. b	24. c
5. d	10. a	15. a	20. a	25. a

Chapter 15: *HEALTH AND STRESS*

Answers Working with Names and Terms

1. hardiness
2. PTSD
3. Holmes
4. daily hassles
5. Lazarus
6. approach-approach
7. arteriosclerosis
8. sedatives
9. Graham
10. Riley
11. avoidance-avoidance
12. Selye
13. psychosomatic-spec
14. lymphocytes
15. risk factors
16. Cannon
17. intellectualization
18. Rosenman
19. Kobasa
20. antigens
21. self-monitoring
22. GAS
23. fight or flight
24. progressive relaxation

Answers for Essay Questions

1. Toward the end, Donna and I argued about almost everything, and I thought my stress would be over when we separated. But it hasn't worked out that way. I am still experiencing a lot of stress, but for different reasons.

    Now that I've moved to my own apartment, I'm so lonely that I would welcome an argument with Donna. I think about our good times, and feel somehow as if I've failed in one of life's big tests. I'm also lonesome for our friends, but most of them were originally Donna's friends, and they probably think I'm an ogre.

    The money situation is really tight. Before we were separated I envisioned leading the life of a dashing bachelor, but it's all I can do to afford having a beer with the boys a couple times a week.

    Then there's the stress that goes with all the hassles of household things. My dark socks are covered with white lint, and my white underwear has a blue-brown tint. I stumbled over the vacuum-cleaner cord and hurt myself, and everything I try to cook either boils over or burns. I have to shop at least once a day because I'm always running out of things--shampoo, razor blades, milk, toilet paper. If I open a can of chili, I don't have any crackers; if I write a letter, I don't have an envelope or a stamp.

2. In my introductory psych class, we've been reading about the relationship between stress and illness, and my limited experience suggests that doctors tend to ignore the mind part of the mind-body system. They would rather prescribe sleeping pills for insomnia or tranquilizers for anxiety than to help their patients deal with the causes of their problems.

    For example, when my mother left my dad a few years ago, he became very depressed. He couldn't sleep, he lost weight, and he almost lost his job because he couldn't keep his mind on his work. The doctor just gave him some pills. I don't think he ever had a heart-to-heart with Dad or suggested that he see a counselor or join a self-help group.

    Our text reported a study showing that surgical patients got well faster when someone took the trouble to talk to them about the surgery and what to expect afterward. When I had my appendectomy, no one told me anything. When the surgeon came to see me after the operation, she had to look at my chart so she could call me by name.

I think people used to consider their doctor as a friend and a person who took the trouble to understand patients and their life situations.

3. Christmas can cause anxiety and fatigue in some people because of the extra work and activity involved--shopping, decorating, cooking, entertaining, and attending social events. Institutions like schools and churches, clubs, and other organization usually have holiday events, and expect members to contribute time to help in preparation for these events. The extra activities that come with the holiday season can be especially stressful for working mothers.

Christmas can result in stress related to the money people feel they must spend for gifts. Some people feel pressured to spend more for gifts than they can afford.

As people get older, Christmas may become more and more a time of sadness as they remember Christmases past that they shared with loved ones who have died.

4. The psychosomatic specificity hypothesis says that people who use the same mechanism for dealing with stress will develop the same physical illness. For example, people who use denial to cope with stress will develop ulcers, and people who use hostility to deal with stress will develop coronary heart disease.

David Graham's research gave some support to the hypothesis, but other studies have not supported it. I expect the relationship between coping strategies and illnesses is complex. In other words, I think the hypothesis is only part of the picture.

It is my observation that people tend to have specific physical symptoms regardless of the type of stress they experience or how they cope with it. It is as if one part of the body or one bodily system is chosen as the scapegoat for stress. My sister gets ulcers in her nose when she is stressed, and my father gets indigestion. Several of my friends get headaches when they are stressed. They have the same symptom, but they are quite different in the things that stress them and the way they deal with stressful situations.

Answers for Multiple-Choice Test I

1. b	6. b	11. c	16. d	21. b
2. a	7. b	12. a	17. c	22. d
3. c	8. a	13. a	18. a	23. c
4. d	9. d	14. b	19. b	24. a
5. a	10. c	15. c	20. a	25. b

Answers for Multiple-Choice Test II

1. c	6. d	11. a	16. d	21. d
2. d	7. b	12. b	17. c	22. c
3. d	8. d	13. d	18. a	23. a
4. a	9. a	14. c	19. b	24. d
5. c	10. c	15. b	20. c	25. b

Chapter 16: *MAJOR PSYCHOLOGICAL DISORDERS*

Answers for Working with Names and Terms

1. Seligman
2. biogenic amine
3. Rosenhan
4. histrionic
5. diathesis-stress
6. agoraphobia
7. multiaxial
8. Freud
9. anxiety
10. Beck
11. Skinner
12. obsessive-compulsive
13. bipolar disorder
14. hallucination
15. secondary gains
16. tolerance
17. undifferentiated
18. dissociative
19. hypochondriasis
20. delusions
21. mood
22. Szasz
23. dopamine
24. anhedonia

Answers for Essay Questions

1. The criterion of statistical deviation defines abnormality in terms of distance from a mean or average. People who have an IQ lower than 68 are diagnosed as retarded by this definition. A criticism of this criterion is inherent in the example. People whose scores deviate from the mean just as far in the opposite direction are envied for their intellectual ability.

    The criterion of social deviance defines abnormal in terms of social values and expectations. This criterion could be used to diagnose mania and antisocial personality disorder. The problem with this definition is that it defines abnormality as conformity to the standards of a particular culture.

    The criterion of maladaptive behavior defines abnormality as behavior that is self-defeating and nonproductive. This criterion could be used to define any type of abnormality. The problem with it is that "normal" people also engage in a lot of behavior and thinking that is self-defeating and nonproductive.

    The criterion of personal distress defines abnormality in terms of feeling miserable, either psychologically or physically. It is especially relevant for anxiety disorders and depression. The problem with it is that disorders like mania and antisocial personality disorder would not be diagnosed under this definition.

2. Many people have symptoms of mood disorder that are less extreme than the symptoms seen in major depression or bipolar disorder. Most people have periods when depression affects their productivity, their appetite, and their self-esteem. Also, many people have times when they feel "on top of the world" and have the overly optimistic outlook and inflated self-image that characterize mania.

    Multiple-personality disorder is apparently rare, but many people display different facets of themselves at different times and in different situations. Consider the young woman who goes to church on Sunday modestly dressed and demure in behavior. Saturday night she was wearing a provocative dress and being suggestive in both her behavior and her conversation. Some people also show one personality at the workplace and another at home.

3. Early last spring I started feeling depressed and thought it was because my grades weren't very good or because I had gained five pounds. But the depression got worse even after I accepted the fact that I'm no genius and lost the five pounds. I started cutting classes because I didn't have the energy to get dressed and go to class. I would just mope around all day and try to read or watch TV. I couldn't sleep very well, and when I did, I had disturbing dreams. And I felt lower than a worm.

   Toward the end of April, my roommate called my parents and they immediately came to visit me. They took me to the student health center where I was assigned to a psychologist and the psychologist arranged for me to be hospitalized.

   When I got to the hospital, I started taking called Prozac and having daily sessions with the psychologist. They also kept me busy helping other patients, painting pictures, and walking around the grounds. I started feeling better almost immediately and think I may be a better, more insightful person than I was before my bout with depression. One thing I learned was that I often expect too much of myself in some areas and that I am often too concerned about what others think of me.

4. The rumination-distraction hypothesis claims that women are more likely to ruminate about causes of their depression and men are more likely to look for activities to distract themselves from their depression.

   Women may get depressed because they have less freedom and personal control over their lives. This is especially true of housewives who are "tied down" with children and who depend on a demanding husband for financial support.

   Women are more likely to have problems that cause depression. They are more likely to be sexually, physically, or psychologically abused, and they are more likely to live in conditions of poverty and hopelessness.

   Women are more likely to make internal attributions for their problems and failures. Child-rearing practices often result in females having lower self-esteem and a lower perception of their self-efficacy.

   Depressive realism is more likely to occur in women. They are not as likely to overestimate themselves or to have overly optimistic attitudes about outcomes.

Answers for Multiple-Choice Test I

1. a	6. d	11. a	16. a	21. c
2. a	7. a	12. c	17. b	22. b
3. b	8. d	13. d	18. d	23. d
4. c	9. c	14. c	19. b	24. a
5. d	10. a	15. a	20. a	25. b

Answers for Multiple-Choice Test II

1. c	6. d	11. c	16. a	21. d
2. d	7. c	12. b	17. b	22. b
3. b	8. b	13. c	18. c	23. b
4. c	9. a	14. d	19. d	24. a
5. a	10. b	15. d	20. a	25. d

Chapter 17: *TREATMENT OF PSYCHOLOGICAL DISORDERS*

Answers for Working with Names and Terms

1. Ellis
2. tardive dyskinesia
3. psychoanalyst
4. congruence
5. deinstitutionalization
6. Charcot
7. Pinel
8. anxiety hierarchy
9. Wolpe
10. manifest content
11. Rogers
12. biofeedback
13. Beck
14. spontaneous remission
15. psychiatrist
16. transference
17. benzodiazepines
18. Breuer
19. lithium
20. conversion disorder
21. Gestalt
22. free association
23. depressive
24. token economy

Answers for Essay Questions

1. Cognitive-behavior therapists believe that depression results from beliefs that are irrational and self-defeating. They also believe that these maladaptive thought patterns are learned and can, therefore, be replaced by more adaptive thought patterns.

    In his rational-emotive therapy, Albert Ellis emphasizes beliefs that something terrible will happen if small things go wrong, that one must achieve mightily, and that one must always have the approval of others. Clients being treated for depression are encouraged to examine their irrational beliefs and to replace them with beliefs that are more realistic and adaptive.

    Aaron Beck's cognitive behavior therapy is similar except that it puts greater emphasis on changing negative beliefs about the self.

2. One reason the peer-counseling center chose Rogers' person-centered therapy is that it is appropriate for the problems students are likely to bring to the center. Serious disorders, like major depression or schizophrenia, would be treated elsewhere.

    Another reason for choosing this therapy is that the assumptions underlying humanistic therapy are likely to be consistent with the assumptions of the therapists and their clients. Specifically, they are likely to assume that people are free to make choices and that they are capable of solving their own problems with a bit of help. College students are generally above average in intelligence and can benefit from therapy that encourages them to examine their own problems and think about solutions.

    Rogers' criteria for therapists are very clear, and this would be an important advantage of his therapy for a center that uses peer counselors. Peer counselors are usually upperclassmen majoring in psychology or graduate students and do not have the experience required to use psychoanalysis or to attempt to modify another person's behavior. Using person-centered therapy, peer counselors are not likely to make matters worse.

3. In choosing a therapist to treat my depression, I would first make a decision concerning the type of therapy I think would be appropriate for my problem. If I

thought it was just a temporary situation resulting from a recently broken love affair, I might just see my doctor and see if she thought some Prozac would help me. If I see myself as having chronically low self-esteem or worrying too much about what other people think of me, I would choose a cognitive-behavior therapist or a person-centered therapist. I might choose a psychoanalyst if my depression didn't seem to result from some specify situation or faulty thinking about myself.

After I decided what type of therapist I'd like to have, I would need to pick a particular person. I think I would like a female therapist who isn't too old and who has a lot of experience. I would also use practical criteria like proximity and cost. I would look for a clinical psychologist rather than a psychiatrist because I don't think I need a therapist who is a medical doctor.

After choosing a name, I would call to make an appointment for a consultation. I think it is important that I like the therapist and have confidence in her ability to help me, and that the therapist seems to like me and be interested in my problem. If I don't feel comfortable with the first person, I will try someone else.

4. Psychoanalysts seem to me to resemble detectives in that they must gather clues from patients' disclosures and behavior concerning the underlying and unconscious roots of the patient's problems. They are also like detectives in that they are attentive and aloof, and do not intrude their own personalities into the therapeutic encounter.

Cognitive-behavior therapists seem to me to resemble engineers in that they attempt to remodel behavior to make it more effective and adaptive. Cognitive-behaviorists are more concerned with behavior and cognitions than with emotions, and are not very interested in the personal history of clients. Their approach is practical and oriented toward solution of specific problems.

Client-centered therapists seem to me to resemble a wise friend because they assume that people can solve their own problems with a bit of guidance and help. Carl Rogers thought therapists could best fulfill their function if they are accepting and empathetic. Client-centered therapists are like a wise friend because they listen carefully and take seriously what you say.

Answers for Multiple-Choice Test I

1. d	6. b	11. d	16. a	21. a
2. a	7. d	12. c	17. c	22. c
3. a	8. a	13. c	18. b	23. b
4. a	9. c	14. d	19. c	24. b
5. c	10. d	15. a	20. d	25. b

Answers for Multiple-Choice Test II

1. c	6. a	11. a	16. c	21. d
2. d	7. a	12. c	17. c	22. c
3. b	8. d	13. d	18. d	23. d
4. a	9. b	14. b	19. b	24. d
5. c	10. b	15. a	20. a	25. b

Appendix: METHODS AND STATISTICS IN PSYCHOLOGY

Answers for Working with Names and Terms

1. spurious
2. Pearson *r*
3. scatter plot
4. variability
5. *z*-scores
6. directionality
7. random assignment
8. descriptive statistics
9. empiricism
10. negative correlation
11. independent variable
12. bimodal
13. measurement
14. skewed
15. inferential statistics
16. mean
17. statistically significant
18. law normal
19. median
20. range
21. confounding
22. third variable
23. standard deviation
24. organismic

Answers for Essay Questions

1. The professor will begin by doing a correlational study. He will compare the number of cavities of children in Aullville with the number of cavities of children in several comparable communities. He might choose to carefully examine the teeth of 9- and 10-year-old children in Aullville and several other towns. If it is true that children in Aullville have significantly fewer cavities, he will formulate hypotheses concerning the cause of the difference.

    As causes, the professor might consider differences in dental hygiene programs in the schools, differences in diets, differences in the educational and socioeconomic levels of the children's families, difference in ethnicity, and differences in the drinking water. Preliminary investigation would allow him to choose the most promising hypotheses for further testing. For example, if Aullville has a vigorous dental hygiene program in the schools, and other communities tested do not, this suggests a promising hypothesis. Because it would be difficult to conduct an experiment testing the effectiveness of a dental hygiene program, the professor might look for communities that are comparable to Aullville that have such programs.

    If he decides that the differences in drinking water is the most promising hypothesis, he will do an experiment in which children are randomly assigned to groups, with the experimental subjects drinking only water from the wells of Aullville for two years. If the professor's hypothesis is confirmed, it will lead to more research and eventually to the use of fluorine in toothpaste and drinking water.

2. The third variable problem occurs when two unrelated variables are correlated because they are both causally related to a third variable. For example, the size of children's feet and their reading ability are correlated because both are related to age, the third variable.

    The directionality problem occurs when there is a causal relationship between two variables, but the directional of the causality is not clear: A could cause B; B could cause A; or causality could proceed in both directions. There is a correlation between watching TV violence and aggressive behavior in children. Does watching the TV violence lead to aggressive behavior? Or do aggressive children choose to watch violence TV? Still another possibility is that causality proceeds in both directions--from TV to aggressive behavior and from aggressive behavior to selection of TV programs.

3. Psychologists use correlational studies in preliminary research because they are easier to do than experiments. For example, if a psychologist thought students do better on tests when music is playing, she could do preliminary research by playing music during some midterms and not playing it during others. If the preliminary research supported the hypothesis, she could proceed to do an experimental study.

    Correlation is also used when any of many variables could be related to the variable of interest. For example, one might correlate reading achievement scores with a number of other variables, such as IQ scores and time spent watching TV.

    Psychologists use correlation when it would be unethical to manipulate the variable of interest. For example, one could not randomly assign children to the "abused" group. They also use correlation when it would be difficult to randomly assign subjects to groups, as in comparing a new teaching method with an older one. And correlation is used to study organismic variables, such as age and sex.

    Psychologists also use correlation for prediction in schools, businesses, and other institutions. Even spurious correlations can be used for prediction. For example, if liking Chinese food is correlated with talent for widget wiring, then liking Chinese food can be used as a criterion in the selection of widget wirers because it is a predictor of performance.

4. Random assignment will usually result in producing groups that have comparable numbers of males and females. However, in situations where there are known sex difference in performance on the dependent variable, the researcher can randomly assign the males and females separately. This is a version of matched random assignment where the matching variable is sex.

    Another possibility is to use only male or only female subjects. This would increase the probability of getting a significant results, but it would also limit the population to which a statistically significant result could be generalized.

Answers for Multiple-Choice Test I

1. b	6. d	11. a	16. c	21. a
2. a	7. b	12. d	17. a	22. d
3. c	8. a	13. b	18. b	23. c
4. c	9. d	14. b	19. b	24. d
5. b	10. d	15. a	20. a	25. c

Answers for Multiple-Choice Test II

1. a	6. d	11. b	16. a	21. d
2. d	7. a	12. a	17. d	22. a
3. d	8. d	13. d	18. c	23. b
4. b	9. a	14. c	19. a	24. c
5. b	10. d	15. b	20. c	25. d

We Want To Hear From YOU!

We need your reactions and ideas about this study guide. What did you like best and least? What would you like to have more or less of? How could it have been handled better? Please jot down your suggestions, cut out this page, fold and tape or staple it, and mail it to us. No postage is needed.

Many thanks!
HarperCollins Supplements Department

• •

Why did you buy the study guide?
   ∆ Teacher required it
   ∆ I needed extra help
   ∆ Mid-term coming, Needed to review
   ∆ It caught my eye
   ∆ Other

Do you prefer answers to the questions....
   ∆ In the back of the book all together
   ∆ At the end of each chapter
   ∆ Right below the question

How many of your classmates also use the study guide?
   ∆ 0%
   ∆ 5%
   ∆ 15%
   ∆ 50%
   ∆ 100%

How did you find out about the study guide?
   ∆ My professor
   ∆ Bookstore
   ∆ Other

Did you feel that you paid a fair price?
   ∆ Yes
   ∆ No

If not, what would you consider to be a fair price?

Do you feel that this study guide helped your final grade in the course?

What did you like best/least about the study guide?

Would you consider purchasing another HarperCollins study guide in the future?

Male_____   Female_____   Age_____

Your final course grade_____
School_____
Major_____
Would you be interested in reviewing study guides and textbooks for us? If so, your valuable time will be compensated with an honorarium. Please fill out you name and address.

_____
_____
_____

••

fold here

fold here

••

2-120408

BUSINESS REPLY MAIL
FIRST CLASS PERMIT NO. 247 NEW YORK, N.Y.

NO POSTAGE
NECESSARY
IF MAILED
IN THE
UNITED STATES

POSTAGE WILL BE PAID BY ADDRESSEE

HarperCollins*Publishers*
Attn: Supplements Editor, Evelyn Owens
College Division-4th Floor
10 East 53rd Street
New York, NY 10126-1111